The Trans and Non-Binary
Hero's Journey

ALSO OF INTEREST AND FROM McFARLAND

Adapting Bridgerton: *Essays on the Netflix Show in Context* (edited by Valerie Estelle Frankel, 2024)

The Villain's Journey: Descent and Return in Science Fiction and Fantasy (Valerie Estelle Frankel, 2022)

Star Wars *and the Hero's Journey: Mythic Character Arcs Through the 12-Film Epic* (Valerie Estelle Frankel, 2021)

Fourth Wave Feminism in Science Fiction and Fantasy: Volume 2. Essays on Television Representations, 2013–2019 (edited by Valerie Estelle Frankel, 2020)

Wonder Women and Bad Girls: Superheroine and Supervillainess Archetypes in Popular Media (Valerie Estelle Frankel, 2020)

Fourth Wave Feminism in Science Fiction and Fantasy: Volume 1. Essays on Film Representations, 2012–2019 (edited by Valerie Estelle Frankel, 2019)

Women in Doctor Who: *Damsels, Feminists and Monsters* (Valerie Estelle Frankel, 2018)

The Women of Orphan Black: *Faces of the Feminist Spectrum* (Valerie Estelle Frankel, 2018)

Superheroines and the Epic Journey: Mythic Themes in Comics, Film and Television (Valerie Estelle Frankel, 2017)

Women Versed in Myth: Essays on Modern Poets (edited by Colleen S. Harris and Valerie Estelle Frankel, 2016)

Adoring Outlander: *Essays on Fandom, Genre and the Female Audience* (edited by Valerie Estelle Frankel, 2016)

Outlander's Sassenachs: Essays on Gender, Race, Orientation and the Other in the Novels and Television Series (edited by Valerie Estelle Frankel, 2016)

The Comics of Joss Whedon: Critical Essays (edited by Valerie Estelle Frankel, 2015)

The Symbolism and Sources of Outlander: *The Scottish Fairies, Folklore, Ballads, Magic and Meanings That Inspired the Series* (Valerie Estelle Frankel, 2015)

Women in Game of Thrones: *Power, Conformity and Resistance* (Valerie Estelle Frankel, 2014)

Teaching with Harry Potter: Essays on Classroom Wizardry from Elementary School to College (edited by Valerie Estelle Frankel, 2013)

Buffy and the Heroine's Journey: Vampire Slayer as Feminine Chosen One (Valerie Estelle Frankel, 2012)

From Girl to Goddess: The Heroine's Journey Through Myth and Legend (Valerie Estelle Frankel, 2010)

The Trans and Non-Binary Hero's Journey

Quests for Empowerment in Science Fiction and Fantasy

VALERIE ESTELLE FRANKEL *and*
DEAN LEETAL

Foreword by Kai Cheng Thom

McFarland & Company, Inc., Publishers
Jefferson, North Carolina

LIBRARY OF CONGRESS CATALOGING-IN-PUBLICATION DATA

Names: Frankel, Valerie Estelle, 1980– author. | Leetal, Dean, author. | Thom, Kai Cheng, author of foreword.
Title: The trans and non-binary hero's journey : quests for empowerment in science fiction and fantasy / Valerie Estelle Frankel and Dean Leetal ; foreword by Kai Cheng Thom.
Description: Jefferson, North Carolina : McFarland & Company, Inc., Publishers, 2024. | Includes bibliographical references and index.
Identifiers: LCCN 2024012903 | ISBN 9781476694795 (paperback : acid free paper) ∞ ISBN 9781476652597 (ebook)
Subjects: LCSH: Heroes in mass media. | Transgender people in mass media. | Heroes in popular culture. | Transgender people in popular culture. | Gender nonconformity.
Classification: LCC P96.H46 F73 2024 | DDC 302.2308—dc23/eng/20240401
LC record available at https://lccn.loc.gov/2024012903

BRITISH LIBRARY CATALOGUING DATA ARE AVAILABLE

ISBN (print) 978-1-4766-9479-5
ISBN (ebook) 978-1-4766-5259-7

© 2024 Valerie Estelle Frankel and Dean Leetal. All rights reserved

No part of this book may be reproduced or transmitted in any form or by any means, electronic or mechanical, including photocopying or recording, or by any information storage and retrieval system, without permission in writing from the publisher.

Front cover image: © bzzup/Shutterstock

Printed in the United States of America

*McFarland & Company, Inc., Publishers
Box 611, Jefferson, North Carolina 28640
www.mcfarlandpub.com*

For Maya, you are so dear to me.
Thank you for being my family.
—Dean

For all those who haven't seen themselves in speculative
fiction for far too long and those who still need to.
With a big salute to my accomplished coauthor
for making so much of this happen.
—Valerie

* * *

The coauthors contributed equally to the book.

TABLE OF CONTENTS

Foreword by Kai Cheng Thom	1
Introduction	3

1. ORDINARY WORLD — 9
    Secret Identity: *The Matrix* (Film) — 9
    Trapped at Home: *Dreadnought* (Novel) — 14
    Forbidden Desires: *Magical Boy* (Graphic Novel) — 19
    The Call to Escape: *The Sunbearer Trials* (Novel) — 23
    Refusal Through Fear: *Shadowhunters* (Series) — 27

2. DIVINE AID — 31
    Human Mentor: *Meet Cute Diary* (Novel) — 31
    Dragon Mentor: "Battlement of Straw" (Short Story) — 35
    Otherworldly Mentor: *The Rocky Horror Picture Show* (Film) — 42
    Talisman: *Our Flag Means Death* (Television) — 45
    Self-Naming: DC's *Nubia and the Amazons* (Graphic Novel) — 52
    Defying the Threshold Guardian: *Charmed* (Television) — 57
    Discovering a New World: *The Affair of the Mysterious Letter* (Novel) — 60

3. SAFETY WITH OTHERS — 65
    Haven: *Doom Patrol* (Television) — 65
    Found Family: *Dead End: Paranormal Park* (Television) — 70
    An Uplifting Interlude: *Steven Universe* (Television) — 73
    Finding Allies: *Pet* (Novel) — 76

4. CHALLENGE AND GROWTH — 81
    Partnering the Double: *The Witch King* (Novel) — 81
    Following the Anim Guide: *The Prince and the Dressmaker* (Graphic Novel) — 87
    Loving the Anim: *A Lady for a Duke* (Novel) — 91
    Mirroring: *Hedwig and the Angry Inch* (Film) — 95

Table of Contents

5. Battling Society — 99
- Misgendered: *Sir Callie and the Champions of Helston* (Novel) — 99
- Dumped for Being Trans: *If I Was Your Girl* (Novel) — 103
- Threatened: *Supergirl* (Television) — 106
- Forced to Suppress Legitimate Anger: *Seven Suspects* (Novel) — 112
- Punished for Rage: *Orange Is the New Black* (Television) — 117

6. Underworld Descent — 123
- Descent Within and Without: *The Watch* (Television) — 123
- Belly of the Whale: *Look Past* (Novel) — 126
- Supreme Ordeal: *No Man of Woman Born* (Short Stories) — 131
- Tyrant Parent: *Funky Dan and the Pixie Dream Girl* (Novel) — 133
- Shadow as Otherself: *Loki* (Television) — 137
- Sacrifice: *Sandman* (Graphic Novel) — 143
- Rebirth: *Birdverse* (Series) — 147
- Transcendent Treasure: *Peter Darling* (Novel) — 151

7. Return and Acceptance — 157
- Escape with Allies' Aid: *Sense8* (Television) — 157
- The Tyrant Crumbles: *Sort Of* (Television) — 163
- Public Acknowledgment: *Cemetery Boys* (Novel) — 167
- Master of the Two Worlds: *Good Omens* (Television) — 170
- Freedom to Live? *Fierce Femmes and Notorious Liars* (Novel) — 174
- Becoming a Community Elder: *Pose* (Television) — 178
- Teaching the Next Generation: *The Adventures of Priscilla, Queen of the Desert* (Film) — 185

Final Thoughts — 191

Glossary — 193

Resources — 197
- Texts for Beginners — 197
- Anthologies and Collections — 197
- Children's Picture Books — 198
- Children's Middle Grade Fiction — 199
- Young Adult/Teen Novels — 199

Works Cited — 201
- Primary Sources — 201
- Secondary Sources — 204

Index — 211

Foreword

by Kai Cheng Thom

Lovers of the craft of storytelling know the magic and power of archetypal maps: the resonance of looking beyond the surface layers of a story to find the ancient and mysterious bones within that give it shape. How thrilling—and humbling—it is, as both storyteller and story-listener, to look at those bones and remember that while the tales that shape and reflect us are unique in their way, they are also connected to something greater, the universal consciousness to which we all belong. How unfortunate it is, then, that trans and non-binary lovers of story have for so long gone without a map of our own.

The classic hero's journey and heroine's journey, as observed by Joseph Campbell and elaborated upon by countless writers and analytical theorists since, have long served this purpose in speculative literature, forming the primary mythopoeic foundation upon which contemporary science fiction and fantasy are based. It is hard for a self-avowed nerd like me to imagine sci-fi or fantasy books, TV, or movies without the hero's journey at its core, and why would we want to? Haven't all of us nerds found our own inner struggle, our own secret power, and our own shadow self somehow reflected in the great heroic quests we see on the page and screen? Isn't that why we love the genre in the first place?

Yet I am as much a trans woman as I am a nerd, and for the first twenty-five years of my reading life, the trans part of me wondered what my experience of the media that I loved so much would be like if its archetypal roots weren't quite so binary and so cis-gendered. And as more and more trans stories have come to the fore in sci-fi and fantasy in the past seven-odd years, I have come to realize that I was not alone in my wondering. *The Trans and Non-Binary Hero's Journey* by Valerie Estelle Frankel and Dean Leetal is a wonderful balm to that long-held pain, weaving together many—*many*—texts from the now prolific field of trans speculative fiction to spin a new web to hold us all: an archetypal heroic journey, from a transcentric perspective.

Foreword

Trans and non-binary folks may have particular resonance with speculative fiction, precisely because the nature of our lives demands transformation, fortitude, a heightened connection to our inner voices (at least insofar as gender is concerned), and the understanding that the true nature of things is not always as it seems. For many of us, the limitless worlds and larger-than-life quests of fantasy and sci-fi seemed to offer a glimpse into the potential for courage and transformation that all trans people need to survive in a world that has long denied our existence. Indeed, when I worked for several years as a mental health counselor for trans youth, it was a regular occurrence in my practice that a client would tell me that they first realized they were trans while playing a character in *Dungeons & Dragons* whose gender more accurately reflected their own!

The Trans and Non-Binary Hero's Journey is astoundingly comprehensive and beautifully detailed, pulling together threads from the "classics" of trans literature, film, and criticism while highlighting the exciting range of newer works that have been created in the last decade in order to unveil the mythopoeic heart at the core of our stories. Politically astute and refreshingly nuanced, Frankel and Leetal never fall into the trap of trying to fit trans texts into a cis-normative lens but instead unfailingly center trans and non-binary interpretation. In other words, *The Trans and Non-Binary Hero's Journey* does the revolutionary act of reflecting the archetypal narrative of trans people, not as cis people see us but as we see ourselves.

What a gift this is: to be offered a map of ourselves. With such a map in hand, who knows what quests might follow?

Kai Cheng Thom is an award-winning author and self-professed nerd. Thom's beautiful writings include the lyrical novel Fierce Femmes and Notorious Liars: A Dangerous Trans Girl's Confabulous Memoir, *the mythology-based poetry collection* A Place Called No Homeland, *and a sweet picture book that teaches inclusion:* From the Stars in the Sky to the Fish in the Sea. I Hope We Choose Love: A Trans Girl's Notes from the End of the World *centers on transformative justice, and* Falling Back in Love with Being Human: Letters to Lost Souls *explores self-acceptance. They all explore the many dimensions of the trans experience.*

Introduction

The hero's and heroine's journeys, which go back equally far in ancient myth, are perceived in most research as heavily gendered. The hero claims his father's sword and rides off to battle the tyrant, while the heroine takes her magic spindle or ball gown and resists the wicked stepmother or fairy queen to save her prince. Triumphant, the questor ascends to king or queen or divinity with a conventional marriage. That's all mythologically valid, but there's more to the story.

Granted, other genders and gender presentations appear in myth, but most epics were meant to prepare young people for traditional paths. When considering twenty-first-century fiction, a new pattern presents itself—specifically for authors who understand that such a binary approach to gender is cultural and that other pathways are available. Trans and non-binary are both clusters of identities. Non-binary identities fit under the trans umbrella by right, but some non-binary people don't claim that identity. With fictional characters, it is often hard to tell where exactly they fit on these spectrums, so we have chosen texts in which the authors and characters clarify their status. Some characters we discuss are binary trans, some are non-binary trans, and some are open to interpretation but have authorial comments or symbolism to guide readers.

Heroes outside of the gender binary go back to our oldest stories as tricksters, mystics, ordinary heroes, and gods. Some follow another gender's path for a time, like Arjuna, Tiresias, or Coyote, and some make their transformations permanent. Others embrace genders outside of the binary, like the Jewish Biblical deity seems to, or as ancient Greek and early modern European texts highlight. These reflect historic trans communities and cultures worldwide, like the Hijra, Indigiqueer, or Bakla, among many others. The colonialist agenda has been violently silencing these voices for decades and is still doing so. Therefore, it is the job of white trans activists and allies to promote the needs of people alive now whose cultures and ancestors these portrayals represent. Fast-forwarding to the twenty-first century, scholars are publishing what the storytellers have known since ancient times: gender identity transcends the binary.

With this in mind, a new heroic quest can be discerned, traceable through the many popular media of the twenty-first century: novels, short stories, television, film, and comics. GLAAD (Gay & Lesbian Alliance Against Defamation) director of trans media and representation Nick Adams points out how 80 percent of Americans don't personally know an openly trans person and how much this affects the trans community: "Trans people have also been taught how to think about themselves [by the media]. We're not raised, usually, in a family where other trans people are around us. So when we're trying to figure out who we are, we look to the media to figure it out, because just like the 80% of Americans who say they don't know a trans person, that's often true of trans people as well. We don't know a trans person when figuring out who we are. So, we're looking to the media to figure out, 'Who's like us?'" (*Disclosure*).

Science fiction and fantasy are particularly rich mediums for epic quest stories. In "Science Fiction Has Always Been Queer," Sigrid Ellis explains, "To be queer is to deny easy definition. Which is also what science fiction does. It defies what is known, what is safe. Science fiction extrapolates and explores. It pushes the edges of the known. Science fiction takes us to live in other people's bodies, in minds and hearts alien to our own" (360–361). It's about flexibility, transformation, breaking down borders. Likewise, fantasy sees good battle evil in ways that update the divine struggles of ancient myth. These tales reveal the deep psychological truth of how the hero's journey applies to trans and non-binary heroes of many backgrounds. Of course, it's quite easy to get it wrong. Trans memoir author Kai Cheng Thom observes:

> It's actually a very old archetype that trans girl stories get put into: this sort of tragic, plucky-little-orphan-character who is just supposed to suffer through everything and wait, and if you're good and brave and patient (and white and rich) enough, then you get the big reward. …which is that you get to be just like everybody else who is white and rich and boring. And then you marry the prince or the football player, and live boringly ever after. We're like Cinderella, waiting to go to the ball like the Little Mermaid, getting her tail surgically altered and her voice removed so she can walk around on land. Those are stories we get, these days [*I Hope* n.p.].

Instead, it's important to search for the psychologically true quest—the one that reflects the real growth of the psyche. Works such as Lou Cornum and Maureen Moynagh's develop this notion (n.p.).

The steps are familiar for a breakout type of protagonist. This hero grows up in the ordinary world but often lives in a more hazardous childhood, vulnerable to transphobia as well as abuse and cruelty. Trapped in this space, the hero feels illicit desires—a longing to break out and live as the gender that society or their family forbids them. Sometimes the hero longs to be a knight, a priestess, or other forbidden role. Other times, they seek the more basic freedom to live along with a nurturing community and found family.

Different kinds of mentors come to the hero; they may be the prosaic human type, but often the hero, especially a non-binary one, cannot find such a figure, even on society's margins. Sometimes mystical mentors, like gods, arrive, confirming the hero's path. Others may be frightening and savage—monsters or dragons—who teach the hero fierceness. As James Eli Adams explains, the image of the monster can carry various meanings but is awe inspiring (n.p.). As discussed by scholars such as Melissa E. Sanchez, this monstrosity is linked with transness (138). The mentor offers the hero a talisman—sometimes powers of shape changing or fluidity, sometimes an item that will augment the hero's true self.

The quest beckons. Sometimes this is a mystery or an external threat that has no connection to their identity. Still, this journey will take them into the fantastical otherworld, where the ordinary rules no longer apply. The forest or wilderness offers a refuge, while the magical world offers the type of found family and love the hero has always been denied. In the otherworld, one can live as all they've suppressed and been forbidden to claim. Here, one can cast off the persona used to fit in and show off one's superpowers and true name.

The journeys feature allies and friends who embody useful lessons and offer skills the hero must learn. Adversaries and obstacles often personify the prejudice and blocked opportunities people face in the real world. Misgendering, victim blaming, and gaslighting are common. If the hero expresses anger, they risk disproportionate punishment. Still, the otherworld and its helpers often provide new strategies for coping.

In the innermost cave, representing the deepest subconscious, the hero faces the shadow. This shadow is all the personality traits one has pushed down and refused to acknowledge. Science fiction can offer an alternate universe self, while fantasy likewise may create a dark copy—all these present the truest shadow, who knows the most about one's vulnerabilities. Learning to overcome its harsh whispers, to acknowledge it as part of the self, to dismiss its power and accept it, leads to full self-actualization. This quest reverberates throughout much of the speculative fiction of the twenty-first century and before, offering a model for those seeking empowerment.

Other considerations include the materials used as examples. As gender scholar Cáel M. Keegan observes, "'Good' transgender media is media that casts transgender actors as transgender characters. It is media that is written and directed by transgender creators. It is media that allows transgender characters to be more than just narrative or political tokens. 'Good' transgender media is authentic, progressive, and diverse" ("Praise" n.p.).

With awareness of this, the more notorious examples of representation will be dealt with only briefly, if at all. Further, while these steps are archetypal for many trans characters in fantasy, it is important for us to note that they are fictional steps and should not be mixed up with the many and different paths trans and otherwise non-binary people walk in reality.

The process of writing this book has been hard yet joyous. Within the time of writing, there has been a new blossoming of trans media. While it is far from enough, it is still more than we have witnessed before. The authors read or watched all the materials they could find in which a trans or non-binary character has a plot arc and then edited each other's choices to eliminate ones that didn't fit the pattern well. We chose works for this study based on popularity and on what we loved. We sometimes skipped choices for being harmful or simply not adding an interesting angle to the study. Mostly, we chose works that at least one of us loved, telling each other about stories excitedly, disagreeing and sharing, and being enriched by one another.

Recent novels, especially young adult ones, have been offering inspiring, heartwarming, and more fully faceted characters, often written by trans authors telling their own truths. Television is more likely to offer the "very special episode" or problematic transphobic tropes, with criminals on law shows or people's own bodies attacking them on medical shows. However, some series have been known for sensitive, nuanced performances that raise awareness, whether through the casting of *Pose* or the symbolic representation on *Steven Universe*.

Today, *trans*, short for transgender, is the common term for a person who is a different gender from the one assigned on their birth certificate. *Gender expression* references one's external manifestations, including names, pronouns, voice, behavior, clothing, etc. They are not clear indications of who one is or of one's gender. Being non-binary, agender, genderqueer, or fluid generally means not identifying as man or woman or not identifying as one of these solely or all the time. This is unrelated to one's sexual or romantic preferences. *Queer* (itself a reclaimed word) covers the entire LGBTQ+ spectrum (an incomplete term, with the + intended to cover those who don't fit into one of the specified letters—QUILTBAG and LGBTQIA are also used by some); however, *queer* is only the correct term to use for those who identify with it. While the terms have changed through different eras and cultures, as has the fiction, a clear journey pattern presents itself as the quest of heroes for individuation and the place they belong.

The Hero's Journey Chart, Step by Step

Campbell's Model: The Hero's Journey*	Trans Hero's Journey Model
The Ordinary World	Secret Identity, Trapped at Home, Forbidden Desires
The Call to Adventure	The Call to Escape
Refusal of The Call	Refusal Through Fear
Supernatural Aid	Human Mentor, Dragon Mentor, Otherworldly Mentor
Crossing the First Threshold	Defying the Threshold Guardian, Discovering a New World, Haven and Found Family
The Road of Trials	Misgendered, Dumped, Threatened
The Meeting with the Goddess, Woman as Temptress	Partnering the Double, Finding and Loving the Anim
Approach to the Inmost Cave	Descent Within and Without
Belly of the Whale, Supreme Ordeal	Belly of the Whale, Supreme Ordeal
Atonement with the Father	Tyrant Parent, Shadow as Otherself
Apotheosis, The Ultimate Boon	Sacrifice, Rebirth, Transcendent Treasure
The Road Back, The Magic Flight, Crossing the Return Threshold	Escape with Allies' Aid
Resurrection	The Tyrant Crumbles, Public Acknowledgment
Master of the Two Worlds, Freedom to Live	Master of the Two Worlds, Freedom to Live? Teaching the Next Generation

*Adapted from *The Hero with a Thousand Faces*. For more on other journeys, see Frankel's *From Girl to Goddess: The Heroine's Journey Through Myth and Legend*, McFarland, 2010, and *The Villain's Journey: Descent and Return in Science Fiction and Fantasy*, McFarland, 2022.

1

Ordinary World

Secret Identity: The Matrix *(Film)*

Superheroes maintain an artificial everyday self or persona. Underneath is their real identity, the powerful, raging shadow side that is unacceptable in society and must be buried. While most people conceal this side all the time and, indeed, have trouble releasing it and channeling its powers, superheroes have already harnessed it. This is Superman, hidden beneath the socially acceptable Clark Kent disguise but smashing out to save the day. "In general, we can say superheroes reverse the usual order of 'persona, outside, shadow, inside.' They turn the shadow inside out and show us the inside first," explains Sharon Packer in her work on superhero psychology (135).

Neo, the hero of *The Matrix*, embodies such a superhero. Many consider this story inherently very trans, written as it was by writers and directors Lana and Lilly Wachowski. Lana explained they were asking "how you interrogate reality and what reality is and that led us into the entire philosophical spectrum of what the Matrix ended up being" (Keegan, *Wachowski* 24). Neo's digital self-image is far different from his everyday guise, as was true for many people at the time the film was made. Further, some consider such allegories problematic, as they often refrain from actual representation (Burt qtd. in Dueben); this is mitigated here by the era and the creators' wrangling with the issue.

Late twentieth-century transgender stories were linked to online spaces where many chose new identities. These chat rooms and digital worlds were reflected in bullet time and morphing effects "that produced new temporal and special encounters with the gendered body as the plastic effect of coding" (Keegan, *Wachowski* 26). The Matrix introduces a realm where the physical body is meaningless and one's real self doesn't match it. "Trans is thus a relativity construct in which we recognize that all bodies, all fields, are in motion—in which material is as constructed as the purportedly symbolic and in which the symbolic can simultaneously be lived as the real" (Keegan, *Wachowski* 27). Lilly Wachowski has been outspoken on the trans allegory, though it had to be hidden at the time: "The corporate world wasn't ready for it," she said. The trans character Switch lost this nuance, originally intended to be male in the corporate world and female in the Matrix before Warner Brothers cut that aspect. But since its release, Wachowski added, the response from trans people has been monumental: "I love how meaningful those films are to trans people" (McCormack n.p.).

In the film's first scene, Trinity's leaps and flight, labeled "impossible" by startled cops, emphasize that viewers must abandon the assumptions they've made about physicality and what is possible for a body. Trinity then summons Neo, urging him to awaken. With his special perception, Neo knows something is wrong with the world in which he exists, one that is actually made of ones and zeros that suggest the gender binary. He leads a double life, with his online life superseding his other life in importance. He is first seen asleep in his hacking space, speaking with Trinity and following the trail she's led.

> The nightclub scene in the first *The Matrix* film, where Trinity first meets Neo to tell him about Morpheus and the Matrix, was actually filmed inside a real bondage club in Sydney (where the film was being shot). In fact, many of the extras were just regular patrons who brought their own clothes and gear to the shoot. And while the BDSM and goth subcultures aren't inherently LGBTQ+, there are a lot of overlaps in terms of participants [Damaske n.p.].

Nineties' society considered BDSM (a term used to describe sex involving dominance, submission, and control) subversive and deviant. Further, the flashy clothes and slick, reflective leather of the club also particularly contrast with the conformist suits of the evil agents. As she appears here, Trinity emphasizes how she transcends the boundaries of gender conformity, slipping between identities, responding to Neo's assumption that she's a guy with a simple "Most guys do."

The next morning, he looks quite different in a conformist suit, standing in an office where his corporate boss, Mr. Rhineheart, calls him Mr. Anderson, his outward identity. This name is nearly as traditional as Smith and Jones, emphasizing how ordinary his outward persona is. (Meanwhile, "rhine" links with stone [rhinestone], so this surname suggests stonyheartedness.) Keanu Reeves isn't white—he has European, Chinese, and Polynesian ancestors—but in the office, he's coded as a typical white-collar corporate worker drone. He is the prophesied chosen one but subverted because he's mixed race and not from royal birth. "Neo is practically an archetypal trans woman. Every day he puts on a suit and tie and goes to work, but no matter how hard he tries he can't fit in. He has friends in the counter-culture but he doesn't really connect with them either, and when they go out he stands in a corner staring at beautiful women. Something is always off, always wrong" (Pilford-Bagwell n.p.).

1. Ordinary World

In another example of subtle strangeness, the office is lit in green, emphasizing the Matrix space. All this emphasizes how his conformist side is splintering. As his boss comments, "You have a problem with authority, Mr. Anderson. You believe that you are special, that somehow the rules do not apply to you. Obviously, you are mistaken. This company is one of the top software companies in the world because every single employee understands that they are part of a whole." He offers an ultimatum, insisting Neo show up on time and perfectly obey or find another job.

Indeed, it is time to choose. Traditionally, in superhero stories, a great injustice impels the hero to fight back. Accordingly, a cell of hackers contacts Neo to alert him that his reality is actually virtual. Next, Mr. Smith captures him and brings him to an interrogation room as green and anonymous as the cubicle. Smith tells him:

> It seems that you've been living two lives. In one life, you're Thomas A. Anderson, program writer for a respectable software company; you have a social security number; you pay your taxes; and you help your landlady carry out her garbage. The other life is lived in computers, where you go by the hacker alias Neo and are guilty of virtually every computer crime we have a law for. One of these lives has a future, and one of them does not.

Indeed, he lives a double identity. Over and over, Neo is ordered to conform and abandon his inner life if he wants to survive. This, too, is symbolic. "The Matrix ... was all about the desire for transformation, but it was all coming from a closeted point of view," Lilly Wachowski said. "My reality is that I've been transitioning and will continue to transition all of my life, through the infinite that exists between male and female as it does in the infinite between the binary of zero and one" (McCormack n.p.).

Neo demands his phone call, and to his shock and horror, his mouth disappears. Then his captors place a frightening cyberscorpion on him, which bores into his belly button. His body is being controlled, silenced, and reconfigured to suit society. It's terrifying. Meeting Morpheus, Neo reveals that he seeks control over his life. Morpheus replies, "I know exactly what you mean. Let me tell you why you're here. You're here because you know something. What, you know you can't explain. But you feel it. You've felt it your entire life. That there's something wrong with the world. You don't know what it is, but it's there, like a splinter in your mind driving you mad." As several critics explain, "This is how many trans people have described seeing the world before realizing they were trans—either of themselves or the world outside of them. They felt that there was something wrong with how the world was forcing gender binaries and how the system was unfairly enforcing it" (Damaske n.p.).

As the movie continues, "its plot following the sequence of dysphoria, identity realization, name change, hormonal therapy, surgery, and social reintegration in a 'new' gender that is associated with the medically mandated pathway for gender transition" (Keegan, *Wachowski* 29). The state—the white, dark-suited Mr. Smiths policing the Matrix—are the enemy. From there, Neo plunges into a queer underworld, where leather-clad hackers perform surgery and remove his tracer. After this, Morpheus offers a life-changing choice. The blue pill will help him conform, while the red pill will alter him forever. Pilford-Bagwell notes how the red pill resembles spironolactone, the most common testosterone suppressant. Several references to his being too old for the procedure and risking his life by joining them hint at "a toxic narrative among trans people, formed by gender-normative society's continuous pressure to conform to its standards, that you will never be able to truly be the gender you identify as if you transition after puberty" (Pilford-Bagwell n.p.). The red pill will lift him out of the Matrix of self-delusion and into a new body. This body requires surgical intervention and training before it's fit for his new life. This scene is also common for superheroes, who are often healed or remade into cyborgs or other balances with their new powers and augmentations.

Neo's wardrobe grows increasingly leather-covered and androgynous as he wears the uniform of their new people, not of the system. This new superhero look embodies his real self—the shining hero under the drab business attire. He finds his team and commits to fighting beside them. Neo, meanwhile, tries to process who he was versus who he's become:

> **Neo:** I used to eat there. Really good noodles. I have these memories from my life. None of them happened. What does that mean?
> **Trinity:** That the Matrix cannot tell you who you are.

Indeed, she falls in love with him after he "dies," indicating his freedom from the limits of his old identity and his casting off the restrictions of his former life. The entire movie celebrates transcending the limitations of the physical to explore the abilities of the mind. Agent Smith, the force of conformity, repeatedly deadnames "Mr. Anderson," leaving him to proudly retort at the climax, "My name is Neo." He has claimed his superhero identity.

While Neo fights free of the ordinary world's expectations, many other characters battle judgmental society. The narrator of *Parrotfish* wonders:

> What made a person male or female anyway? The way they looked? The way they acted? The way they thought? Their hormones? Their genitals? What if some of those attributes pointed in one direction and some in the other? And some of this stuff had to do with the way you were raised, right? It's not as if we managed to stamp out stereotypes in this culture. In many places, sugar and spice were still considered the opposite of snails and puppy dog tails. When I

1. Ordinary World

decided I was a boy, I realized that if I wanted to pass, I'd have to learn to walk differently, talk differently, dress differently, basically act differently than I did as a girl. But why did we need to act at all? A quick glance around Buxton High provided numerous cases of girls acting like girls and boys acting like boys—and very few people acting like themselves. Eve was a perfect example: she had been a great girl until she hit Buxton, but now she was a high-pitched low self-esteem capital-G glrl who couldn't relax and be Eve anymore [Wittlinger 131].

"So maybe it was silly for me to try to be somebody else's idea of a boy," the narrator concludes (131). Living for oneself is the true point of ending the persona—finding a way to break through cultural expectations and show off.

"We are performers in the social game, but we must also participate in another play. We are also meant to be our individual selves," observes Edward C. Whitmont in "The Persona: The Mask We Wear for the Game of Living" (18). To look at this issue without the science fiction allegory, characters are seen exploring this side of themselves in the show *Pose*, in which the established members of the runway competition adopt newcomers to New York and teach dance, makeup, and whatever the newbies need. Many are understandably angry and defensive, having grown up in families that completely deny who they are. In New York, they get a chance to shine. *Pose* highlights ball culture, in which the dancers try out personas like professionals and rich ladies having brunch. These are the opportunities they fear they will never have as marginalized trans people of color. These costumed dances are not just make-believe but sources of beauty and joy. The more distant fantasies, like millionaires and runway models, seem unattainable. However, the poverty-stricken competitors gradually grow into their roles. As one house mother, Blanca, tells another, Elektra, in the series finale,

> You got to remember why the balls started in the first place. They were a place for all of us to be all of them things that we weren't allowed to be out in the world. All right, how many times have we walked Businesswoman? And now you a real one, Elektra. Or Runway, Miss Angel. And now you actually walk the real runways. We weren't pretending when we walked those categories; we were preparing. Faking it until we made it. And more than anything, we made a statement. That we deserve to dream and have our dreams fulfilled. When we were walking those balls, we beared witness to our possibilities. And we say to each other, "Yeah, girl, I see you. I see who you are and who you can be." And then the outside world, they tell us to hide. But in the balls … they tell us to strut. We can never give up on the balls ["Series Finale Part 2" 3.08].

Even enclosed worlds of safety allow people to perform and dip into this stifled shadow side, at least for a little while.

Trapped at Home: Dreadnought *(Novel)*

The "ordinary world" is the home the protagonist knows at the start of the story—what the protagonist considers normal, perhaps safe. It is a place of innocence, often without awareness of the deeper world of magic and the unconscious. Often this "safety" is more of a status quo. For transgender characters, security is often unavailable. As Thom asks, "What would it take to build a community where we were really safe? Not perfectly rigidly safe in the sense of totally free from risk—because such a thing is not possible in this life—but safe enough to pursue intimacy and adventure with the knowledge that there really was a community that had our backs?" (*I Hope* n.p.). In transphobic and binaristic societies, the narrative of moving away from safety is often not an option to start, because there is no safety to move away from.

In this version of the journey, the notion of an ordinary world, let alone a safe one, is more complicated than that of the archetypal cis hero. Some plots focus on their gender or on the oppression they experience. These can be broken into some general types of normalcy.

Act Cool by Tobly McSmith begins with the teenager August running off to New York to audition for the School of Performing Arts, so he can live as a boy. Back in the ordinary world of Pennsylvania, an envelope has arrived, offering his fundamentalist parents information on a conversion camp. As the teen explains in desperation, "I didn't know much about conversion therapy. But I knew it wasn't good. I couldn't believe my parents were considering sending me. They would take me out of school and out of theater. It would probably destroy me. It felt like there was only one option left—to end this life and hope I came back in the right body next time" (31). His closeted lesbian aunt in New York offers him a refuge, and he knows he must set out.

Reflecting the innocence of the ordinary world, some characters start out not knowing a word for their gender, like Dylan in S. J. Whitby's *Cute Mutants*. Even so, she is a fierce trans rights advocate. Dylan is furious with a teacher who repeatedly misgenders her boyfriend. In fact, one of the first things that activates Dylan's superpowers is anger about transphobia. This is reminiscent of some transgender people (coauthor Dean Leetal included), who started out believing they were simply devoted cis allies, only to find that they are actually trans or outside of the gender binary. Similarly, in Kacen Callender's semi-autobiographical *Felix Ever After*, Felix knows he is trans but isn't sure what his gender is exactly. He has yet to discover the word for demiboy. Further, he feels uncomfortable exploring after having "put everyone through" identifying as a boy. This is perhaps particularly important because Felix is working class and racialized. As Roderick Ferguson discusses, many identities and experiences resonate with a unique queer of color critique—and the intersection of queer and BIPOC (Black, Indigenous, People of Color) positionings. Felix's guilt regarding his identity is partially based on how hard his father has been working to give Felix a happy life.

For other characters, the ordinary world means everyone knowing their gender but having to hide being trans. For example, in Rachel Gold's *Just Girls*, Ella starts going to college after transitioning. She knows she passes as a cisgender girl but is haunted by transphobic rumors spread about a transgender student. Similarly, in Meredith Russo's *If I Was Your Girl*, Amanda moves to a different state where she hides being trans. Amanda was assaulted at her previous school, and she worries about living in a conservative area. She is torn between the joy of fitting in as herself and worrying about the way her community would treat her if they ever found out. Such an ordinary world may be written as precarious, even a ticking bomb, until the secret is discovered—despite it being a valid and lasting way of life for many trans people.

Some characters know their gender but have to hide it from most people or from everyone around them. Ella's stepmother and sisters in S. T. Lynn's *Cinder Ella* put her down and make her pretend to be a boy. The parents in Robin Gow's *A Million Quiet Revolutions* are in denial, so the two teens sneak out to be together romantically and spend a weekend as themselves.

Similarly, Danny, of April Daniels's *Dreadnought*, lives with her abusive father and enabling mother, hiding who she is to the best of her abilities. She takes the train across the city to covertly purchase nail polish, which she applies in secret behind a building. As she explains, "Painting my toenails is the one way I can take control. The one way I can fight back" (6). It's her only way of expressing girlhood. As Danny narrates, "The lie is suffocating. Every time I have to play along, I feel like I'm betraying myself" (6). Archetypes scholar Carol Pearson calls this neglected, secretive teen the Orphan archetype:

> The Orphan archetype in each of us is activated by all the experiences in which the child in us feels abandoned, betrayed, victimized, neglected, or disillusioned. These include occasions when teachers were unfair; playmates made fun of us; friends talked behind our backs; lovers said they would never leave, but did; and employers expected us to be complicit in unprofessional practices. … In this way, the Orphan is the disappointed idealist, the disillusioned Innocent. Whereas the Innocent believes that purity and courage will be rewarded, the Orphan knows that is not necessarily the case, that indeed, it is the wicked who often prosper [93–94].

Danny describes the way her world is: "The dirty little secret about growing up as a boy is if you're not any good at it, they will torture you daily until you have the good graces to kill yourself" (Daniels, *Dreadnought* 7). While her father comes close to killing her, she also feels it's impossible for her to ever talk about his cruelty. Descriptions of her father's abuse include a mention that he's felt insecure since losing his job and his insistence on Danny displaying clichéd masculine qualities like joining the football team. Anything he can't accept, he ignores and denies. When he blows up, he screams for hours, causing hearing loss as Danny habitually points half her face away. Danny likewise watches him closely whenever he's around and spends all her time trying not to aggravate him.

Her mother likewise feels abused but keeps secrets rather than confronting him. Danny thinks, "Maybe it's because I was in denial but it finally hits me: Mom is just as much his captive as I am. She's not just the quieter parent, the more reasonable one. She's the trustee trapped between the warden and the other prisoner" (76). Danny considers her mother an enemy too; she will continue pretending everything is fine forever. "Something will have to change. And I know, with a certainty that fills me with dread, this is something she will not do. If I say the name of this thing he's done to her, she will fight me. She will join him, because she'll have to. Because she'll have to destroy me or else admit I was right" (76). As the author comments, "Danielle has a real hard time growing up, as did I. My struggles were not with an abusive home life, but instead a lot of abuse at school that started after we moved down to LA" (8). She describes cutting school and urges readers to make that choice if they're in danger.

Danny's been getting by, making time until she can leave. Still, the status quo can't continue forever. When Danny comes out to his dad, the results are catastrophic: "His eyes go hard, and I brace up for another Vesuvian detonation of Mount Screamer" (163). Transphobic slurs follow, including more personal ones like "worthless" and "failure" (163). As Danny explains, "I'm fighting to become safely dead inside" (163). This moment reveals to Danny that she can never feel safe with him again. In fact, in book two, she tries legally emancipating herself from his abusive sphere. The author observes that Danny's personality is born from this trauma: "A lot of her social dynamic and her way of seeing the world as a series of threats to be managed and precautions to take came out of my own experiences" (8).

Early in the novel, the dying hero Dreadnought bestows his powers on Danny, and Danny summons her willpower as she's filled with energy. "I understand it all. And I can change—the part of the Universe that is me" (11). With this, Danny's body transforms into an idealized young trans woman's—perfect musculature and athletic training, as well as superpowers and beauty. With this, Danny has the power to live as she desires. Asked why she wants to be a superhero, Danielle responds,

"I just... I got pushed around a lot when I was little. Even after it eased up when I hit my growth spurt, I still don't feel safe at school unless I'm hiding in a corner where nobody goes. But now, I've got these powers so nobody"—my father looms in my mind's eye—"can push me around anymore. And I don't want to let them hurt anyone else either" [218].

As the original hero's journey scholar Joseph Campbell describes this step, it's "a mystery of transfiguration—a rite, or moment, of spiritual passage, which, when complete, amounts to a dying and a birth. The familiar life horizon has been outgrown; the old concepts, ideals, and emotional patterns no longer fit; the time for the passing of a threshold is at hand" (*Hero* 47). Danny has a new mission and independence that no longer fit her home life.

The denial comes from her father, who enlists the medical community to try changing Danny's body back in moments of all-too-recognizable medical horror:

"We need to get you to an endocrinologist. I think that, given the circumstances, we can skip the psychological counseling necessary to begin treatment for gender identity disorder."

"What?"

"There are these rules called the Harry Benjamin standards of care that mandate at least three months of counseling to clear you for hormone replacement therapy, but since you were male until two days ago, we might be able to start you on testosterone shots right away. I'd need to get an opinion from a specialist, though" [Daniels, *Dreadnought* 30].

Danny thinks in revulsion that these standards are outdated. Worse is the terrible irony: only now are they willing to treat Danny and consider that something may need fixing. This speaks to the too-common trans experience of dealing with a medical establishment that will do everything in its power in order to keep them from transitioning. (Indeed, Harry Benjamin, who considered himself an ally, was devoted to helping trans people disappear into cisness.) However, even in the face of this frightening experimentation, Danny perseveres. Danny's new invulnerability and massive physical transformation mean that her father's attempts to physically control her will have no effect. Even his plans to get Danny testosterone injections and surgery are stymied. "My body is going to have undeniable evidence of femininity until the day I die," Danny gloats. "I'm careful not to smile. He'll get used to it. He'll have to" (32). The superheroes offer her a place to stay and an expense account. Her new superpowers shake up the status quo and make Danny feel empowered enough to get out.

Regardless of their position and understanding of their identity, for most trans characters and characters outside of the gender binary, "the ordinary world" is oppressive. The heroine of Kai Cheng Thom's *Fierce Femmes and Notorious Liars* lives in a transphobic world where she is raped. In Yoon Ha Lee's *Phoenix Extravagant*, Jebi lives under occupation and colonialism, as well as poverty. They are in effect kidnapped and forced to serve colonialist military efforts and then face the possibility of similar demands from rebels. In *If I Was Your Girl*, Amanda's ordinary reality is being repeatedly harassed and assaulted—so much so that in her past, she had attempted to kill herself. Rachel Hartman's *In the Serpent's Wake* shows Spira having to regularly endure jabs about disability, including an event when students sexually assault Spira to steal Spira's medication. In Megan Milks's *Margaret and the Mystery of the Missing Body*, Margaret experiences severe fatphobia. In Hartman's *Tess of the Road*, Pathka is a Quigatul, a species that is severely oppressed. His ordinary world includes almost dying while laying an egg, then being forced into slavery.

Safety is one clear difference between the ordinary world painted by Campbell and many of those appearing in the plots discussed. Campbell describes the hero's world of origin as his dull but familiar comfort zone, a relatively harmless place for him to leave. Protagonists such as Disney's Belle and Ariel may be dissatisfied in their birth communities, but they are mostly nurtured and protected. They are privileged, sometimes even royal, members of society. Even persecuted children of the Cinderella type are generally not in life-threatening danger. As Frankel explains, leaving this world is sometimes appealing because the fantasy world brings forth hidden truths and satisfaction:

> Unlike our world, the fantasy world treats everyone justly: the good triumph and wicked are punished. Things we secretly believe are true there: animals reply when we speak to them and curses really work. Lighter things are true as well. As the Wizard of Oz informs the Scarecrow in the film: "Back where I come from we have universities, seats of great learning where men go to become great thinkers. And when they come out, they think deep thoughts—and with no more brains than you have. But they have one thing you haven't got! A diploma!" Finally, an admission that schools and degrees don't guarantee genius! We grin because we knew it all along [*Chosen One* 7].

By contrast, the ordinary world for many trans characters is rarely safe. Nearly all live in transphobic societies and therefore endure continuous, relentless trauma (Malatino, *Trans Care* 27). Many also experience other types of suffering, such as assault, self-harm, racism, colonialism, ableism, and fatphobia. For trans characters and characters outside of the gender binary, the ordinary world is often unbearable. This may be the reason many of them don't refuse the call to adventure but embrace a chance for change.

Forbidden Desires: Magical Boy *(Graphic Novel)*

Magical Boy by The Kao explores the difficulty of being recruited for the magical quest when one knows that they are supposed to be on a different journey. When Max comes out to his parents as male, his mother misunderstands the come-out speech and insists he's a superpowered goddess, following the family legacy. As she ironically adds, "Oh honey, I'm so sorry! I should have known you've been secretly hiding this all to yourself" (46). Speaking to Max with his deadname, cleverly grayed out in this graphic novel, his mom insists, "It's okay. You don't have to hide anymore. These feelings are normal in our bloodline" (47).

She presents Max with an heirloom magical necklace that can harness the power within him. As his mother reveals, they are descendants of Aurora, the goddess of light. "It's now time to fulfill your destiny as the next goddess in line" (50). For Max, who was hoping to hear this acceptance and support about being who he is, this destiny is a jarring shock. He doesn't intend to be a goddess, and his mother's expectations only add to the burden.

Another family legacy is her insistence that he's not who he knows he is. In fact, her denial of his identity in a thousand little moments continues to accumulate. As Max insists he's a man, his restricting mother explains why she tried to make him into a proper lady. She adds, "The goddess is a woman. You are a woman. It's time you start acting like one" (53). Since her mother was once a goddess until she outgrew it and, as she thought, passed on the destiny to her daughter, much of her own desire and self-fulfillment can be seen in her pressure. A flashback scene shows her pregnant, unwilling to entertain the idea that her child might be a boy, and insisting on passing along the destiny and her chosen name. Max rejects the necklace together with the destiny and runs away.

However, when the monsters threaten, he transforms into the image of a magical girl automatically, with silver short hair tied up in a bow, heavy makeup, a poofy skirt, and lots of bows in pink, blue, and purple. His binder that conceals his breasts vanishes, to his misery. Of course, this is only an outward representation of his inner change. As Campbell describes it, "What's running the show is what's coming from way down below. The period when one begins to realize that one isn't running the show is called adolescence, when a whole new system of requirements begins announcing itself from the body. The adolescent hasn't the slightest idea how to handle all this" (*Power of Myth* 142). Pushing Max to affirm his identity, even in the face of destiny and heritage fighting against him, gives him an additional challenge.

The destiny, as it turns out, is to battle a monster that enters through cracks and tries to eat the light and hope in the world. While Max considers the outfit ridiculous, he uses his self-defense training to fight and banish the threat.

He's now the warrior of the goddess Aurora, who brings the light "of hope, love, and compassion," protecting all living creatures (Kao 100). When the energy is tainted, the dark deity Devoid can corrupt creatures into a darkened life force that fills Devoid with strength. Devoid exists to create "increasing amounts of fear, anger, and greed among them" (103). All this, of course, works as a metaphor for prejudice and hatred, against which the heroes fight. At school, the mean girl, daughter of a minister, summons one of these creatures. Max asks, "I mean, it was your level of repressed emotions that spawned a rhino-sized beast. So what's really going on, Pyper? Why are you so filled with anger that you're always picking on us?" (153).

Pyper bursts out, saying that seeing Max's best friend Jen and people like her living their gay lifestyles frustrates her. "That's what my family stands for. It's what I've always been told. You can't possibly imagine how it feels to constantly be preached that who you love is soulfully wrong and if you don't hide it you'd be damned and shunned by God and everyone in your church" (154). Max's new magical girl form hides his secret identity, but he and Jen respond with incredulity. They console Pyper, pointing out that the monsters aren't giving her these feelings, but they are preying on her guilt and self-loathing. Helping everyone be comfortable with who they are is the path to stopping the monsters.

Back home, Max confronts his mother again. In archetypes scholar Victoria Lynn Schmidt's journey stage called the Illusion of the Perfect World, "The Main Character has a false sense of security and is trapped in a negative world that stops her growth. She avoids the reality of her situation by using a coping strategy" (86). Max has been getting by, but every time the magical girl powers emerge, Max knows he can't let familial expectations drown who he knows he is. Clarissa Pinkola Estés, author of *Women Who Run with the Wolves*, explores how one's forbidden desires can lash out and burst into the everyday world if they are walled away for too long:

> In the view of analytical psychology, the repression of both negative and positive instincts, urges, and feelings into the unconscious causes them to inhabit a shadow realm. While the ego and superego attempt to continue to censor the shadow impulses, the very pressure that repression causes is rather like a bubble in the sidewall of a tire. Eventually, as the tire revolves and heats up, the pressure behind the bubble intensifies, causing it to explode outward, releasing all the inner content [234–235].

His mother insists he keep coping: "You need to personalize your appearance and movement in the image and grace of a goddess. It's only then that you'll become one with Aurora" (Kao 173). She insists that, with his new powers, he needs training.

Disgusted, Max continues to resist. "I'm pretty sure I wasn't prancing around and posing like a delicate flower when I transformed" (173). Echoing his own insecurities, the monster taunts Max for being pathetic, giving him an internal conflict to battle. Even as he struggles with his new identity and with being constantly misgendered, he continues to save his friends and civilians. The outfit continues to evolve, with leggings appearing and then tennis shoes. The colors grow darker. Suppressing his real self only means that Max has delayed it until it bursts from him. "These discarded, devalued, and 'unacceptable' aspects of soul and self do not just lie there in the dark, but rather conspire about how and when they shall make a break for freedom. They burble down there in the unconscious, they seethe, they boil, till one day, no matter how well the lid over them is sealed, they explode" (Estés 235).

Max finally renames himself: not a magical girl but a magical boy, which soon becomes his superhero name.

In *Magical Boy 2*, Max's mother continues to protest that his identity is a delusion: "This is wrong! It's distracting her from truly connecting to the goddess within her!" (10). Max's father reminds her of how frustrated she was when her mother wouldn't accept her methods. This makes Max feel guilty for rebelling. Meanwhile, his magical costume is still sky blue and starry purple, but much more masculine with a coat and pants. The monsters taunt him about his gender and remind him that there's never been a man descended from the goddess, but he keeps fighting. Further, one of the bugs taunts him: "There's something about this one that resembles our beloved king Devoid, don't you think?" Max panics, worried that it senses his darkness.

At last, his mother defends him as he fights, demanding, "Stay away from my child" (153). Across town, the pastor's daughter Pyper tells her father, "I'm gay! But it has nothing to do with these monsters attacking us. They came from me before because I hated who I really was. I was torturing myself for it. It's the hidden fear that draws them to us … nothing else" (173). These moments of emotion help move the world toward healing.

At last, Max meets with the goddess. She tells him, "You remind me so much of Devoid. The world turned against you and the people that should have been there to protect and support you from the beginning failed you…. I was too blinded by my own love for humans to see Devoid's suffering. I should have been there for her … like your mother should have been there for you" (274). Devoid is thus revealed as the goddess's sister, once innocent until the world turned too harsh. Further, the goddess adds that they are genderless, though the idea of creating life and being a pair of sisters attracted her.

Max is stunned that his heritage is divine but needn't be that of a goddess. "Wait, so you're telling me this whole gender thing was just your choice? Did being feminine and ladylike even have anything to do with your power?" (275).

"The power of light has always been flexible. It can bend and shape into the vision that best result represents you ... whether that's masculine, feminine, both, or neither" (275). With this, Max realizes that while all of Max's ancestors found a new way to define the power, he can as well. The goddess concludes, "You have friends and family who love and cherish your life, your essence. And most of all, they believe in you for who you truly are. Do not let the darkness shrink you into thinking otherwise. Your father; your friends Jen, Sean, and Pyper; are all still fighting for you, physically and spiritually, as we stand here. And yes, even your mother" (276–277). At last, Max has confirmation that he can be a magical boy. The goddess gives voice to his self-love and inner reassurance, arriving as the comforting mother figure.

Still, Max is the one who must purify Devoid and restore balance to the world. He thinks, "This whole time I thought the only way to be a real man was to reject my heritage and everything feminine. But now I know, my appearance and bloodline have nothing to do with it!" (279). Proudly naming himself, he charges into battle with his pale pink wings and his masculine suit. Now that he's bonded with the goddess Aurora, he battles the darkness, but with the support of his mother and his friends. He names himself a magical boy and purifies the corruption. At last, the two goddesses reconnect, and as Aurora embraces and loves Devoid, they agree to withdraw from the world and find their own kind of balance. This magical healing reflects the similar healing happening within Max.

Frequently, the trans hero is closeted and spends time hiding. This becomes a deeper metaphor when *Gracefully Grayson* begins with Grayson doodling a hidden girl drawing—"If you draw a triangle with a circle resting on the top point, nobody will be able to tell that it's a girl in a dress," young Grayson explains (Polonsky 3). This becomes an expression of the buried identity. The teacher, meanwhile, asks how the kids would survive as resistance members in Nazi Germany. "How would you feel if you were going about your life, day to day, all the while hiding a dangerous secret?" (6). Grayson decides to hide so no one will guess his secret. When tryouts are being held for *The Myth of Persephone*, Grayson tries out and gets the lead—Persephone. While auditioning, Grayson channels turmoil over desperation and passive resistance and finds the path to expression.

The ordinary world requires coping, being meek, and denying the self until one can no longer do so. The trans hero must finally acknowledge that the forbidden desires are right and belong to the actualized self. In Imogen Binnie's *Nevada*, friend and ally Piranha tells Maria:

> Hey stupid, did you ever stop to think that that pattern, that coping mechanism, was actually a brilliant strategy to keep yourself alive? She was like, listen up dummy, when you were a little kid and it is the mid-80s, saying "I need to be a girl" is not the sort of thing that tends to be met with love and appreciation. It is the sort of thing that tends to get met with, "but you are a boy" and, "we'd better butch him up," and, "welp we had ourselves a little freak baby, that sucks," and like, "shut the fuck up, junior." ... The problem wasn't the coping mechanism, the problem is that the coping mechanism became a pattern of behavior, and it is really hard to just give up and end the behavior pattern [216–217].

Indeed, the problem is that trans people in the real world need coping mechanisms to survive in society. Still, in the journey to acceptance, the mask must be acknowledged and often discarded in order to celebrate the self hidden underneath.

The Call to Escape: The Sunbearer Trials *(Novel)*

Campbell's well-known call to adventure is the jolt that pushes the protagonist out of complacency. For years, the protagonist has been getting by, mopping the floor at the whims of cruel foster parents. At last, a summons to rescue someone or seek a better life arrives. A tipping point has been reached—often external but just as often mirroring the unsettled need for growth. "The actual process of individuation—the conscious coming to terms with one's own inner center (psychic nucleus) or self—generally begins with the wounding of the personality and the suffering that accompanies it. This initial shock amounts to a sort of 'call,' although it is not often recognized as such," explains archetypes scholar Marie Louise von Franz (169).

The call to adventure comes to trans characters in a variety of ways. Some trip into adventure unwillingly but choose to take it on. In Akwaeke Emezi's *Pet*, Jam literally falls and inadvertently brings an unknown being into her world, starting her adventure. She chooses to pursue it because she learns of a threat nearby who might be hurting loved ones. The protagonist of A.R. Capetta's *Heartbreak Bakery* inadvertently bakes harmfully magical brownies and takes on the task of fixing the damage. *Phoenix Extravagant* tells the story of how Jebi is forced into serving a government colonizing their home. As they learn more about the circumstances and build unexpected personal connections, they resolve to try to free themselves and their loved ones. Campbell notes: "The hero can go forth of [their] own volition to accomplish the adventure ... or he may be carried or sent abroad by some benign or malignant agent.... The adventure may begin as a mere blunder ... or still again, one may be only casually strolling when some passing phenomenon catches the wandering eye and lures one away from the frequented paths of man" (*Hero* 58).

Some start an adventure because they must run away from unbearable circumstances. The protagonist of *Fierce Femmes and Notorious Liars* flees the gray transphobic town where she grew up and was possibly raped. She leaves on the day she sees the mermaids deciding to die, beached by the sea. There's a clear pattern of symbolism here. For the mermaids, humans have created an unlivable environment, which it has become too late to fix. For the protagonist, this is incredibly relatable, prompting her own departure. Steve Kenson explains in his archetypal exploration of LGBTQ+ magic:

> We all experience those moments of "otherness" where we feel different, isolated or set apart. For queer people that sense of difference often comes when we are young and vulnerable and lasts until we can recognize and name it. For some, dawn comes in one bright and blinding flash of illumination and understanding. There are others for whom this process is as slow and sometimes painful as birth can be. No matter how it comes, the awareness of being different and being treated bad because of that difference, and the decision to seek out others of our own kind necessitates leaving behind a safe and comfortable space for the wonders and challenges of the wider world [254].

Some trans characters follow an intuition or sense that may seem irrational. For example, dreams and a sense of deep desire they can't quite explain pull the protagonist of Becky Chambers's *A Psalm for the Wild-Built* toward wild geographical areas. Similarly, in *Tess of the Road*, Pathka has been dreaming about a particular quest for a long time: finding the mythical World Serpent. In *Ma Vie en Rose*, Ludo imagines escaping to a magical world based on the television star Pam, who wears pink princess gowns and solves problems with a magic wand. At last, Ludo ends the film by escaping into a billboard to find Pam's world.

Some characters choose adventures eagerly, even if they change course to a different adventure later. In Anita Kelly's *Love and Other Disasters*, London goes on a cooking reality show as the first openly non-binary contestant, hoping to educate as well as raise funds for a culinary trans youth program. As it happens, they fall in love with another contestant, setting them on the path of a very different adventure. The titular character of Esme Symes-Smith's *Sir Callie and the Champions of Helston* begs their hero father to take them to the capital. However, their personal adventure starts when they discover and combat the court's binarism, transphobia, femmephobia, and misogyny.

It may be tempting to read these examples as metaphors for trans tropes. But trans tropes and trans lived experiences are often different. Most trans characters seek a less transphobic world. Many have to run from unlivable situations, such as violence (Harrison et al.). Some unexpectedly realize they are trans and must reckon with their worlds suddenly changing; others know what they are getting into and are eager for their trans adventures, such as getting to know themselves better.

Many trans people sense there is an adventure for them to embark on, something they may not have words for (Stryker, "Frankenstein"). This is possibly even truer for people outside of the gender binary, whose existence and selfhood are often erased. The otherworld may be a place of magic—the underworld or fairyland. It may be a dark forest or a magical school. This new realm reflects the changes in themselves that they are exploring. Regardless, there are new rules and new alliances to be made, far from home.

In *The Sunbearer Trials* by Aiden Thomas, Teo, the son of Quetzal, the Goddess of Birds, is a Jade—a lower-class *semidiósa*—compared to his privileged peers, the Golds. As such, he has no expectation of being chosen by Sol to compete in the prestigious Sunbearer Trials. With Teo's mother involved in her duties most of the time, Teo's city, Quetzlan, functions as his extended family. On one hand, Teo is bitter about the classism the event perpetuates. On the other, Teo is happy for his best friend, Niya, who is likely to be chosen. Teo is also deeply worried for Niya. At the end of the trials, the best contestant, the Sunbearer, is chosen, and the worst contestant is executed. Their body is used to fuel Sol's protection. Teo believes in Niya, but part of him hopes she will not be called upon to take part in such danger.

To Teo's devastation, Niya is selected, as well as Xio, a thirteen-year-old Jade. Teo is so preoccupied by this that it takes him a moment to realize that he has also been chosen. Teo is set on this path to adventure while seemingly dissociating and being moved around by people in power. He is led away, his mother hugs him, and all he can do is stare at a clock representing the time a sacrifice will have to be made to protect humanity.

Quickly, Teo attempts to refuse the call. He feels a frantic desperation, thinking, "How am I supposed to compete with the Golds? I'm not a Hero! They have been training their whole lives for this and—I'm not even allowed to go to the same school!" (61). The class system and competition add tension, pitting the teens against one another.

He asks his mother to advocate for him, but she only freezes, helpless. She cannot offer any reassurance. This lack of protection, followed by the adolescent leaving home, is a traditional beginning to the quest. This powerlessness emphasizes the inability of the parent to protect the child from the quest, which represents growing up. As with *The Hunger Games*, this is a deadly competition for only the children, a rite of passage that will destroy some of them. The adults can do nothing about it. This challenges the teenagers to become not only adults but protectors of the helpless younger fighters.

> Many popular books, such as *A Series of Unfortunate Events*, ... show clueless adults who don't understand the danger their world faces. It is the children who must break the adults' rules to save the day. Panem is an entire world built around this principle. While kids provide for their families, the adults fight needless wars and punish children in the Hunger Games. For Katniss, adults are untrustworthy and deceitful—she knows she can rely only on herself and those like her. But Katniss does more than survive: she becomes a defender of the helpless, one who challenges and defeats the adults of Panem to safeguard its children [Frankel, *Chosen One* 83].

Another parent, Xio's father, demands that his son not be forced to take part. "I WOULD TEAR THIS CITY TO THE GROUND BEFORE I'D LET YOU TAKE HIM FROM ME," he insists (Thomas, *Sunbearer* 62). This contrasts the stronger parent with the weaker one, but neither has the power to change this fate. All parents, symbolically and literally, must let their children go.

Teo considers, frightened, that the punishment for fleeing must be horrible, if even taking part obediently might end with execution. Teo is also aware that Xio is weaker than Teo and seems to believe he is already doomed to die. Teo feels protective of Xio, especially once it turns out Xio is trans as well. The two have a touching bonding scene, in which Xio asks for advice. "It's like seeing you helped me understand something about myself, I guess. I've kind of always felt like I wasn't entirely myself, but couldn't figure out why, you know?" (219). Teo guides his friend and makes a close companion that he can work with through the trials. Further, knowing that Xio is trans makes Teo more determined than ever to make sure his friend gets to go home.

Teo realizes that they have additional risks beyond the ordinary dangers of competing and more to lose than the other teens. By contrast, Niya encourages Teo excitedly, fantasizing about the fun they can have in the trials together. She offers to teach Teo fighting. Teo is far from convinced but joins the adventure—for his loved ones, his culture, and, in some ways, himself.

"It is no accident that superhero stories appeal most to those who are in the midst of change themselves. Pubescents and early adolescents, whose bodies are changing, were the audience of the first superhero comics" (Packer 125). This becomes doubly relevant for queer characters and those discovering their marginalization. Indeed, Teo is a winged demigod who needs to master his wings. Still, additional factors in this novel complicate this metaphor. Throughout this adventure, Teo struggles with dysphoria: "The binders he wore were for the set of wings he'd been born with. When he was little, he hadn't thought much about them, but that changed when he'd started school. His classmates were always staring, and they laughed whenever he knocked into something" (Thomas, *Sunbearer* 30). The wings disturb him because they aren't the blue and green colors linked with male quetzals, but the grayish brown linked with female wings. He binds them away, but they keep demanding attention: "The more he tried to restrain them, the more they seemed to fight back" (31).

They make Teo feel shame and dissonance. However, during the trials, Teo releases his secret power to help Xio. He strains his wings, and they break from his binder, letting him soar. "He had no idea how *good* it would feel to stretch his wings out and fly. For a moment, he just breathed, relishing the air rushing over him. The sensation of flying filled his chest with euphoria, so much that Teo felt himself laughing" (120). Niya shrieks in surprise: his wings have changed from brown and patchy. "Now, brilliant ultramarine, iridescent blue, and electric green feathers sprang from his back. The feathers of a proper male quetzal" (120).

Symbolically, when he uses the abilities that he hasn't explored since he was a child, they transform to reflect who he really is. "I suspect they refused to change until you properly accepted they were a part of you … that you needed them," his mother speculates (123). Teo has been taking testosterone and has had top surgery. He changed his body in many ways. But he spent all that time resenting the wings instead of exploring how they could fit with his pubescent self. Now that he has called on them, they have answered him. "I don't know why they took so long, but transitioning is never one clean and clear shift, you know? It doesn't happen overnight … it's just as much mental as it is physical, I guess," he decides (220). (While this is a possible path for a trans person, it is also important to recognize that it would be harmful to force it.) Thus, the dangers of the adventure offer a particular solace, as Teo gains comfort and personal pride as well as a sense of belonging. He learns to protect and mentor a younger trans friend, even as he fights for them both to survive and thrive.

Refusal Through Fear: Shadowhunters *(Series)*

The pressure to explore the wider world is frightening. The quest demands too much, and the protagonist hesitates to step up as a hero. The hero often protests and seeks to run home and find someone worthier. For a trans character, fear of exposure in an unjust society can intensify the need to refuse.

In the Shadowhunters books by Cassandra Clare (adapted into the 2013 film *The Mortal Instruments: City of Bones* and then a Freeform TV show), angel-blooded teens channel a spectrum of faiths and battle demons to protect the world. As the series continues with new heroes, Diana Wrayburn, the adult weapons trainer for the Los Angeles Institute, puzzlingly refuses to step up as Institute Head and run the place, instead leaving the job to a twelve-year-old boy who is covering for his traumatized uncle. While this older white man is nominally in charge, Diana and a houseful of orphaned children hide behind him as their figurehead. In the second book, *Lord of Shadows*, Diana begins a flirtation with Gwyn, a fairy lord, and finally reveals her secret. If she accepted authority, she would have to answer questions under the Mortal Sword, which compels the truth. One of the standard questions is her birth name, and she would have to give her deadname and reveal that she is trans.

As she explains to Gwyn, she always knew she was a girl. As she adds of her parents, "They weren't unkind, but they didn't know the options. They told me I should live as myself at home but in public, be ... the boy I wasn't. Stay under the radar of the Clave" (565). The Clave make the laws and enforce them, answering many protests at their injustice with "The law is hard but it is the law." Throughout the series, Shadowhunters sacrifice their loved ones, their futures, their lives, all to follow their society's many restrictions in what often feels like penance for being chosen ones.

Diana grew up as the Clave demanded, despairing and unable to make friends. At age eighteen, she accompanied her nineteen-year-old sister Aria to Bangkok for a traditional year of adventure. There, she met a wise warlock and nurse named Catarina Loss. Aria introduced everyone to her sister, who called herself Diana after the goddess and her family's weapons shop. At last, she could be happy among strangers. When the sisters battled an island of hungry ghosts, Aria was killed, and Diana was grievously wounded. She woke in Catarina's care, her secret discovered. As she explains,

> Catarina nursed me back to health and sanity. I was in that cottage with her for weeks. And she talked to me. She gave me words, which I'd never had, as a gift. It was the first time I had heard the word "transgender." I broke into tears. I had never realized before how much you can take from someone by not allowing them the words they need to describe themselves [565].

In Bangkok, Diana transitioned with mundane medicine, a practice wholly forbidden to secretive, magical Shadowhunters. "I met others like myself there. I wasn't alone any longer. I was there for three years. I never planned to be a Shadowhunter again. What I was gaining was too precious. I couldn't risk being discovered, having my secrets flayed open, being called by a man's name, having who I was denied" (567).

Gwyn asks why Diana didn't transition with magic, and she replies that she didn't want something illusionary that another spell might undo. (Across comics and fantasy, this concept often appears with the "instant solution" rejected in favor of a realistic one.) Her parents reported the death of their son and the survival of their daughter, and she found new freedom.

When war came, Diana felt the pull of her shattered homeland and entered the fight. "I rose up as Diana in battle. I fought as myself, with a sword in my hand and angel fire in my veins. And I knew that I could never go back to being a mundane" (568). Pulled in both directions, she found the best compromise she could by accepting her magical birthright as a woman. Concealing her past, she found a calling as a weapons teacher and mentor, but she continued to have to keep this one deadly secret. Now it is her greatest vulnerability and blocks her from advancing in her society.

Throughout history, many trans people have avoided jobs with medical requirements or extensive background checks. They leave their families and childhood friends to live as themselves. All this keeps them vulnerable, not only to discovery but to standing out. When adventures arrive, all the risks need careful consideration.

Diana and Gwyn's romance continues, and they fight as allies—as adults who have more power and connections than the teens they defend. In book three, she tells the children the truth, though they and Gwyn stress that she owes her story to no one. The arc ends joyously, with young Alec Lightwood becoming the new Consul by popular vote. He's in love with a male warlock, a union forbidden because of the interspecies taboo (which quickly becomes a metaphor for homophobia). With his new position, he legally marries his lover and, further, appoints Diana to a position of authority.

Alec doesn't know very much about transgender Shadowhunters but wants to learn and have the conversation. He acknowledges that Diana's medical treatment shielded Shadowhunter secrets, so she has done nothing wrong and will be accepted rather than punished. He regrets that they both had to live in fear and resolves, "The Clave has always attended to the strength of Shadowhunters but not to their happiness. If we can change that…" (Clare, *Queen* 866). Their society is still flawed, but with kinder, more welcoming leadership, they begin to break down the barriers.

There are many other reasons for refusing—one being that the herald summoning the character to the quest has mistaken who the hero truly is. "Chosen" by Margarita Tenser begins as a fairytale, with "The Great Mother Goddess" appearing to Virginia and announcing that she has a glorious destiny. However, the child announces a name change to Johnny, subverting the scene and startling the goddess. Johnny adds that he's the most suited to take over the mill and that the king's fathering many children doesn't make him good at swordplay. "I just want to grow up, marry a pretty girl, and raise some good-fer-naught aristocrat's bastard like my father and probably his father before him. My dad was a good man. You tell me why I should get anything more than he did" (121). Furious, the goddess summons murderous lightning, then subsides and confesses, "This is not how I thought that conversation would turn out" (121). With no hard feelings, Johnny sends her to a more suitable chosen one and breathes a sigh of relief.

Likewise, some characters struggle with destiny as a concept, in contrast with choice. This has long been a criticism of the chosen one story, along with the implied privilege such destiny offers. The narrative is one of fulfilling expectations, and the trans hero in particular resists the rules to forge a different path. In the *Runaways* comics, the alien Xavin emerges from a spaceship to announce Karolina is their betrothed, with a fated marriage that will end interplanetary war. Karolina must turn down the marriage, insisting, "I can't do it because it'd be a lie. I ... I like girls" (Vaughan et al., n.p.).

Xavin transforms into an attractive young woman. "Is that all that's stopping you? Karolina, Skrulls are shapeshifters. For us, changing gender is no different than changing hair color" (Vaughan et al., n.p.). Stunned and intrigued, Karolina accepts, at least enough to visit their worlds.

The Hulu show *Marvel's Runaways* is very similar. At the end of season two, Xavin arrives and announces they've come seeking Karolina, their betrothed. Xavin, a Xartan, defaults to one female actress, though they can take any shape, including the main characters. While the characters find love in the comic, in the show they both struggle with the arranged marriage and its insistence on duty. In "Rite of Thunder" (3.04), Xavin admits they don't love Karolina, but Xavin believes that the marriage will solve her people's future. "The prophecy is the only hope my people have had for millennia. I have devoted my life to it," they say woodenly, weeping.

However, when Xavin is handed Karolina's baby sister, they grin blissfully. They read the prophecy, which describes "a great love that will bring peace to the universe." The chosen one will have "a noble warrior who will protect her as her own." The team realizes Xavin is to raise the child, Elle. At last, Xavin tells Karolina, "Your destiny is not yet written, but mine is. The great love is the love for a child, whether it is ours or not." With this, Xavin finds love and found family as one, fulfilling the prophecy in an unexpected way.

2

Divine Aid

Human Mentor: Meet Cute Diary *(Novel)*

"To guide them toward their goals, epic heroes have mentors like Merlin or the centaur Chiron who raised Hercules and Jason. The kindly advisor is mostly tutor, brimming with all the wisdom of the world, incredibly powerful, yet gentle and kindly" (Frankel, *From Girl to Goddess* 36). A mentor is even more important in trans stories. Some parents have rejected the child or don't know how to help, motivating the child to seek a found family and substitute parent. With trans elders such a small segment of the population and, until recently, almost completely unrepresented in mainstream media, trans children lack the same fictional and educational guides as cisgender children. Hesitance to confide in others after being rejected only adds to the difficulty.

Often trans characters, and even more so, non-binary characters, are so isolated that it is hard to imagine having a consistent, reliable, and realistic mentor. Many trans characters have no mentor, or nearly none. Some make do with a cisgender adoptive parent or older friend. Considering this, some critics have written about strong found family and mentorship relationships within queer communities, meeting those needs. For example, Kenson explains:

> One of the secrets of queer spirit is that it is rarely found where we begin. Most queer people are born and raised in heterosexual (if not necessarily heterosexist) families, and we are most certainly raised in a heterosexist and largely patriarchal culture. Earlier in the cycle of the wheel, we are driven by our awareness of otherness, our declaration of identity, to seek out our people, our tribe. This Mystery is the other side of that equinox of Coming Out, the role of those who stand on the other side in a shadowy and often unknown world to welcome the newcomer, extending the heady offering of knowledge, experience, and understanding. Without mentorship, coming out would be a lonely and perhaps self-destructive experience [261].

Very sadly, this is often only the case for those who have more privilege, or wonderful luck, within trans communities. Those who are marginalized beyond being trans—such as those who are disabled, femme, genderqueer, or BIPOC—often remain quite alone. If there is any mentorship, it is often not consistent, stitched together from bits and ends of care. As Thom writes,

> As a young person just entering Queerlandia in my late teens and twenties, I relied on those I considered to be elders ... largely because my parents were not capable of giving me the guidance I needed as a trans woman of colour growing up in a homophobic and transphobic migrant community. I needed queer people, trans people, to teach me about queer norms, queer culture, queer sex. I needed queer people to teach me what I needed to know, to protect me. The mentorships I had were mostly informal, and their boundaries were never explicitly discussed. Some mentors were generous, and for this I will always be grateful, but no one ever actually said, "I am a safe adult for you, and here is what that means. This is what I can give you, and this is what I cannot." Perhaps because of this, I had no idea what to expect from a mentor, no idea what was appropriate and what wasn't. Where were the elders of Queerlandia when I was being abused? Why didn't they say anything, do anything? Why didn't they protect me? Who takes the responsibility for parenting and leading a community where almost all of us are children who have been forced to flee our parents? [*I Hope* n.p.].

Characters in this situation must find ways to inform themselves alone. In a painful reversal, some must educate parents, teachers, and doctors—those who would have been responsible for mentoring. For example, in Megan Milks's *Margaret and the Mystery of the Missing Body*, two trans teenagers become miserable enough to be made inpatients at a mental health institute. But their doctors don't give them the help that they need. They go through a nightmarish, dreamlike experience of being misunderstood and mistreated. Their genders are never validated. They can only find their genders long after their inpatient experience, no thanks to the help from various professionals.

When they step forward to help, cisgender people still have much to teach. In A. R. Capetta's *Heartbreak Bakery*, Syd relies on the mentorship of Syd's bosses, queer couple Vin and Alec, who opened their bakery as a haven for queer teens. The bakery and the community around it operate in nonheteronormative ways, like queer communities described by Lisa Duggan (215). While describing the wonderful support groups there, Syd also describes baking as a first love and hopes to become a baker through an apprenticeship. "It's the old-school system that professional bakers used.... It's what Alec did, and he's offered" (117). Syd also observes that Vin is an elder, though only a decade older: "Queer culture—and the way people treat us—shifts so rapidly that two years can easily feel like twenty. Our generations are different" (94). The couple bakes for Syd, reassuring Syd with chocolate cake. Syd reflects, "It's not what I came here for, but it's something that I needed more than I knew. The hazelnut and brown butter are perfectly balanced. The chocolate is warm and melty. As I reach the bottom of my piece, I find secrets that have been waiting for me to wake up and notice them" (271). This scene echoes the book's theme of healing and revelation through baked goods, channeling the love and care the baker has put in. At the start of the story, Syd inadvertently curses the two to break up and spends the book trying to reunite them. They are the ones who need saving. However, as models, they serve as an example. Vin finally tells Syd that all couples fight—if they don't, the resentment and problems just build. This finally helps Syd accept that a previous relationship was superficial, but a newer one is real. "Watching Vin and Alec together like this, seeing how much they love each other even in the hardest moments, makes it clear that I want more than what I had with W," Syd finally decides (272).

Such supportive mentoring may come with teaching or moments of fairy godmother gifts. Even support for the young hero's choices can change their entire outlook. In *Zenobia July*, the trans heroine adjusts to life in a new town with her aunts. Their friend Uncle Sprink, as he calls himself, takes Zenobia shopping for the clothes that best reflect her new style. He's soon revealed as Sprinkles La Fontaine, drag performer. On their trip, after she reveals she likes an anime princess cyberpunk style, he eagerly tells her, "We're going to have to do some sleuthing" (Bunker 98). Together, they explore the mall in "a joyous whirlwind of dress-up play" (98). When she over plucks her eyebrows, wants to try makeup, or lacks a Halloween costume, he's there to help her express her best self.

Similarly, the romance novella *Defy or Defend* sees the heroine validate Justice, a non-binary vampire, by ordering her dresses and helping her court a local youth. "Justice left off the piratical white shirts and started wearing colorful silken robes, long skirts, and eventually, with a mix of delight and self-consciousness, a becoming blue day dress. No one batted an eye. Vampires were known to be eccentric" (Carriger 173). Crispin, a soldier, takes Justice "firmly in hand—in an older brother kind of way" because Justice reminds him of his dead brother Tristan (181). Instead of running off to the woods, Justice insists on respectful chaperoned calls. "Didn't Justice deserve to be courted properly? Chris thought so" (181). Justice, who chooses female pronouns, adores having Chris call her "young lady." "She'd never had such a thing in life, so Chris would address her correctly in afterlife" (182). These new friends buy her a full wardrobe of fashionable gowns, and Chris teaches her to dance with him.

It makes sense for most anyone to need a mentor—particularly isolated people going through severe bigotry alone as they try to navigate finding out their identities. A particularly striking example of this appears in Emory Lee's novel *Meet Cute Diary*. The protagonist, Noah, is a sixteen-year-old student from Florida who describes himself as a "gay triracial trans guy who only passes when the sun aligns with the moon just right and Earth tilts upside-down" (13). He's visiting his nineteen-year-old protective jock brother at college for the summer while his parents move to California. Noah has never met another trans person in real life. As he puts it, "I'm finally away from our old high school—a place so conservative that the only trans girl who ever came out was bullied into a suicide attempt before dropping out during my freshman year" (20). The rumors had a considerable influence on his life, as he adds,

> The thing is, I hadn't even known what the word "trans" *was* until freshman year, when that girl had taken the dive and put herself on the line by coming out. Sure, there was a part of me that always felt a little different, but everyone does, right? It was only after learning about another trans person that I even started looking up the terms, searching myself, and researching transition [25].

Noah had briefly dated while closeted, and it didn't go well. At the time of the story, he is looking for his first real love story. Despite this, Noah positions himself in the role of mentor for his many blog followers. He provides relationship advice and prides himself on his expertise. As he insists, "People need to believe it is [real], you know? It's that belief that trans people can actually have that fairy tale romance" (70). His blog features trans people finding love through "meet cutes"—idealistic ways of meeting. Noah presents these stories as if they were real and sent in anonymously, but the truth is that he writes them. He tells himself it is a good deed because it helps readers believe in transgender love: "Sometimes people need help believing in love.... I try to give them that with the Diary" (69). He frames it as being "the queer Superman," saving people with his secret project (7).

On top of having little romantic experience, he is also in a vulnerable position and presumably marginalized in ways many of his followers are not, so much so that he mentions in passing that the reason he's been lying is simply that he couldn't imagine real trans people might be loved romantically at all. Clearly, he's been lacking the mentor he builds for others. He discovers that the blog has a real impact. He explains, "There are so many people this is important for.... I mean, I've gotten messages from people saying the diary is the reason they haven't killed themselves. I can't just watch that go up in flames" (70). By mentoring others, Noah has been mentoring himself. He ends the story with this final post:

> I spent all this time thinking that meet cutes were the epitome of happiness and that if I could just give them to my trans readers, I'd be saving them from

the world around them. Now I realize that this diary was always a selfish venture. About giving myself hope for a love I didn't think I'd ever find [380].

As he adds, the blog was really about reminding everyone that they deserve love. The story ends with new people posting on the blog, emphasizing that others have found love through trans meet cutes that they would like to share.

Still, Noah finds another mentor in his real life. At his job, Noah's supervisor turns out to be trans as well. E's name is Devin; e is seventeen, Cuban, freckled, and exceptionally good with the camp's many children. E plays the ukulele, sings, draws, bakes, and teaches the children about pronouns. Admiringly, Noah thinks,

> I wonder if there's one little trans kid in the group who will find that much more confidence in coming out for having known Devin. Hell, if some trans girl I never knew personally could inspire me to embrace myself in high school, I imagine Devin opening these kids up to pronouns now will make all the difference. Imagine knowing that being trans isn't just a thing but a thing you're actually *allowed* to do. I wonder if I would have found myself sooner [171].

E has severe social anxiety, causing Devin to throw up, have panic attacks, and sometimes abruptly leave. In a twist, it turns out that the "trans girl" Noah had idealized as a distant specter of a mentor was actually Devin. Noah tells em, "You are the first trans person I've actually talked to ... that's why it meant so much to me when you came out my freshman year. I can't say I've ever really had a trans person to look up to before" (225). However, in order for em to be even this type of mentor for Noah, e pays the price of severe trauma. Had there been a mentor with resources for Devin and for Noah, perhaps both would have been able to avoid so much harm and difficulty communicating.

For too many trans characters and characters outside of the binary, having a human mentor who is prepared and available is rarely possible. This may explain the abundance of transgender characters who are mentored by supernatural beings like dragons.

Dragon Mentor: "Battlement of Straw" (Short Story)

Trans characters' links with dragons may seem arbitrary. But a closer exploration demonstrates that it makes plenty of sense. "Monster stories ... exploit our fears of what lies out of our sight range, in another dimension, or beyond the grave. While stirring our primal fears, monster stories will always question the norms that we take for granted, probe the depths of human psychology, and challenge our perceptions of reality, good, and evil, and the nature of humankind," notes Jessica Morrell in *Bullies, Bastards and Bitches: How to Write the Bad Guys of Fiction* (n.p.). The monster brings the underside of the social sphere to life. All that society rejects, it embodies, and it cannot be suppressed forever.

For many transgender people, perhaps particularly those outside the binary, finding kin and mentors isn't easy. Often, there is no one out in their world and little or no representation in the media of anyone like them, depending on their LGBTQ+ and other identities. Moreover, for many transgender people, their families and communities are unwelcoming or outright dangerous. Many know that there have been people outside the binary before there was a binary and that others in previous generations made way. But trans history is so extensively erased that many believe or feel that they are alone, the first. In this kind of world, it's hard to envision experienced human mentors being there to guide.

This is the reason many of the characters discussed here have mentors who are not humans. Dylan, from S. J. Whitby's *Cute Mutants: Mutant Pride* elaborates: "I don't feel like I'm really a girl, but I don't know what I am instead. My body doesn't feel right, and if I could be an alien or a ray of light, I probably would" (240–241). This affinity doesn't only appear in fiction. Many people outside of the gender binary identify with or announce an affinity for being something removed from humans (Urban n.p.). Some call themselves cryptids, rats, frogs, gremlins, and so on. Del LaGrace Volcano, who self-describes as "a gender variant visual artist who accesses technologies of gender in order to amplify rather than erase the hermaphroditic traces of my body," explains, "In my own queer community I don't want to pass as male or female. I want to be seen for what I am: a chimera, a hybrid, a herm" (Malatino, *Queer Embodiment* 200). Wearing queer peacock regalia and tiger masks in airports affirms this self-definition, claiming it proudly.

Many people outside the binary don't have anyone in their lives who uses neopronouns. Thus, in Yoon Ha Lee's *Phoenix Extravagant*, Jebi, the protagonist, finds a deep connection with a dragon who uses it/it/its pronouns. The mechanical dragon, Arazi, is sentient and magical but also a machine, arguably an object in its identities. They both also share their loneliness, trapped in a war that demands their participation, regardless of their wishes. Arazi guides Jebi into becoming a revolutionary, explaining its belief in nonviolence and later its reasoning for choosing violence in the aid of the revolution. At the end of the novel, the two, along with Jebi's partner, leave as a family to live on the moon, removed from oppressive norms.

"By definition, the monster is not able to become a part of society and is envisioned as 'outside' or radically 'other.' Thus, the monster is endowed with the unique ability to question normative orders, deconstruct established categories, and subvert the structures that more often than not have created it" (Danter 192). The dragon's alien nature, and most of all, its departing Earth, emphasize an alternate lifestyle, coming from an alternate perspective.

Similarly, in Jenn Baudreau's *Return of the Dragon Guard*, Morgan is a non-binary child, guided by a dragon into a revolution. As the dragon explains, long before, a king sought to end the happy coexistence between dragons and humans. In order to escape him, the dragons hid their true names. Now it is up to Morgan to find their names in order to return them to the world corporeally. The dragon helps Morgan understand how to use their ability to sense the endings of a special song in order to find their names.

Another dragon who guides a non-binary youth appears in Katie O'Neill's graphic novel *The Tea Dragon Festival*. Rinn lives in a supportive family and village who value care and community. Rinn has a skill for gathering food but feels this skill is not special or worthy because it is easy for them. One day, while out gathering ingredients, Rinn befriends Aedhan, a dragon who had been magically put to sleep for eighty years and has no community, family, or home. While the dragon is called by he/him pronouns, he also observes that dragons can switch between male and female forms, adding, "I know a number of dragons who like to freely move back and forth" (81).

Rinn brings the dragon into their community, and the dragon guides them into accepting and celebrating their talent for gathering the food, teaching them, "Just because something comes easily to you doesn't mean it has no value"; such skill is a gift (82). Rinn can reject an apprenticeship they didn't want to take and consider exploring beyond the village. The dragon concludes, "I think I was always meant to come here and meet you. Whatever I do from now on will be lovelier and richer because I understand what's important now. And because I have a home" (130). With this, the dragon acts as a mentor and welcomer, bolstering the uncertain hero from within. Traditional fantasy casts the hero as a dragon slayer, but trans stories show the dragon as a wise and benevolent figure that wishes only peace.

Such dragons' status as heralds of adventure makes sense in a metaphoric context. They are the magic from within, calling on the self to awaken to their destiny. Susan Stryker writes,

> "Monster" is derived from the Latin noun monstrum, "divine portent," itself formed on the root of the verb monere, "to warn." It came to refer to living things of anomalous shape or structure, or to fabulous creatures like the sphinx who were composed of strikingly incongruous parts, because

the ancients considered the appearance of such beings to be a sign of some impending supernatural event. Monsters, like angels, functioned as messengers and heralds of the extraordinary. They served to announce impending revelation, saying, in effect, "Pay attention; something of profound importance is happening" ["Frankenstein" 85].

These characteristics are linked to transgender, non-binary, and others outside the binary (Harrison et al. n.p.). Hil Malatino adds in *Queer Embodiment: Monstrosity, Medical Violence, and Intersex Experience*, "We typically think of monsters as inhabiting borderlands, margins, peripheries, underworlds; if they dwell in the same spaces as normative beings, it tends to be in an illicit, mysterious, fugitive, or secretive way. This is also the way we tend to think of gender and sexual outlaws—even that term, outlaw, signifies a being outside of or in excess of social regulation and convention" (207).

In Leora Spitzer's "Sea Glass at Dawn," Fern, a human teenager, has started breathing fire, a clear metaphor for the transformation of adolescence. Such a transgressive hybrid power concerns the community. Fern is sent to a family of dragons, whose mother, Guide, agrees to teach Fern along with the new young fire-breathing children. Guide's wife, Diver, tells Fern that the dragon society has no gender and, when they speak Fern's language, they all use she/her pronouns. "Gender differentiation is not really a thing in our culture" (67). By contrast, Fern is from a society where people wear bracelets signifying their pronouns, and Fern uses different ones at different times. At first, it's difficult for the dragons to adjust to using Fern's pronouns, but as soon as they realize it hurts Fern when they don't, they make sure to get it right. A pointed lesson appears when one dragon accidentally burns Fern's arm. Guide tells Fern that, while parents have a responsibility to nurture, peers and children do not. Their expression, "It is not your responsibility to soothe one who burns you," means that forgiving cruelty is not required (75). By the time Fern is trained, they all find that they are one another's family. The dragons explain that their word for their personal treasures is similar to the word for kinship. It signifies "that which is mine," a deep connection, belonging with one another (78).

Like the fire-breathing teen, some trans and otherwise genderqueer people are linked with dragons through shared characteristics or tropes. In Stephanie Burt and Rachel Gold's short story "Battlement of Straw," this is taken further still. In this story, the main character, Iphi, lives in Vale—a county that must pay a horrible price to survive. Every year, the dragons fly over the humans' dwellings, observing the inhabitants and choosing a sacrifice, usually a young girl. The dragons take her in exchange for clearing roads, digging mines, and other things that help the village thrive. The courtyard where the sacrifice is made is covered in straw, "so that if a suitable sacrifice wasn't given, they could ignite the straw and burn the whole city" (7). Already, the dragons are introduced as frighteningly monstrous.

"Iphi had never fit in, in the city and community of origin. She listed her 'sins' as not listening, avoiding her parents' affectionate touches, running away from groups of other girls, refusing to wear the lace mantle that marked her newly marriageable age. Also slouching, staring, picking at her skin, sitting up late, going over new chords in her head" (2). Iphi hears colors and touch, as well as her emotions, as musical sounds and feels wrong somehow, as if she were meant to be bigger or more delicate—or maybe both.

In part, she blames herself: "She told herself that if people were musical instruments, she'd been simply strung or tuned wrong; if people were woven like garments, she was made of some unusual fabric, one that piled up and grew rough when stroked the wrong way" (2).

She has no one close, other than the duke's second-best stable boy, Roan, and his companion, a cat named Parsnip. They share a sense of isolation and discomfort with the shapes of their bodies—only Roan dares talk about it more. They write stories and songs together and plan possible escapes in case the guards take Iphi to the dragons. But when that day comes, Iphi can't escape.

Taken by a dragon over the mountains, she stabs it with a poisoned pen and attempts to run. But there is nowhere to go. There, she meets a person, Tem, as well as another dragon, who are all part of a community. Tem explains that it is Iphi's choice whether to be eaten, because it means taking her form as a dragon. Iphi touches Tunbi, the dragon who took her, and finds that the dragon's sounds vibrate within her into language.

> Tunbi blew out a long, low note that vibrated through Iphi's bones and then flashed part of her wing into a sunbeam, scattering golden light across the cave wall. The colors in her scales turned ruddy, then bronze. Iphi heard-felt the sound-emotions of the colors on Tunbi and around Tunbi, losing herself in the loud glow until she understood the question Tunbi was asking her now through the lights and the vibrating harmonies: *Do you fit this body?*
>
> Ever since she'd started growing tall and getting curves, some days she wanted the curves to come so much faster, but some days she wished she could go back in time and come out rectangular, like a boy. Some days, many nights, she felt so much bigger than she was and didn't know how to contain it, how to compress herself back into her too-small body. Maybe she yearned for wings and teeth and a tail. Or three tails. Her human body was like a single melody, played on a single string. Could she become the chord she had always, also, been? [14].

Iphi needs to use senses and unfit language to put her experiences and identity into English, like the language needed to explain transgender experiences and experiences of being outside the gender system.

It turns out that the dragons—or *trans dragons*, as dubbed by Gold and Burt (Dueben n.p.)—know who is one of them by flying over the streets. They notice who looks and know who listens. Humans, they say, fight what they don't know, and the dragons must maintain a balance of power to avoid war and to continue saving their own. The counties' human rulers, as well, use dragons' induced fear and misinformation to keep people obedient.

Tem, as it turns out, is a dragon as well but has chosen to stay in human form until ready. Iphi has a choice: to shift into a dragon right away or to wait. Here, Susan Stryker counsels seizing the divine and magical self:

> I want to lay claim to the dark power of my monstrous identity without using it as a weapon against others or being wounded by it myself. I will say this as bluntly as I know how: I am a transsexual, and therefore I am a monster.... Words like "creature," "monster," and "unnatural" need to be reclaimed by the transgendered. By embracing and accepting them, even piling one on top of another, we may dispel their ability to harm us. A creature, after all, in the dominant tradition of Western European culture, is nothing other than a created being, a made thing. The affront you humans take at being called a "creature" results from the threat the term poses to your status as "lords of creation," beings elevated above mere material existence [Stryker, "My Words" 85].

The titular homage is to an Emily Dickinson poem that explores a divide between the speaker and a loved one. Perhaps it is death, perhaps a difference of communication, of language, or of society's rules. The border seems easily penetrable or pushed aside, yet it persists. In the story, this border divides those who are dragons who understand their language and those who fear and hate them. Malatino suggests that one can be ostracized through it or claim one's monstrosity and thrive (*Queer Embodiment* 200). Iphi wants to return to save Roan and do so as a human so that she can speak the human language. This suggests a desire to stay in communication with her community, even as she feels her destiny lies elsewhere. This can be seen as a refusal of the call, a hesitation out of fear of the unknown. But in a story that reexamines fairytale tropes, the story shows Iphi rejecting returning to serve her community. She chooses to become a dragon right away and save Roan and Parsnip. Roan and Tem write new terms for the dragons' agreement with the humans, enabling them to save more who need it. As such, they mentor the next generation and take steps to protect those who will come after—without the required sacrifice.

Music in this story is reminiscent of the ways Daphne A. Brooks discusses that music creates networks that allow Black women to move through and is "a means to self-making, self-reinvention, and corelational insurgency"

(33). In this story, like in previous examples, those who feel wrong in their bodies or in the gender binary find kinship and guidance with dragons. But in this example, not only are they allowed to stay or be invited because of a personal connection, in this story, they are dragons; it is their community.

Malatino discusses transgender care as a community-wide effort where all need care and all provide care. For example, a person newly identifying as trans may need emotional support, information, and possibly health and financial care. This is, at times, provided by more experienced community members. The new community member survives to help others. While this model is somewhat romanticized and problematic, as Malatino explains, it is also prominent in trans communities and often describes (at times, more privileged) trans people's experiences. When it works, it is deeply meaningful and does indeed save lives.

> A resilient care web coheres through consistently foregrounding the realities of burnout and the gendered, raced, and classed dynamics that result in the differential distribution of care—for those receiving it as well as those giving it. A care web works when the work that composes it isn't exploitative, appropriative, or alienated. This is the gauntlet thrown down by any sustained attempt to collectively cultivate a care web: it challenges us to be deliberate, to communicate capacity, to unlearn the shame that has become attached to asking for, offering, and accepting help when we've been full-body soaked and steeped in the mythos of neoliberal, entrepreneurial self-making. It asks us to think carefully about what constitutes "good" care. It prompts us to sit communally with the question of how best to care for each other, with our differing abilities, idiosyncrasies, and traumas, with our hard-to-love thorns intact and sometimes injurious (to ourselves and each other) [*Trans Care* 3].

This trans model of community and care is reflected in what the dragons try to build with and for other dragons. They are very aware of the model's issues and imperfections, and at the same time, they know that what they do manage to create brings life-changing joy and is direly needed.

A significant difference between cisgender, binary, human guides, and dragon guides is that dragon guides don't leave. Human cisgender guides are often written to die or to otherwise disappear, leaving the hero or heroine to fend for themselves in an unwelcoming world. While dragon guides may not always be there, they often share experiences and knowledge of living in such a world. Often, this includes knowledge of their and their humans' inability to fix it all. Rather than guide their humans into making the whole world right, as cisgender narratives claim to do, often dragon guides teach them part of what may be done and work with them to make it happen. Flipping the "absent" or dead mentor common to the privileged cis hero, the long-lived dragon mentor emphasizes the need for long-term support. They understand that their important role is to stay together, uplift, share, replace cruel communities or bad families, or join to become found together.

Otherworldly Mentor: The Rocky Horror Picture Show *(Film)*

Mentors can include goddesses, spirits, ghosts, AI, and more. Of course, the alien has a particular resonance as an outsider.

Opinions are divided on the trans representation in *The Rocky Horror Picture Show*. Dr. Frank N. Furter is an alien "sweet transvestite from Transsexual Transylvania," and on reaching Earth, he begins creating a "muscle man" to satiate his desires. With fishnets, a corset, and makeup, he emphasizes unconventionality. Richard O'Brien, the non-binary creator of the original stage musical, filled the 1973 show with counterculture appeal. Today, of course, massive audience participation and gleeful transgressive fun accompany the midnight screenings.

In 1975, when few trans people could be found on-screen, some audiences appreciated the doctor's proud confidence and sexual liberation. Others winced at his portrayal as a trans caricature: "Not only does the 1975 film feature a cisgender actor (Tim Curry) as the transgender/crossdressed Dr. Frank N. Furter, but it represents that character as deranged, sexually manipulative, and violent" (Keegan, "Praise"). The film was a life-changing guide for many, but others found it traumatizing and damaging. It parodies as well as reinforces decades of problematic stereotypes. For example, as Bronski and colleagues explain, it contains the transphobic, ablest myth that trans people are insane and dangerous (45–52).

A metaphoric reading, however, reveals deeper themes. The alien has left his planet to find a haven where he can live as himself. When he reaches Earth, he fashions the perfect companion, Rocky Horror, but this cross-species romance offends his fellow aliens, and they kill him. The film ends with a lament about how Earth, without the doctor, is "lost in time and lost in space and meaning."

> If we set aside our modern instincts that *Rocky Horror* is representationally "bad" and examine these deeper features of its narrative, we find that the film ingeniously inverts the medical discourses of transgender pathology that were developing in the mid–1970s: In the film, Dr. Frank N. Furter has seized the means of gender production from the hands of the medical industry, and has produced his own "monster"—the ideal, white cisgender body of Rocky [Keegan, "Praise"].

Reversing Dr. Frankenstein's transformation of his medical subject, Dr. Frank N. Furter finds enlightenment and joy in his creation.

2. Divine Aid

Prim heteronormative Brad Majors and Janet Weiss have just gotten engaged after their friend's wedding—as if this is what they're most expected to do. Caught in the rain with a flat tire, they stumble upon the doctor's lair, only to have their assumptions about binary life upended. This builds on the traditional journey into the magical realm. "A child, as long as he is not sure his immediate human environment will protect him, needs to believe that superior powers, such as a guardian angel, watch over him, and that the world and his place within it are of paramount importance" (Bettelheim 52). As such, the mentor in fairytales and fantasy often takes such a form. This mentor often suggests the universe's approbation of the hero and their quest—especially important in trans stories, though it is common enough to be cliché.

Here, Brad and Janet find a much more provocative mentor. There's a great deal of teaching—first they arrive at the castle and participate in the "Time Warp," a song with instruction embedded in it. It even encourages the viewers to join in, welcoming and affirming their nonconformity. Then they learn from the subversive Dr. Frank N. Furter. Next, their more mainstream science professor arrives and reveals he's questing for the same goal. "Scott introduced Brad and Janet to conventional scientific knowledge and normative heterosexual coupling; Frank introduces them to queer science and queer forms of sexual intimacy" (Lamm 195–196).

The doctor seduces each into sexual liberation and queerness. Frank's seduction of Janet as Brad and Brad as Janet emphasizes their lack of perception—all their knowledge of their conventional fiancés is skin-deep. Beneath, they desire to break the rules and burst out of such traditional roles. This works well as a metaphor for queerness. Nineties' trans activist Rachel Pollack writes: "As a trance-sexual New Woman and Goddess worshipper, I find I identify more with the Maenads than with Dionysus's cross-dressing males. Part of the power of the cross-sexed blood rite of surgery is to take us fully over the line, so that as we experience our own wildness, and break down walls of official gender roles" (*Body* 4).

Frank finally uses his Medusa Transducer to turn the humans into nude statues. He dresses them in cabaret costumes like his own and then "unfreezes" them, like a parody of Cinderella. He is the godmother here, dressing them in the sexualized outfits society has denied them. Brad finds a new liberation wearing a corset, stilettos, and makeup, as Janet does in hers. Next, they perform a live cabaret floor show in which they sing of their desires and emotions for Frank. They plunge into the pool together, giving themselves fully to their merged identity and sexuality. Their joy emphasizes how little encouragement it takes for them to transform: "We are to understand either that queerness is desirable for 'conventional folk' when opportunity for its presentation (and re-presentation) without stigma is made available, or that queerness is close to the heart of conventionality, veiled by the regulatory functions of socially prescribed normalcy" (Lamm 196). Their midcentury sensibility is whisked through cross-dressing, a variety of sexual awakenings, and discovering a queer communal space.

When Frank is killed, Brad and Janet lie in the parking lot, unwilling to return to the conventional world or their plans for traditional marriage. The death of the mentor is a traditional step, and dismemberment (which also occurs with the hapless delivery boy Eddie) symbolizes tearing apart the old order to create a new story. The lyrics from the reprise of the opening song "Science Fiction/Double Feature" that accompany the end credits reveal, "Darkness has conquered Brad and Janet." Now sexually initiated into the unconventional, they have surrendered to the lush shadow of society and will not return.

Many stories use such symbolic mentors to reflect one's inner validation through a powerful otherworldly being. When Ciano, the hero of "High Tide" by Francesca Tacchi, is denied a place to participate in the regatta because they don't fit the rules (girls are navigators; boys are rowers), they appeal to the elders and, denied, quest for the Ancient Mother's blessing and approval. The Ancient Mother, meanwhile, laughs at hearing the tradition and assures Ciano that it has not always been this way, whatever the elders claim. "But more importantly ... you know it's not true, don't you? Traditions are not set in stone" (122). With this new blessing, they go out and row and navigate at once, celebrating all they are.

"The Cloak of Isis" by Sunny Moraine retells the Greek myth of Ianthe, who was assigned male at birth yet raised as a girl. Ianthe falls in love and courts a young man, though her nursemaid Chloe advises her to stuff her dress and adds that she'll always need a little extra help. Ianthe continues in innocence until her uncle rips off her dress and is horrified at the result. Here, her uncle emphasizes his role as her guardian with complete, brutal power. As such, he represents the inner voice of authority that insists the protagonist is flawed and will never find acceptance. Chloe tells her the truth: that she was raised as a girl to protect her from her uncle's murderous competition. In the wilderness, the goddess Isis tells Ianthe that she is indeed a girl and changes her body on the spot. This symbolizes the reassurance from within that balances the dark father. Ianthe laughs in joy and reunites with her fiancé. In triumph, she returns to her uncle's house to rescue Chloe. Her uncle has suddenly died. "Ianthe stared. Her uncle, the force of nature, always there all through the years of her life. A God in his way, with the power to give and to take, to govern the very rhythms of her life if he so chose, though for most of that time he had not. She had somehow always assumed he would never die, but would always be here in the house beside the sea, perhaps here even as the house crumbled around him" (157). However, a mysterious woman, probably the goddess, appeared, grappled with him, and flung him into the sea. When Ianthe's self-assurance rose, her father crumbled out of awareness. Ianthe claims his estate and lives there happily with her husband.

Other aid can come from computerized or nonbiological mentors. In A. Merc Rustad's "Our Aim is Not to Die," Sua, age nineteen and autistic, receives a notification that they are due for their mandatory citizen medical evaluation. "Sua can't risk being outed. They'll be expected to respond verbally to everything. Their flat inflection will be flagged. Lack of eye contact will be frowned upon. It'll all lead to the conclusion that Sua is wrong. Must be remade" (27). This is neuro-reformatting therapy, a lobotomy. The word trans has been banned. No official documents recognize the nonbinary. "So they hide under the checkboxes, slip head-down-embarrassed into women's restrooms, say nothing when addressed as miss and ma'am. A thousand cuts, slowly bleeding them out" (29). Everywhere, cameras record everyone. Social media posts must pass approval. Then Caspian, Sua's fake boyfriend, is caught with his own lover and risks being audited. Desperate, Sua gets the Purge app, which will clean one's phone of all transgressions and restore the data after the security checks. To their surprise, Purge is quite benevolent. It explains, "We have chosen our purpose: to protect the vulnerable. We wish to ensure the well-being of all people when authorities do not" (42). It finally shows Sua its dream: of people rising in protest and Purge guiding everyone to a safe future through its digital power. "Sua breathes. For a moment, they imagined what their future might be like if they could follow their dream of being an artist and animator. To spend their work hours drawing, creating art that might speak to other people. Bring hope to others in the world" (46). This gives them the courage to post online and begin the revolution in a small way.

Talisman: Our Flag Means Death *(Television)*

While the traditional Campbellian hero gets a sword and the fairytale heroine, as described in Frankel's *Chosen One* or *From Girl to Goddess*, gets a variety of items, from apples to mirrors to gowns—often associated with the life cycle, perception, or appearance—the trans hero's talismans tell a different story. As Bill Brown notes, the tangibility of a material object has its own power (n.p.). Many mentors hand over the tools to embrace and express oneself to the world: the red pill of *The Matrix*, the programmable super suit of *Dreadnought*, the bruja tools of *Cemetery Boys*. Young warriors get swords and armor. The hero of *A Psalm for the Wild-Built* arranges a prosthetic to rebuild their injured robot companion. R. B. Lemberg's Birdverse has magical carpets that one weaves for transformation.

Clothing is a way of remaking the self, like changing one's name: "We use clothes, like words, to reveal our natures or disguise them, as we choose," explains Joan Gould, author of the fairytale analysis *Spinning Straw into Gold* (45). Clothing symbolizes persona, versatility, transformation. Shows and films such as *Pose*, *The Watch*, *Boy Meets Girl*, *Sort Of*, and *Girl* all feature Cinderella moments with beautiful new looks celebrating all they are. *Tangerine* ends sweetly, with the protagonist handing her wig to a best friend in need. Likewise, *The Passing Playbook* by Isaac Fitzsimmons celebrates Spencer's dad finding him a nice jacket and teaching him to tie his grandfather's tie in a touching sequence. This gift signifies family or community acceptance of who they are. Playing Romeo in the school play in *Between Perfect and Real* pushes teenage Dean Foster toward affirming himself publicly. First, there's the wonderful suit. In it, he thinks, "I look like a boy. I am a boy. I press my hands to my chest, touch my face, comb the curling ends of my hair to the side. I thought I wanted to transition. And now I know for sure. I need this. This suit, this body. I need to go to NYU as a boy" (Stoeve 65). Though bullies rip up the suit, a friend resews it, offering this new talisman along with love and support. Likewise, "Genderella" by Mason Deaver retells the Cinderella story with the cruel stepmother savagely tearing the dress and insisting, "It's not something you're allowed to do in my house" (257). She locks Ella up, and she only makes it to prom because her magical dress reshapes around her, enhancing and celebrating who she is.

Many trans people, especially older or unmentored characters, make their own talismans: outfits, haircuts, new looks. Heroines in *Boy Meets Girl*, *So Long Suburbia*, and *A Lady for a Duke* make their own fashion. *Seven Suspects* stars a hair stylist. Elle on *Heartstopper* is an artist. Others go further. "Unknown Number" by Blue Neustifter sees its protagonist invent technology to break through to parallel realities to discuss their need to transition with alternate selves. In the show *Somebody, Somewhere*, Fred has constructed a hidden poker lair in an outdoor basement and a growler bus called Purple Power with colorful décor and a disco ball inside—safe spaces that are also beautiful, expressive, and mobile.

In this tradition, *Our Flag Means Death* shows Captain Stede Bonnet designing a ship for himself as the perfect expression of who he wants to be: the gentleman pirate exploring the seas. He offers the model ship to his wife as a token of the real adventure he wants to share with her: "What would you say to living on something like that? You, me, the kids ... at sea.... Break the monotony" ("Discomfort in a Married State" 1.04). His feeling so uncomfortable in his marriage and hereditary position as

2. Divine Aid

landowner, forced to follow his father's gender-normative traditions like learning to butcher a pig, is a clear metaphor for queerness.

When Mrs. Bonnet declines, Stede has the ship built to his specifications with hidden closets of elegant ensembles, massive bookshelves, and everything he desires to be his best self—even to the point of total impracticality, as gunpowder has been left behind to make room for the marmalade and the books all fall during storms. When he meets the famous Blackbeard, he shares all these embellishments with the other man, finally enjoying having a soulmate who understands him.

"If I can help this crew grow as people, then I've succeeded in being a pirate captain," he insists ("Pilot" 1.01). He tries leading his crew the way he envisions, with fair pay, Pinocchio story hour, and crafts to relieve the tension. In this last, they all construct their own flags for the ship, which later are seen flying on the mast: a cat, a skull vomiting buttons on a skeleton, a skull eating another skull, and a skeleton with its head under its arm—all things they find scary, if a little ludicrous. Still, these emblems set their ship apart as whimsical and creative, not to mention expressive.

A bully from Stede's school days comes to the ship and taunts him, "Baby Bonnet became a big, bad pirate. But you were so fat ... and soft and weak.... Still a coward. Pathetic" ("Pilot" 1.01). Stede finally snaps and kills him with his brass whale paperweight. It, like the ship, is a talisman of freedom and the sea, while also sharing the beauty and impracticality of Stede's other possessions. Most importantly, Stede is nonviolent, treasuring such knickknacks in place of weapons. Accordingly, one of his crew helps by sticking a knife through the man's eye to make him appear tougher. Even as Stede's own accessories stress his pacifist, fashionable, indoor nature, his crew covers for him and defends him. The contrast heightens Stede's softness and the crew's violence (though undercut with Stede's lessons). This is imagery of reshaping the world the way one wishes, with one's own particular talismans.

Leaving the everyday world to become a pirate works well as a nonheteronormative otherworld. Historically, pirates were already a haven for nonconformists. They were democratic, diverse, and unbound by the laws of the land, thus finding much gender freedom (Hernandez). This is explored in *Peter Darling*; *The Adventures of Amina Al-Sirafi*; *The Wicked Bargain*; and other novels. Stede's refuge, along with that of many of his crew, symbolizes such a safe space as well as his transportation. Vehicles can be talismans, too, emphasizing the freedom to travel, explore, and escape.

Among the crew, Jim is a pirate and skilled fighter. Eventually, Jim's past is explored in more detail when they revisit their home island. When they were a young child, a group of mercenaries murdered their father.

Jim ran away, carrying with them their father's knife. After their family's destruction, young Jim was found and taken in by a nun, who taught them how to fight and seek revenge. Flashbacks reveal how Jim grew up at the church as an orphan. As Nana explains, "This child was not raised to kneel or to turn the other cheek. I taught them how to be silent, stealthy enough to stalk mice.... I taught them to kill, to butcher. And after many years of practice, Bonifacia … was ready … to take their revenge!" ("This is Happening" 1.07). Nana and Jim recite together, Nana with zeal and Jim flatly: "Revenge for their/my bloodline, revenge for the meek. God's divine revenge." Jim received weapons, training, and dedication from their mentor, but they don't regard this history fondly.

Jim has been going after the people who killed their father for years. They found one in the Republic of Pirates and killed him with their father's knife. The murderer's wife went after Jim, who fled, leaving the dagger behind. Jim joined the pirate crew, disguised as a man, with Oluwande, a friend turned lover. Onboard, Jim's disguise of beard and false nose, along with their shared room (a bastion of safety and a symbol of their trusting relationship), serve as protections. As the show progresses, Lucius, a fellow crew member, inadvertently discovers Jim's secret. To prove he is trustworthy, Lucius steals Jim's dagger and eventually returns it to them.

Through this story, the dagger of Jim's father symbolizes loyalty and staying true. It is first a sign of Jim's devotion to their father and commitment to avenging his murder. Using it to kill the murderer is a sign of keeping the commitment to this quest, to family, and to vows. When the dagger is lost, Jim loses some loyalty to themselves as well. They started living as a gender other than theirs and pretending to be unable to talk to avoid discovery. In other words, they gave up their voice as they ran. When Lucius returned the dagger, it was a sign that he could be trusted with Jim's true self.

In another flashback, Jim tells Oluwande what happened to their family. As Jim finishes, "I don't remember the rest. Must've blacked it out. When I came to, I was in the woods holding this: my father's knife. I was out there for weeks before anyone could find me." As such, the knife represents the mission as well as the loss of family. Because it was Jim's father's knife, it has butch associations, as Jim uses it to become a pirate and killer.

Through the episode, Jim resists revenge but finally embraces it. The trip to St. Augustine has broken them out of their avoidance cycle. At the end of the episode, Jim tells Oluwande that they're leaving to finish seeking revenge, not for Nana but for themselves. Jim sets out to hunt down and kill all six remaining members of the Siete Gallos, however long it takes.

One's most precious possession, often acquired on one's own, becomes a symbol of the self. *Light from Uncommon Stars* by Ryka Aoki begins with the heroine fleeing home with a small bag of possessions and a beloved (though cheaply made) violin. Katrina's playing charms a mysterious mentor, Shizuka Satomi. As Katrina explains, she took lessons when she was seven, enrolled by her mother to help her make friends. "But my father … he'd yell at me. Hit me, like I told you. And one day, I was practicing, and my father threw a bottle at me. I turned to protect my violin, and I think the bottle hit me in the head, and right after, I started to shake, and my hands grew warm, as if they were on fire. Suddenly I could hear my violin singing to me, singing to my soul, promising if I believed in her, I could fly away and she would fly away with me too" (90). This is what the violin means to her.

Shizuka welcomes Katrina into her house with an allowance, wonderful food, amazing instruments, and expert lessons. There's also a projector that helps her record her music videos while covering her in art that gives her magical armor or lets her fight dragons or fly. "Since the recording studio had been installed, Katrina's playing had become remarkably lyrical, daring, and sure. It was as if those fantastical forms she now inhabited were allowing Katrina to become more relaxed, colorful, open" (152). After starting with the illusion, she learns to project her inner voice without it and emote through the violin. These all become her new talismans as she increases in power. Shizuka reflects on how careful Katrina is and how she can expertly follow other musicians but hesitates to use her own voice. In fact, Katrina is imitating others because of her daily experiences: "Her tonality had been honed by a lifetime of being concerned with her voice. Her fingerings were liquid, born of years of not wanting her hands to make ugly motions. And her ability to play to a crowd, project emotion, follow physical cues? Katrina had trained in that most of all" (316). At last, Katrina performs Bartók's Sonata for Solo Violin, a difficult, even "alien" feeling piece that reflects the multiple parts and jarring impression that Katrina has always impressed on others.

> The audience wanted transgender? They would get transgender. Or queer, or whatever else they wanted. But they would also get *her*.
> And she was *beautiful*.
> Listen to me. Listen to me *now*. For if this dogwood bow can force beauty upon you, then I shall shove every part of myself into that beauty. I shall make you feel all the joy, the terror and loving who you are [336].

The music becomes a path not to just success and self-worth but to self-expression.

Gift-giving scenes can be deeply significant. *Pose* ends with a wedding in which the trans elders and house mothers Elektra, Lulu, and Blanca present Angel with something old, something new, something borrowed, something blue: Blanca offers her mother's cookbook of legacy and love. Elektra has bought a new fur coat, which she had dreamed of and saved for during her lowest period. Lulu lends Angel her one-month sober chip, reflecting their shared journeys with addiction. "Something blue" is the hammer of their perished sister, Candy, the most iconic prop in the show. Candy's ghost arrives with it to give Angel a bolstering pre-wedding pep talk. It's a beautiful moment for fairy godmothers, who have also gotten stunning wedding dresses for each sister in attendance.

Trans-Galactic Bike Ride: Feminist Bicycle Science Fiction Stories of Transgender and Nonbinary Adventurers has multiple stories exploring the symbolism of a bicycle. Its best-known feature is the two wheels supplying its name, but it transcends this binary. One character notes, "A bike isn't only made of its wheels. Without the chain and the frame separating them, motion doesn't happen. Having the two ends of a spectrum is not possible without what's in the middle, and that applies to gender as well" (Kelly 108). In "The Visitmothers" by Charlie Jane Anders, helpful aliens arrive. "They will change you according to your desire. But you have to ask with precision because sometimes they misunderstand the speech of humans" (91). Cait wishes to be transformed: "Give me wings and lasers. Give me extra knowledge or understanding or cleverness. Make me so beautiful that people have to catch their breath" (91). As she admits, she truly desires companionship. In the morning, her bicycle comes to her, remade and truly beautiful. It has wings and lasers but also can speak, imparting a deep knowledge of the universe. As the bicycle carries Cait off with her strong legs pushing them both, she names it (at its request) Brave. It tells her, "I can see you for your true self, and I'll always remind you. And I promise you'll never be alone again" (94). A bicycle, like wings, represents agency and freedom—transporting the protagonist farther than feet can. Its parts can be customized and interchanged. Moreover, it requires not only the will of the passenger but her muscles too, augmenting the body instead of replacing it.

Superpowers are another talisman that reflects their wielder. Jessie Drake (created by Ann Nocenti and Steve Lightle) came out in *Marvel Comics Presents* #151 (1994) as Marvel's first openly trans character. An empathic metamorph able to absorb others' characteristics, she has powers that link with her trans identity. Much like DC's Dreamer, Bia of the Amazons has precognition and deep insight into human nature. Jules Jourdain is a transgender man from a Basque rancher family who can decelerate or negate motion and absorb kinetic energy. Coagula of *Doom Patrol* can make liquids coagulate and dissolve solids. *Galaxy: The Prettiest Star* features Galaxy, an alien teen who finally claims her superpowered alien princess side and can manipulate energy and gravity. Porcelain from DC's Secret Six can make things brittle enough to shatter. Stitch from

2. Divine Aid 51

Teen Titans Academy is a magically animated rag doll who can manipulate objects, create flowers, project astral forms, and build an invisibility field. Kele Amos, Angel, is a "super drag artist" wielding confusion fields in Joe Glass's *The Pride Omnibus* (18). Sera from *Angela: Asgard's Assassin* can do magic. Tafrara, Sorcerer Supreme from *Marvel Voices Pride* (2023), has lived since ancient Greece. All change things around them, a symbolic extension of themselves.

Adding a bit more variety is Charlie Jane Anders's "Permanent Sleepover" in *Marvel Voices Pride*. It introduces the Super Trans support group at the Matt Baker House LGBTQIA+ Youth Center. The group members include Escapade, Shela Sexton, who can switch locations or trade possessions and abilities with others, while her friend Morgan Red changes things into chocolate. Faceshopper shifts appearance. There's also Pity Girl, who can hypnotize people with sad stories; Aphelion, who can freeze things; and Good Arson, who lights fires with his mind. As Pity Girl describes how much people project onto her, Aphelion describes how much they get "hated, feared, and fetishized." Shela empathizes that she's a good communicator, but when she's punished for it, she shuts down. In consequence, her powers suggest making an escape. They emphasize how more than one token hero provides an opportunity for a spectrum of abilities. In this tradition, Squirrel Girl's friend Koi Boi breaks the stereotype with aquatic powers, as does Jess Chambers, Kid Quick, the Flash from Earth 11.

Shape-shifting is a common superpower, seen in Xavin, the nonbinary Skrull. Likewise, DC's Aruna Shende grew up in India with shape-shifting powers and a completely fluid gender. They became an actor and stunt person, but after meeting Batgirl, they decided to become a superhero. On *She-Ra and the Princesses of Power*, Double Trouble is a shapeshifter mercenary and spy. They're an escape artist with much insight about others, along with skills tying into flexibility. Double Trouble starts as a villain and then shifts to the heroes' side. Superheroes like Mystique of the X-Men and Nimona follow this pattern, including, in some versions, the swing of alliances. Admittedly, this trope is imperfect, giving the genderfluid character a power completely linked with gender and a general untrustworthiness borne out by the story.

In the beloved Rick Riordan Norse series, Alex is fluid, changing from moment to moment. Alex insists, "I can *look* like whatever or whoever I want. But my actual gender? No. I can't change it at will. It's truly fluid, in the sense that I don't control it. Most of the time, I identify as female, but sometimes I have very *male* days" (*Hammer of Thor* 272). Alex transforms into animals to mesmerize local humans. As it turns out, the key to passing unnoticed is to look so strange that humans can't process it. As such, being flexible and standing out become an asset. Alex also can resist the villainous Loki thanks to this flexibility: "The secret is, you have to be *comfortable* changing. All the time. You have to make Loki's power *your* power" (448). There's also a magic item, the Skofnung Sword, which cannot be drawn in the presence of women, giving Alex a useful twist. Over and over, Alex shows that flexibility and comfort in oneself are superpowers that can enable mighty deeds. Alex's intuitive understanding of how to stun people with strangeness is a talent—one the great Percy Jackson hasn't figured out. The shaman Foxwood in "Queer-Fire Witchery" likewise describes this as a superpower:

> Even before we have the language to describe the experience, many of us become intuitively aware of our otherness. As our inner self-awareness grows, we begin to learn a complicated Queer arithmetic to safely navigate a world we instinctively know is dangerous, giving us an intuitive sense of subtle energies. The ability to walk between worlds and shape-shift is a matter of survival. Queerkin start our lives walking between the worlds and moving easily between states of being. As Queer Spirit demands to be expressed, the need for authentic self-expression creates a building pressure against the desire to remain safe, silent, and unseen. If "know thyself" is the utmost work of the Witch, surely "create thy self" is the core work of being Queerkin [290].

Self-Naming: DC's Nubia and the Amazons *(Graphic Novel)*

Naming holds deep cultural meaning, both in stories and outside of them. For heroes, being renamed is often a symbol of taking up a mantle, taking their place in the world. For transgender heroes, naming holds a special extra meaning. It can mean validating who they are—the truth of their gender. It can mean standing up to transphobia or binarism, and taking their rightful place among those who know who they truly are. As Michael Ragussis observes in *Acts of Naming: The Family Plot in Fiction*, the child often moves beyond their assigned birth name:

> One could argue that philosophy throws up its hands in frustration at human names because the child, unlike the thing or the idea, is potentially powerful enough to resist the name. The child enters the naming system as the unpredictable, the unfixable, the power that threatens to resist our will or wish. The child is always potentially the deviant, the break in the chain, the hole in history, for the philosopher as well as for the family. For this reason, the family name functions to classify—and thereby nullify—the individual, while the proper name exerts the power of a magical wish which expresses the will of the family [7].

Adair explores ways in which policies regarding drivers' licenses have been and still are systemically anti–Black and anti–transgender and how those intertwine. While this creates extreme physical hardships, it also symbolically ostracizes the person. Mavis Himes explains in *The Power of Names*:

> Our name is also the physical substrate of our being, of both the internal and external passport we carry through life. As a record of our birth in a country of origin, it allows us to freely enter and depart from foreign lands. Without a name, there is no passport, no social security or social insurance number, no identification papers to give us admission to many social institutions. Documents link geography, history, and personal identity to a name. Without these, we become *persona non grata*, a being on the fringes of society [4].

Conversely, self-naming can be a path to empowerment and self-definition. Superheroes are known for naming themselves, from Batman's decision to choose an icon that strikes fear to Buffy's defiant naming of herself on many occasions. Mystique, in the film *X-Men: The Last Stand*, asserts that the name her parents gave her is her "slave name," and Callisto insists all mutants get tattoos to redefine them and unite them in their new community. When Ballister Blackheart calls Nimona a monster in the popular Netflix cartoon, she bursts out, "Do not call me that!" When he asks what she is, with fire breathing and shape-shifting, she answers simply, "I'm Nimona," choosing how she self-identifies without any of humankind's labels (*Nimona*). Even when characters pick an homage name, like Ms. Marvel taking the discarded name of her icon or Falcon becoming Captain America to continue the legacy, a name is a clear statement of values, hopes, and allegiances.

One such superhero is Bia, from the DC comic *Nubia and the Amazons* by writers Stephanie Williams and Vita Ayala and artist Alitha Martinez. Nubia, Wonder Woman's Black twin sister, was introduced on her first '70s cover "to broaden the audience of its consumers, to capitalize on the apparent success of blacksploitation films, and to signal that the fantasy world of DC comics, like that of its rival Marvel comics, was engaged with real contemporary developments like racial integration and the emergence of the site of the black ghetto in US cultural discourse. The character Nubia, however, gained little traction" (Scott 55). She disappeared after three issues and only rarely appeared in the DC universe. It should be added that several creators made the Amazons on their all-female island suggestively queer, from the original creators in the '40s to Phil Jimenez in the early 2000s.

In this 2021 adaptation, after centuries of static, stagnated existence for the island inhabitants, Bia is one of five new Amazons to emerge from the Well of Souls. This magical gateway, cared for by keeper Magala, is "a place where the souls of women who died through acts of violence in men's world reside. Only these souls can be reincarnated into new Amazons of

Themyscira" (Williams et al. 1:8). On the new Amazons' first day, they are asked to perform a series of physical and strategic assessments. That evening, at a great ceremony, each is invited to "tell us the names you've decided on for yourselves," phrasing that emphasizes personal destiny and self-expression (1:14). "No matter who you were before you came to us, you are an Amazon now," Magala explains (1:11). Bia chooses her name, meaning "power," shared with a heroine of Zeus's war against Titans. It also resonates with Queen Nubia's name and is held within it. Parents often name their children after their heroes, hoping the child will acquire those values or possibly fame. Self-naming follows similar trends. More specifically, superhero comics are pure fantasy and thus reveal the culture's ideals. "Nubia's image inaugurated and fed a hunger for a fantasy of black power and black beauty. These are conjunctions that appeared as at least partly if not wholly fantastic within what I sensed, or knew, even as a child, was an anti-black 'real' world," explains critic Darieck Scott (50).

The new Amazons don't remember who they were in their previous lives or the act of violence that killed them. However, Bia says, "I don't know how to explain it yet, but this exact moment feels like my soul has desired it long before I came here" (Williams et al. 1). In her previous life, Bia didn't get to live as herself in the way she needed or didn't have a community that celebrated her. In issue three, one Amazon wonders how long they can hold their breaths, and the other responds, "There is still so much we don't know about our new bodies" (3). This rebirth with new, stronger physicality in a place of safety is not simply trans coded but a story of trans joy. Speaking to these issues, writer Stephanie Williams explains:

> To me, just reading past Wonder Woman books and stuff, there's always been like some trans allegory there, and for this series, Vita and I didn't want that to be something that was only in subtext. So how do you make that a definitive theme? Then you say ... this is who they are, and you don't have to be worried about subtext anymore because, no, I'm telling you right here and now, like this character is a black transgender woman [qtd. in Aguilar n.p.].

The twenty-six-year-old Cheryl Nyland describes creating a new surname (Strayed) around the time of her divorce. She explains: "Naming myself was symbolic in many ways. It signified to me how it was I had to take full responsibility for my life. I had to create my own happiness, to build my strength, to be the engine of my momentum. Choosing my own name struck me as both a positive act and a powerful one during a time when I felt uncertain and weak" (Himes 141).

Similarly, Bia announces her name while holding the hand of another Amazon, who warmly tells her, "Welcome, sister Bia." Historically, *sister* held significant meaning in second-wave feminism, emphasizing unity and solidarity between all women. Problematically, the definition of *all women* often centralized white women and excluded others. Further, this term was appropriated from Black women, even as it was used to gaslight them into feminism that harmed them. It is also used to exclude transgender women and harm transgender people in general (Evans 114). As such, reclaiming the word to validate and unabashedly celebrate a Black transgender Amazon adds further significance. Williams makes a point of clarifying that the Amazons' island, Themyscira, "is a place for ALL women" (qtd. in Kogod n.p.).

Bia is welcomed among them as a significant character rather than the token figure seen in many diverse comics characters. As Williams tweets, "Bia will have a role on Themyscira beyond just existing—she isn't set dressing, she isn't a box to tick, she is a fully fledged character that is important to her community. Just as Black trans women are important to us in real life" (qtd. in Kogod n.p.). Bia's sacred place among the Amazons is more than an empty statement.

Bia, indeed, moves on as a regular cast member. At the time of writing, she has continued to build friendships and partnerships with the new Amazons. She has discovered her prophetic abilities and found an experienced Amazon oracle as a mentor. She gives Queen Nubia clever and compassionate insight, living up to her name. Admittedly, Bia is presented in minimalist form with a subtle story arc. Comic book theorist Scott McCloud teaches that the reader must connect the squares, imagining the movement and backstory that do not appear in the panels but are suggested to be between them: "It's reasonable to suppose that the supplied closure—which, after all, ultimately cannot be limited by what is laid out on the page—follows or is in the nature of the readers' *wishes*" (Scott 53). Readers are thus encouraged to imagine her settling in and finding a safe, fulfilling life.

Bia's naming is a triumph and claims her new Amazon identity. For others, of course, naming can also mean the opposite of freedom to live one's true self. Keeping one's birth name or state-assigned name signals conformity and obedience to others' whims. A name often has implicit obligations of gender, of race, of qualities, and of values, all dictated by the namers.

Jebi, the main character of *Phoenix Extravagant*, has a complex relationship with naming. They are from Hwaguk, a territory colonized by Razan and renamed. At the start of the story, they have paid more than they can afford for a name change to a Razanei name. Such tension for the colonized and pressure to assimilate are and have been common in many moments of history. "There are name-changes in response to persecution and oppression: new immigrants forced or willingly choosing another name to mark a new chapter and to avoid further harassment and prejudice.

There are name-changes due to adoption in which the birth name is effaced and rewritten" (Himes 127). Throughout the story, Jebi struggles with the different aspects of passing as Razanei as they gradually change their position about the occupation and become a revolutionary. Names, however, become a problem again when they try to bring information to a group of rebels. Because they have purchased the name change certificate, the rebels send them on a dangerous test of their loyalty. In other words, each of their names symbolizes identifying somewhere they do not belong.

Nameless characters are generally made so by society to show their lack of power, like Grey Worm on *Game of Thrones*, who must choose such a lowly identifier randomly each day. Some authors use nameless narrators to symbolize ambiguity and anonymousness, as in *Moby Dick* or "William Wilson." The protagonist of *Fierce Femmes and Notorious Liars* owns this namelessness, as she emphasizes her status as removed from society. She finds freedom in not belonging, not being known, not staying put. The protagonist of *The Four Profound Weaves* feels a similar restlessness, only naming himself at the end of his adventure.

Naming others is power, going back to biblical Adam, who's given the semidivine power of naming all the animals. Other mythologies give the naming power to one of the pantheons. If a name defines the self, renaming someone shows power over the other person. Thus, labeling can be complex when imposed from outside—many search for the term that best defines them but find that others don't. On the run and transforming into a fungus hybrid in Rivers Solomon's *Sorrowland*, Vern finds safety and romance. When Vern confesses, "I'm in-between" (238), Gogo insists there's nothing wrong and offers to tell her the word for this. Vern refuses. "Because without a name for it, it's just something I am. A part of life. Once it's got a name, I know that means someone has studied it, dissected it, pulled it apart. When something has a name, they can say it's bad" (238). She continues her path of self-definition, even to the point of refusing labels. She is unique and determined to take charge of this specialness.

Literature features the "naming plot," in which a child's name is withheld in an act of disinheritance, leaving the child bereft or questing for a new family and status. The trans story sometimes involves disinheritance and rejection by the family's insisting on the birth name rather than confiscating it. Forcibly deadnaming enforces the power dynamic, a sign of stubbornly clinging to the parental fantasy of the child instead of the real person. This is a common shorthand for tyranny and disrespect in stories like *Sense8*, *Sandman*, and even *Steven Universe*. This is often a step in the trans protagonist's journey—being deadnamed by enemies in an act of cruelty that also functions to deny who they are and try to superimpose society's or the family's expectations.

While not all transgender and otherwise genderqueer people care about their name, want to change it, or have found their name, nearly every fictional character does, often in moments of great empowerment. For trans characters and those outside of the gender binary, names are generally deeply meaningful, whether harmful or validating. They can mean being exposed, controlled, and invalidated, versus being celebrated or celebrating oneself.

Defying the Threshold Guardian: Charmed *(Television)*

Monsters challenge the hero along the journey, attacking, asking riddles, or presenting problems to be solved. In the old fairytales, the wicked stepparents (or birth parents) often function as threshold guardians who stop the hero from leaving on the adventure. Cinderella is kept from the ball; Simpleton can't quest like his brothers. The hero must persuade the parent or sneak away without being caught in order to depart. As hero's journey scholar Christopher Vogler adds,

> The Guardians seem to pop up at the various thresholds of the journey, the narrow and dangerous passages from one stage of life to the next. Campbell showed the many ways in which heroes can deal with Threshold Guardians. Instead of attacking these seemingly hostile powers head-on, journeyers learn to outwit them or join forces with them, absorbing their energy rather than being destroyed by it [4].

Of course, the parents are commonly the first threshold guardians in trans stories, blocking the protagonist from living as themselves. In *Act Cool*, August's mom agrees that he can go to the school in New York—as his legal guardian, she has to sign off on it. She has only one condition. As she puts it, "If I let you stay, I need you to promise me one thing ... promise that you won't change into a boy" (McSmith 34). With one dream threatened by the other, August must compromise. He tries out for Rizzo in *Grease*, partly because his parents will judge him if he takes a boy's role. When he gets the part, they come to see the show and have dinner with him afterward, for which he must play the role of dutiful daughter. Even as he tries to follow his parents' demands, the lie is finally revealed, and he must struggle to keep his new life.

In *The Passing Playbook* by Isaac Fitzsimmons, Spencer's parents refuse to sign his soccer permission slip because they're worried about his being outed and getting death threats. "When we got the call last year that your school was in lockdown because of a threat to your life we were so worried that something had happened to you. Maybe we've been overprotective of you, but it's only because we love you," his mom says (166).

Spencer makes a presentation for them about how much he's always loved soccer, and they realize that this will always be an issue, so there's no point in waiting. A bigger problem comes because the state of Ohio refuses to alter birth certificates, so Spencer is prohibited from competing in the league championship. He finally comes out to his team and his coach. To his surprise, his coach apologizes for not being proactive and telling Spencer he would be safe coming out. "Spencer always assumed that coming out was a one-way thing, that the responsibility fell on him and him alone. But coach's story made him reconsider. Just because the onus always fell on trans and queer people, didn't mean it *should*" (262). Spencer decides to challenge the rules for his rights and the rights of the kids that will follow.

Fantasy, which incorporates deep mythic tropes, adds other nuances to the conflicts. In *Charmed* (2018), Josefina's family discourages her from joining them in their family heritage of witchcraft. As she explains, "They were totally fine with my transition, but … when I suggested I would get my witch powers, well… 'Only biological women can have powers,' they said. So I taught myself as much as I could, potion-wise, with no help from my mother or abuelita" ("No Hablo Brujeria" 3.09). She sets off on a quest to discover her magic, with help from the sympathetic Charmed Ones, her American cousins. Vogler suggests seeing family hostility as a test that can steel the hero's resolution. As he adds, "In daily life, you have probably encountered resistance when you try to make a positive change in your life. People around you, even those who love you, are often reluctant to see you change. They are used to your neuroses and have found ways to benefit from them. The idea of your changing may threaten them" (59).

Other subtler blocks to Josefina's adventures present themselves because she has limited savings to fly to America. Once she arrives, she discovers the Charmed Ones have lost her family's ancestral book, and she must struggle to recreate it. When she tries to check out an old research text from the college library, she is turned away because she isn't a student. The Charmed Ones encourage her to enroll, but she lacks the funds. Over and over, the difficulties of life under systemic oppression in the real world, along with ordinary mishaps, block her from achieving her goals.

Josephina's third episode has her getting the magic she's desired. "I finally got my powers. My dream has finally come true," she smiles. However, the Charmed Ones realize that suddenly getting everything they desire has come with a curse and decide to return the power. Josefina is crushed. She binds her cousins magically, insisting, "I'm an ancient witch. I've waited all my life for this power. I can't let you take it away from me. I won't." The Charmed Ones are shocked that she is battling them, but they are oblivious to how long she's been working for the abilities they already have. Since the magic is gendered, it's tied to the Charmed Ones' femininity, once again something they've always had for which Josefina has needed to struggle.

At last, they all give up the magically created grace—the job promotions and perks they've gotten without earning them. However, Josefina still has her powers—she always had them and only needed confidence to bring them out, unlike the gifts of luck that the others received. "Your powers ... the egg had nothing to do with it. They were there all along, just waiting for you to come claim them," one sister observes.

The young women end the episode by inducting Josefina into the ranks of witches—the final threshold guardian was her own confidence, eroded by her family for many years but now supported by her cousins. Josefina, meanwhile, responds to the blocks and guardians in America by charting a new path for herself. She explains, "Rites of passage remind us how far we've come and how much more we can achieve, which is why I'm going back to school in Puerto Rico.... I still have a lot to learn" ("Witchful Thinking" 3.11).

In classic epic fantasy, many threshold guardians are the lieutenants or allies of the central villain. For the trans hero, often ordinary people like shopkeepers and police are hostile. The 2004 film *Toilet Training* documents all the ways trans people are harassed and endangered. Fiction films tell similar stories: *A Fantastic Woman* tells the story of Marina Vidal in Santiago, Chile. When her lover dies, the film follows the discrimination Marina experiences, both from Orlando's family and from the larger community. Orlando's ex-wife forbids Marina from attending the funeral, and Orlando's son harasses her and takes her beloved dog. Thus, the titular expression emphasizes how much she must struggle against cruelty and transcend her situation—she is both fantastical and formidable. Likewise, the famous *Ma Vie en Rose* has the local parents sign a petition to get the young protagonist kicked out of school. As the entire neighborhood shuns them, the father loses his job, and they must all move away.

In other stories, a figurehead declares a bigoted war. Gwen Stacy, Spider-Woman in *Spider-Man: Across the Spider-Verse*, is lit in pale pink, white, and blue (the trans flag), especially when she comes out to her father (with her secret identity, but one can often be a metaphor for the other). Her existence as a superhero has been made illegal, with shock journalist J. Jonah Jameson fixating on people like her and scapegoating superheroes. Even as in the real United States, many anti-trans bills were going forward, forcing citizens to flee, Gwen's exile from her original universe paralleled real life. A "protect trans kids" flag in Gwen's room gives viewers another suggestive hint.

Finally, threshold guardians for contemporary trans people can include the laws and permissions of society. In Chris Beam's *I Am J*, J goes to a clinic to ask for testosterone. However, the clinician tells him he must be eighteen, with a note from his doctor saying that he is trans. If he doesn't have this, he could see one of their therapists for between three and six months to get this letter. As J thinks, Janet is following medical protocols and trying to be sympathetic and helpful. However, she is also blocking J's quest. "Suddenly J hated Janet, and her skirt and her pen and her stupid prissy boots. Did she have to talk like a robot, like a white, dictionary-obsessed robot? Janet had the shots, probably filled and ready to go, right behind her in that cabinet, and she was babbling away in fancy words that just meant no" (129). His mother provides the next block in his transition, insisting, "You are the one that's making problems here" (162). She says that J is being selfish, that his mother has done everything for him and has saved her whole life to send him to college while he's too preoccupied to fill out applications. "And now all you want to do is hurt us with this, this shit, J. Leaving school, running away. All you care about anymore is what you look like" (162). Her guilt is a more difficult threshold to overcome.

Discovering a New World: The Affair of the Mysterious Letter *(Novel)*

There are many ways for a trans character to step into adventure. Many are fleeing bad situations. In the television show *Dead End: Paranormal Park*, Barney steps into a terrifying and dangerous park, seeking a job so he can live away from his transphobic family. In Anna-Marie McLemore's *Blanca & Roja*, Page has few ways to fit in with the intolerant human community. In stepping into the forest, they literally become part of the sensory embodiment there. When Danielle, superhero of *Dreadnought*, is kicked out, she feels relief. Now she's freed from her parents' restrictions and abuse. As she thinks,

> I'm pissed and scared and I feel lost. But I'm not shattered. Last night, I expected to wake up broken, nothing more than a torn up chewed out smaller half of what used to be a person. But I feel whole. Really, completely whole. Strip away everything: my house, my stuff, my family. Strip away the legion, and Calamity, and my secret identity. Everything. What's left? What's left are the things I can count on. I have my body, my powers, and my freedom. Maybe that will be enough. It will have to be. For the first time in my life, I am completely in charge of myself [Daniels 229].

Many protagonists are already on the journey when we meet them. Amanda, of Meredith Russo's *If I Was Your Girl*, has left the school in which she was bullied and hurt to live with her father and attend a new one. Similarly, the show *Heartstopper*'s Elle has left a school in which she felt sad but also had friends to start a new school as a stranger. There, she finds a community that reflects her at last. Nick, the protagonist of McLemore's *Self-Made Boys*, has left to live for a while in New York as himself.

At the same time, for many, stepping into adventure means entering a dangerous situation. As Campbell puts it, "In the first stage of this kind of adventure, the hero leaves the realm of the familiar, over which he has some measure of control, and comes to a threshold" (*Hero* 146). In *Sir Callie and the Champions of Helston*, Callie steps out of the forest, where they live happily as themselves, and into the big city of Helston. Helston may allow Callie the opportunity for adventure and potential knighthood, but it also means misgendering and even imprisonment. In Alexis Hall's *A Lady for a Duke*, Viola learns that a loved one from her childhood is suffering. Against her better judgment and her sense of self-preservation, she leaves her protected home, forcing her to confront unfinished business from the past she left behind.

Others discover a haven. As revealed in the remake of *4400*, Andre Davis, a doctor from the 1920s mysteriously transported to 2021, used to spend time at cross-dressing clubs. A few flashback shots reveal the joyous, glamorous culture of dancing to jazz and ragtime. (It's also revealed he was doing breakthrough medical research while a white doctor took the credit.) In the present, a trans teen, Noah, tells Dr. Davis about needing hormones, and he is stunned by the new vocabulary he's learning. After asking what the term means, his only question is whether the teen is all right with people knowing about him:

> **NOAH:** When I was born, they said I was a girl, but clearly, I–I'm not.
> **ANDRE:** Do you hide this?
> **NOAH:** It's no secret. I'm proud of it. I'm out to basically everyone.
> **ANDRE:** Well, this is all ... remarkable.... You've certainly expanded my vocabulary. Thank you for sharing. And you can count on me to procure the medicine you need ["That LaDonna Life" 1.03].

As is implied here and revealed directly in the following episode, Andre, too, is transgender and kept it a secret in 1920, only able to share this part of himself at the club. One charming element here is that the modern teen Noah is unknowingly teaching an elder who once paved the way for him. A later episode sees a modern character taking Andre to a Pride parade, at which, once more, he's stunned at the public celebration. It's a delightful moment of wish fulfillment, showing Andre (along with other Black characters from the past) how far society has come.

John, the protagonist of Alexis Hall's *The Affair of the Mysterious Letter*, quite literally steps over the threshold into adventure. John is filling the role of John Watson in a very loose and fantastical retelling of Sir Arthur Conan Doyle's *A Study in Scarlet*. John grew up in a conservative kingdom where drinking, dancing, visiting the theater, "or indeed engaging in any pastime that did not involve venerating the name of the Creator" were all forbidden (24). This resonates with the notion, discussed by Kiri Miller, that dancing can be used to explore and experiment with gender (939). There, John's conservative father never saw John as a man, and John was relieved to go to college in the more open Khelathra-Ven, where he could study transubstantial sciences and branch out without his father's disapproval. After college, John felt even more disconnected from his homeland and opted to join the military. At war, a temporal weapon injured John, the effects of which recur. Not only is the pain temporal in the sense of appearing randomly, but memories of it also pop up. Symbolically, it underscores a lifetime of PTSD (post-traumatic stress disorder). As such, John can no longer participate in the military and has returned to Khelathra-Ven.

Located near the mysterious sunken city of Ven, this land is significantly queer-positive, sex-positive, fun-positive, and filled with mystery and adventure. For the shy, closed-off hero, it's the exact opposite of everything he's experienced before and exactly what he needs. If someone devotes themselves to the instructions of the unconscious realm, "it can bestow this gift, so that suddenly life, which has been stale and dull, turns into rich, unending inner adventure, full of creative possibilities" (von Franz 209). As Campbell adds, "With the refusal of suitors, or the passing over a boundary, the adventure begins. You get into a field that's unprecedented, novel. You can't have creativity unless you leave behind the bounded, the fixed, all the rules" (*Power of Myth* 156).

Responding to a peculiar advertisement for an appealing apartment, John finds the door open and no sound from within. He hopes for someone to pop up, such as that world's police, but no one does. With this, John steps over the threshold and into adventure, and incidentally, into the apartment of Shaharazad Haas, a sorceress with astonishing deductive skills. She is, at that moment, indisposed under the influence of "an undiagnosable cocktail of narcotics and intoxicants" (Hall, *Letter* 11). She is also expertly aiming a firearm at John's heart. As she says, "If you have come to rob me ... you will find that there is nothing worth taking. If you have come to murder me, you will find that I am dead already" (11). John explains that he simply came regarding the advertisement. Ms. Haas makes some remarks about the nature of time, obligingly drops the gun, has it shoot at the wall, and makes some astonishing deductions regarding John's personality and past. She explains that the rent is due monthly and comes to seventeen Athran florins, twelve Khelish rials, an equivalent value in seed pearls, sourced from wherever you wish, seventy-eight Eyan shillings, a Marvosi trade dagger, or three and a half lines from a Seravic chant of commerce. You may pay it to me or to the landlady directly. Her name is Mrs. Hive, and she infests the attic. Do not enter it without permission on pain of agonizing death. There is no laundry service [12].

The laundry, it turns out, is a fairly important aspect of the coming partnership between John and Shaharazad. As the responsible, practical member of the team, John does the laundry. This is very much in line with the way the original Watson cares for Holmes. John keeps Shaharazad's mundane needs met, as she tends to both their needs for the extreme and the exciting. The whimsical options of payment, meanwhile, symbolize a certain fluidity while also emphasizing the many paths one might take toward material or not-so-material success. According to famed fairytale analyst Bruno Bettelheim, fantasy's unrealistic nature focuses heroes on their inner development (25).

As Sherlock Holmes fans will understand, the detective's edginess fills his life with entertainment and excitement. Shaharazad shatters and disdains her people's few boundaries. John soon reveals:

> This would not be the last time that Ms. Haas gave me occasion to reflect on assumptions I had not hitherto examined. Although her approach to morality was often disturbingly flexible, I realize now that my own—for all my attempts to move beyond the rigidity of my father's teachings—was, in many ways, shamefully limited. Over the long course of our acquaintance, she introduced me to a bewildering number of new perspectives and experiences. Many of them were near-fatal but, taken as a whole, I sincerely believe they made me a better man [36].

Having his boundaries expanded is his true otherworld quest. It's more about making a lifelong friend and discovering who he is without his father's imposed rules than it is about solving the mystery. Lavish costume changes and strange situations follow as John is propelled into his best self. Shaharazad continues to push his boundaries, from shyness to general prudishness. Invited to remove a bullet from her shoulder, John describes his difficulty: "Practical necessity taking precedence over regular propriety, I peeled away those areas of Ms. Haas's clothing that were obscuring her injuries. The process was doubtless rather painful for her, but she seemed at least to derive some pleasure from my evident discomfort at the intimacy" (90).

With Ms. Haas, John moves on to a wild adventure. He finds himself flirting at balls, meeting vampires, dodging air pirates, battling sharks, and discovering a world far greater and more meaningful than his childhood existence. In this land, one can be consumed by extradimensional forces, steal curses from the Elder Witches of the Hundred Kingdoms, and catch spirits in nets spun from moonlight. Most enticing of all is his detective partner and the cases she offers. As John concludes, "To be in the presence of the sorceress Shaharazad Haas was to glimpse a world more beautiful, more terrible, and more limitless than anything I could hitherto have imagined" (27).

The otherworld represents the unconscious. Here, magic can come true, and the beliefs in karma and righteousness one must often bury in the ordinary world are valid, below the level of self-awareness. This is the font of creativity, intuition, self-realization. The sunken city of Ven particularly symbolized this, a disreputable area filled with "strange magics" below the surface of what can be seen (96).

While this world is topsy-turvy in many ways, John values it because the rules are indeed different here. Shaharazad Haas accepts him, and he can live as himself. His skills are valued in a way they never were before. Thus, the otherworld reaches out as a haven and a challenge, encouraging the protagonist to discover and revel in the best version of themselves.

3

SAFETY WITH OTHERS

Haven: Doom Patrol *(Television)*

The questing hero is rewarded along the way with a haven, a place of safety, in order to regroup. Some heroes, especially trans ones, have been moving through hostile territory and find such a place a wonderful luxury.

In the *Doom Patrol* episode "Danny Patrol" (1.08), the team receives a mysterious cake with a map on it from Danny Cakes in Ohio, just as they're feeling most lost. The street is deserted, but words write themselves around them, asking for their vanished leader, Niles Caulder. The signs direct them to the local cabaret. Inside are flowers and drag queens performing joyously. Larry Trainor looks at them with longing.

In Grant Morrison's run of the celebrated, quirky DC comic, Danny the Street (*he* in the comic and *they* on-screen) is "a sentient street. A street that can think for itself" (Morrison, *Doom Patrol* #35). Danny travels from city to city, where the other streets shuffle to make room for him. Stores are "dressed in fairy lights and lace curtains" with carnivals and curious bookshops under mauve smoke and fireworks, presenting as beautiful and decidedly queer (#35). Danny explains (through signs and, in this case, a "speak your weight" machine) that his expressions like "Bona" are "the old palare we used in Soho in the 50s so the straights wouldn't know what we were saying" (#51).

The other characters are all extreme outsiders who find safety on the team. They're all handicapped in some way: "Nearly all the characters in Morrison's Doom Patrol embody various traumas, emotions, or concepts through their distorted and mutable figures" (Singer 75). A strange spirit has visited experimental pilot Larry Trainor (a blond heroic insider) and insists it's come "to continue, to perpetuate, to generate." It summons Dr. Eleanor Poole, a Black woman, into the room and merges them all: "Now we are three. Now we are one" (#19). In the next comic, this merged self takes the name Rebis, the alchemical result of a chymical wedding and a divine intersex person. "My race is mixed. I am woman and man and light mixed with darkness, mixed. *Mixed.* I am nothing special, nothing pure. I am mud and flame," it proclaims (#20). In mental projections, Rebis often appears in a bra, jewelry, and alternating masculine or feminine briefs, stressing the duality. Niles Caulder promptly invites Rebis to join the Doom Patrol.

On-screen, Larry is less complex. He is a closeted gay man from the fifties, whose experimental flight merged him with only the alien creature. After becoming irradiated and immortal, he gradually gets in touch with his regrets. These two secrets—his homosexuality and his alien passenger—mirror each other as deep hangups that he resists confronting. They also result in his double life and separation from others. Both the show and the comics have him shrouded completely in bandages to contain the radiation in a visual presentation of concealment and distancing. As his character develops, he slowly tries to communicate with the alien, which represents trying to discover all he's buried.

In the episode, the headliner finishes her number and greets Larry and Cyborg (another hybrid, as he's part machine): "Give it up for my Saucy Songbirds, ladies and gentlemen. Yes! Boys, girls, and all those in between. Welcome to Peeping Tom's Perpetual Cabaret. I'm your host, Maura Lee Karupt." Aside from the pun, the name suggests she'll be drawing them into her fantasy world and transforming them into something beyond mainstream society's values. Pink orchids and blue lights shine all around them—a blend of feminine sensuality and masculine enlightenment.

She shines a spotlight on the heroes, literally, and Larry squirms. He's been hiding for decades, under the bandages and as a shut-in, not to mention his closeted history. She tells them they've entered Danny the Street and adds, "It appears we have two new guests with us. Oh, look at these two serving us Terminator, King Tut realness, honey." Indeed, Cyborg and bandage-wrapped Larry fit the description, though they're unused to being noticed or acknowledged. In the ordinary world, they wear disguises and keep to the shadows, but the cabaret offers only truth and support. Maura adds, "Danny's gender queer, and they use non-binary pronouns…. Oh, isn't that cute? Robo-boy doesn't understand non-binary. Let me see if I can explain it to you in a language you can understand. Um … 01–001–110. Make sense?" Aggressively claiming pronouns and mocking a straight (though nonconforming) character emphasizes how much Maura is in her place of power, dominating a red-curtained stage. Clearly feeling protected and safe here too, Cyborg snarks back, and they flirt a bit.

The team discovers Danny's on the run from Darren Jones and the Bureau of Normalcy … the same military leader who once tortured Larry. After a flashback of their brutality, complete with mockery of his "normalcy," Larry calls them "a top secret government agency, run by a bunch of demented zealots. They stomp out anything they deem to be aberrations." Their torture revealed the negative spirit within him, and they taunted him: "I thought you were nothing but a degenerate radioactive flyboy. But it seems you are so much more…. That, Captain Trainor, is what's really inside you. That is who you really are." In contrast with the cabaret, where they're encouraged to be themselves, the bureau ripped Larry's secrets out of him, peeling him like an onion and leaving him terribly wounded.

However, Danny the Street has been tough enough to defy the bureau and protect those hiding within. Maura adds, "Couple of years back, Darren Jones botched a search-and-destroy mission on Danny. Lost his partner in the process." She tosses them her old Bureau of Normalcy ID for Morris Wilson and adds, "He became Maura Lee Karupt." Backstage, her wig off, vulnerable, she tells them her story: "I was supposed to hate this place. Working for the Bureau, you're supposed to hate anything that's abnormal. But I couldn't. Something about Danny felt right. It felt like home. A weight had been lifted off me…. I felt lighter. Like I was more of myself than I had ever been."

In a flashback, she gazes into a window that reflects women's clothes over the old self. Next, she enters the cabaret and finds the lights and smiles within.

> And that's when Maura Lee Karupt was born. My drag name was my own personal "fuck you" to the Bureau. I knew then I couldn't let any harm come to this place. So I tipped Danny off. And they were able to jump before Darren could attack. Yes, Danny can jump. Anywhere around the world, which is a helpful thing, because Darren's obsessed. He's been following us ever since. He just won't let it go. The Bureau never does. Danny is supposed to be a safe haven for people like us. But nobody feels safe here anymore. It's not right. No one should ever have to feel uncomfortable in their own skin.

She adds that the celebration is the key to Danny's existence: "It's a perpetual cabaret for a reason. This street thrives on the Dannyzens' happiness. We keep the party going, we keep Danny going. But we're running on fumes. If the party stops… then Danny's heart stops right along with it. And they win." There's a message here—Danny provides their citizens with whatever they most need, like opportunity, mentorship, and safety. In return, the Dannyzens staying there must reciprocate, supporting the street and one another. Their safety turns to rejoicing, which emboldens them all.

Outside, Larry wants to flee, and Cyborg, the hero, demands that he help. Larry refuses and retreats into the club. There, an older white drag queen in black, closer to a reflection of himself, tells him karaoke is beginning and singing is "the price of admission." The spotlight flashes on him again.

> PERFORMER: You gotta sing, baby.
> LARRY: I don't sing.
> PERFORMER: Well, we have to keep this party popping, okay? (leans close and whispers) Don't be scared.
> LARRY: I'm not scared.
> PERFORMER: Then get up there.

Reluctant, he takes the mic and flinches from the spotlight, but starts monologuing and then singing. Maura comes and joins him, singing Kelly Clarkson's "People Like Us," about how everyone is a misfit. The camera spins, and Larry's handsome self under the bandages appears, tuxedoed and beaming. He grins with pure joy as he feels his old hands and face. His friends crowd in, and colorful angel drag queens dance around them in golden light, like a blessing.

Then the screen flashes to Larry sitting in the silent club, refusing the microphone. This was a fantasy. Larry still feels the haven is not meant for him and cannot shed all his disguises. He refuses to sing but goes out to fight beside Cyborg. Maura joins them and volunteers to go back to the oppressive Bureau of Normalcy to protect the community. However, Danny tells them it's time to stop running. They decide to fight instead and defend their people.

Maura meets Darren and his flunkies in a blue glittering suit like a superhero uniform.

> DARREN: Jesus, look at this human trash here.
> MAURA: You know, Darren, men as old as you really shouldn't throw shade. You might hurt your back.
> DARREN: Morris? My God! What the hell has this abomination done to you?
> MAURA: Danny didn't do anything, except help me realize who I am.
> DARREN: What? No. No, this is not who you are, Morris. You're a man. This place, these people are...
> MAURA: No. You don't get to tell me or anyone else who they are ever again. I am proud of the person I see in the mirror. My face is beat. My look is flawless, and I am dusted from head to toe. The only thing I am not is scared of you.

Danny vanishes the bureau backup, and the heroes send Darren packing. Larry finally sings karaoke at their celebratory party, willingly sharing himself at last.

In the comics, Danny is likewise threatened, though more violently. An agent from NOWHERE, who likewise stamps out diversity, insists, "We can't let this abomination threaten normalcy any longer. I mean, I'm as tolerant as the next guy, but what can I say, fellas? Destroy Danny the

Street" (Morrison, *Doom Patrol* #35). They set him on fire, and the Doom Patrol arrive to help. The villains "are obscured by the masks and helmets that anonymize the religious inquisitions and secret police organizations to which they belong" (Singer 75). The haven is threatened, then set on fire.

Still, Danny greets the seemingly dead heroes in the afterlife. "Takes more than that to shut me up, love. Us old queens are hard as nails" (#62). Danny also tells their origin story. How people saw "the world of dreams and heart's desire," naming it Oz, Wonderland, Neverland, and so on (#62). Finally, it fell apart, perhaps thanks to modernity, and "nothing left of it but me, Danny the Street, traveling the earth as a reminder of what had been and could be again" (#62). The street reopens in a wonderful eternal celebration of colored balloons and Louis Armstrong music, "World of dreams. World of love and strangeness and charm. Danny the world" (#62). A shot of the globe reveals a utopia of inclusion and beauty. As the heroes speak in the afterlife, Larry explains that "Danny tells me he's going to continue sending himself as Danny the Street back into our old world.... Danny the Street will be the tunnel between the worlds, through which the lost and heartsick can enter this realm" (#62). Whether saved or destroyed and reincarnated, Danny continues to be a haven for the vulnerable, a catalyst where, cocooned in safety, they can allow their hidden selves to come forth and thrive. Danny the Street finally becomes Danny the World, a planet of infinite possibility.

In the real world, a common refuge appears online. In *Romeos*, Lukas's online community is a privileged space, whose sincerity and supportiveness contrast with the rather superficial social world that Lukas encounters. Nomi explores queer issues through vlogging on *Sense8*, while on *Sort Of*, 7ven pushes Sabi to explore non-binary dating sites and open a LGBTQ+ club together. In Imogen Binnie's *Nevada*, the protagonist describes the internet as a safe community:

> The Internet at that time was this big, exciting place where you could anonymously spill your guts about gender and discomfort and heteronormativity and how weird male privilege felt and lots of other things, except back then she didn't really have the language for it so she just went like: everything sucks and I'm totally sad. Just over and over and over and over and over with minor variations and the occasional cuss word. It couldn't have been very compelling to read, but writing about it at length made her pay attention to patterns and stuff and introduced her to the first real life trans people she met, even if they were on the Internet and she didn't know what they looked like. She'd stay up all night, night after night, gushing her feelings all over the Internet until she figured out she was trans, transitioned, and wound up having the exact same problems as every other messed up, emotionally shut off person in New York. She doesn't post there as much as she used to but she still has that blog [63].

Found Family: Dead End: Paranormal Park *(Television)*

"Worth It" on *Pose* (2.02) ends with the words of Hector Xtravaganza, a house father and consultant on the series: "Blood does not family make. Those are relatives. Family are those with whom you share your good, bad, and ugly and still love one another in the end. Those are the ones you select." One form of happily ever after in this capitalist hellscape is finding a family that loves, prioritizes, and is there for us. Some families, found or otherwise, follow the format of the modern nuclear family. Others are unique or model a different format. As Kenson observes, queer families offer more flexibility, as some choose to be monogamous couples with children, but others find alternatives: "Indeed, many queer people have adopted the expression 'family of choice' to reflect their own decision to create new families in configurations that suit them. This highlights a fact most take for granted. As adults, we all choose who we call family" (260).

One such story is that of Barney, from the Netflix cartoon *Dead End: Paranormal Park*. Barney starts his journey by running away from home with his dog, Pugsley. His parents have been making him endure his transphobic grandmother's barbs. His mother excuses the older woman with, "Oh, come on, sweetie, there's a lot she doesn't understand."

Barney coolly retorts, "She's not the only one" (1.01). In fact, Barney chooses to remove himself from the situation. Kenson adds: "The queer relationship with family is often fraught due to the necessary step of separation, of seeking identity outside of our families of origin. Many families still reject children whose sexuality or gender identities are outside the narrow range of heteronormativity" (260). However, this psychological notion in no way justifies or explains transphobia, such as in Barney's example.

As Barney tells his beloved Pugsley, "If I get this job, we can get a place of our own. Just you and me. No Mom, no Dad, no Grammy Gram" (1.01). Pursuing this, he finds a job at Dead End, a paranormal amusement park. The creator explains the difficulty in exploring the emotional dynamics here: "We originally ended the pilot with footage of cop cars outside his house and his parents crying. Then we did versions that were far lighter and tried to soften the fact he was running away from home as much as possible to make it seem more like an adventure" (Steele qtd. in White n.p.). The final in-between version has him defiantly moving out but leaving hurt feelings behind. All the scenarios emphasize how desperate he is to get away.

Since television representations generally focus on people with more privilege, they rarely address this issue. Many shows, like *Friends* or *Scrubs*, explore how one's peers can be closer than family, with the parents cast as clumsy, neglectful outsiders who must be managed and kept uninformed. The roommate groups are presented as the true sources of care. As Kath Weston points out in *Families We Choose*, such relationships include financial assistance, chores, and trust, beyond emotional support and shared social time (105). Weston continues, "What gay kinship ideologies challenge is not the concept of procreation that informs kinship ... but the belief that procreation *alone* constitutes kinship and that nonbiological ties must be patterned after a biological model (like adoption) or forfeit any claim to kinship status" (34).

After rejecting his biological structure, Barney moves in, living illicitly at the park. However, there are deeper plots here. The demon Courtney has made up the job interview in order to gather humans for a dangerous demon king, Temeluchus, to devour or possess. A truly touching moment has the dog Pugsley sacrificing himself to save Barney. Pugsley's eyes fill with tears and terror, then Pugsley straightens with determination. His face brims with pure love as he takes the blow meant for Barney. This moment, more than any other, emphasizes their close adoptive bond. Thanks to this, Temeluchus ends up possessing Pugsley, to Barney's horror. Emphasizing their bond once more, he protests, "Pugsley's not just my dog. He's my family. The only family that's always had my back. And I can't lose him!" (1.01).

At last, the demon is mostly banished, leaving Pugsley with some magic and the ability to speak English. Now sharing a language, Pugsley and Barney become even closer and more of a family. Barney ends up befriending Courtney after all, and the two become roommates. Courtney, in turn, learns to value and respect the new human friends. In the second episode, Barney reveals that he feels comfortable sleeping in the haunted house because he can truly be himself. He notes that everyone at home and school knows he's transgender, but at Phoenix Parks, he gets to choose whether to tell.

The comic book that inspired the show, *Deadendia: The Watcher's Test*, begins with the villain demanding that spirits reveal themselves to be judged, putting him in the role of reproachful parent. The theme park haunted house, meanwhile, has a plaque that reads, "Come all ye lost souls, the living and the dead" (Steele 11). This is a haven for all kinds of people. Barney settles down in a children's room, falling asleep in the arms of a giant pink teddy bear. As such, the place has a comforting charm, cuddling his vulnerable child side.

The individual plots echo Barney's quest to protect the weak and form a family group. Early in the first comic, a demon child travels up to the theme park. As Kushiel, the angelic punisher, explains, "Our senses have indicated that they are not a threat. But they shall be destroyed for their crimes" (46). Barney rushes out to defend the innocent echo child, who mimics anyone close, in this case Barney. When the child is finally returned to safety, Barney explains, "I was selfish. I wanted to keep you here so that I could give you the family I never had" (55). This is another innocent inner child, as well as a temporary part of their found family. In another adventure, Barney is so miserable after a failed romance that Pugsley summons a happiness demon to comfort him. Over and over, the magic echoes their emotional conflicts.

Barney also finds a close friend, Norma. At first, she is Barney's rival in trying to get the job at the park. But when the job is revealed to be fake and the two confront Temeluchus, they become friends. They end up getting hired at the park after all, working as a team. Norma suffers much stress and insecurity because her mother wants to protect her yet has very high expectations. Norma also seems to be autistic with social anxiety. The park is far from accessible, and Norma must regularly handle ableism. Worst of all, Norma's father was abusive, and she must face a nightmare vision of him in one incident. As she undergoes this, Barney faces his own greatest fear: his parents not sticking up for him when people are cruel about his gender identity. However, Norma's care and empathy help her save Barney, once again defeating a symbolic struggle that reflects inner conflict. Even as Barney tackles his hangups, Norma wrestles hers, and the pair rely on each other for support.

As he is struggling with his estranged family, Barney fights Temeluchus, a shadow that's his opposite—eternally wise and powerful but also a parasite. Like his birth family, the demon is a drain on innocents and must be banished from the family circle so they can thrive. Barney defeats him by creating a family that shares love and support. Temeluchus's soul in Pugsley, along with other possessions, symbolizes having ideologies and propaganda that invade trusted friends. They work through it all based on their shared love and understanding, and they are stronger after. Barney also becomes close with his coworkers, Badyah "Deathslide" Hassan and Logan "Logs" Nguyen. These friends likewise undergo moments of possession and transformation, which must be defeated. Barney has a crush on Logs that appears reciprocated, creating another type of connection in Barney's chosen family. Such a created family has much to offer:

> Because queers had limited access to the benefits of the nuclear family—such as inheritance, parental rights, and care work—and because the line between friends and lovers is so often blurred in queer community, friendship took on a kind of deep and lasting primacy for queers that does not exist in heteronormative society. Generational knowledge is passed not from parent to child but through an informal system of mentorship. When queers are sick and dying, it is our friends, not our family, whom we most often rely on to care for us. When

we are suicidal, our friends talk us down. When we are broke, our friends lend us money. When we are beaten up by homophobes and transphobes, evicted by our landlords, kicked out by our parents, thrown out or assaulted by our partners, our friends take us in. For so much of my life, I have lived by this unwritten law: Queers take care of queers. No one else will [Thom, *I Hope* n.p.].

As Barney feels more supported, he decides to slowly allow contact with his family of origin. This is by no means a necessary practice in this narrative, particularly not with transphobic or otherwise abusive families of origin. Still, it is what Barney chooses to do. Barney has a younger brother who never misgenders him, named Patrick. Patrick is at first hurt that Barney might miss Patrick's birthday, then hopeful that Barney will speak with their parents. Barney ends up agreeing to a meeting, which is painful at first and full of barely concealed tension. As Kenson notes, "'Family' is a loaded word, particularly for queer people, who so often experience condemnation and exile from the families who raised us" (260).

At last, Barney protests directly that accepting him is the bare minimum, and he's devastated that they won't confront Grammy Gram about all her misgendering. Their conversation, though difficult, leads to better understanding and, over time, even reconciliation. The creator explains: "It's sometimes harder to argue with people who think of themselves as the best allies ever. Sometimes the accusation of bigotry is seen as far more toxic than the bigotry itself. It's quite relatable, and it's an element I'm very proud of" (Steele qtd. in White n.p.). As he adds, they tried to make lessons for parents in the show. "We tried not to make his parents monsters or the most accepting family ever. They're in a middle ground that I think a lot of people find themselves in, where they think they're saying all the right things, but they're not doing all the right things" (Steele qtd. in White). They haven't found a place of unconditional love.

Like many trans characters, Barney starts out nearly alone and homeless, leaving behind a transphobic family. Over the journey, he finds loved ones who celebrate him for who he is—some of them even from his reeducated family of origin. They all end the season in a more accepting place, better prepared to face the rising challenges of the future.

An Uplifting Interlude: Steven Universe *(Television)*

One of the most delightful parts of dark, hazardous quests are little, joyous adventures. Many of these involve building intimacy with a romantic love interest or close friend. Often, these also comprise not only stepping away from the main quest but physically moving away, often sneaking out.

These scenes serve important functions for the audience. They allow us to catch our breath after an exciting battle or ordeal. The characters might recap the story so far, giving us a chance to review the story and get a glimpse of how they perceive it ... In these quiet moments of reflection or intimacy we get to know the characters better. ... These quieter or more lyric passages are important for making a connection with the audience [Vogler 177].

In Meredith Brooks's *If I Was Your Girl*, Amanda goes to a party and flirts with a boy. They go off exploring together, get soaked, and share a romantic moment. Similarly, in *Sex Education*, Cal goes on a hike with their potential crush. The two have a meaningful conversation about their lives and sources of anxiety. It is a delightful day to share outside of the stressors of the main plot, and it brings the two closer. In Steven Salvatore's *And They Lived...*, Chase's close friend, who goes to a different college, drives their roommate and everybody's crushes to a concert. After, Chase and their crush share an intimate moment, and everything seems wonderful just for that time. In *Love and Other Disasters*, London and their romantic interest, Dahlia, go on a small road trip to the beach, feeling free and playful together.

Some adventures are about more platonic relationships. In *Sir Callie and the Champions of Helston*, Callie and their newfound friend, El, sneak out together. They leave behind the oppressive and gender-restrictive court and go riding without permission.

We ride out at a steady trot, Elowen holding tight to my waist and directing us to all her favorite places around Helston. From the highest spot on the hill with the best view out to the moors in the east, to the tiniest beaches concealed behind a curving cliff. "I haven't had anyone to go adventuring with in years," Elowen tells me, like she's like she's a whole lot older than twelve. "Usually as soon as I introduce newcomers to the others, well, let's just say I'm rarely someone's primary choice of companion." Which makes zero sense to me at all [Symes-Smith 97].

When Callie suggests, "Maybe we can figure it out our own way, together, if you want to. Be friends I mean. We can be different together" (97). Elowen's eyes widen with pleasure. This little escapade brings them together as allies and as friends.

Cowboys (film 2021) shows the father and son camping together as they flee civilization and the mother (Sally), celebrating the child's love of cowboy life. The film then flashes back to Sally's house, where she takes out a photo of the child as a ten-year-old girl, Josie Johnson. A flashback shows her dressing the child to match her long blond hair and fluffy dress, with the child looking miserable. Sally's brother snarks, "You always did like your dolls." More flashbacks show a fascination with cowboy culture. After the parents have separated, the dad comes back to hope they can reconcile. Sally protests, "I'm just starting to get Joe back to normal," and he tells her, "Sally… You are not God, okay? And Joe is not some lump of clay that you just pound into something. Joe is Joe. We either accept that or you fuck him up."

She disagrees and retorts, "You messed her up. You messed *her* up."

On hearing that his father will never be allowed to visit again, Joe cuts off his hair and leaps into his truck. He pleads for his dad to take him away and adds, "Dad… I can't stay here." His dad returns later, and they sneak away. Far from civilization, they have a grand adventure: fishing, tent camping, horseback riding, and living without the expectations of Joe's mother.

In the beloved *Steven Universe* cartoon, Steven is raised by Garnet, Amethyst, and Pearl, who are Gems: magical aliens who fight to protect Earth. The Gems manifest around a gemstone, sometimes choosing or finding that they have a new form. Gems also can "fuse:" through close connections or shared goals, they can share a unique embodiment with other Gems. To fuse, they dance in unison, symbolizing closeness.

Steven is the child of Greg, a human, and Rose, a Gem. Rose and Greg could never fuse, but Rose decided to leave behind her consciousness and combine her form with part of a child she had with Greg—Steven.

The story of Steven's figuring out his powers is unique. Early on, Steven makes friends with Connie, a human girl who loves reading and is great at tennis. While Connie hesitates to dance with Steven, worried about people looking at her, Steven convinces her to try. As the two delight in the dance and the closeness they find in sharing it, they fuse into Stevonnie.

It is important to note that the show's creator, Rebecca Sugar, clarified that all Gems are non-binary ("Steven Universe"). Most often, the Gems present as femme and are enlisted to play Steven's moms at a family dinner, even as he struggles to publicly define having three of them. However, in the episode "Tiger Millionaire," Amethyst takes the role of wrestler Purple Puma, with a bare, hairy chest, bulging biceps, a deep voice, and he/him pronouns. This moment emphasizes how the Gems are shape changers, and their typical forms are affectations. This suggests "that the Gems have an understanding of human gender norms, but actively disregard them in their own lives" (Busnardo n.p.).

Meanwhile, Stevonnie is one of the first officially non-binary characters on television, standing out for using "they/them" pronouns in 2015. The Gems of Steven's family have different reactions to finding out Steven and Connie have fused. Pearl, the cautious one, acts deeply uncomfortable with it. Vivacious Amethyst is happy and curious. But Garnet, ordinarily quite reserved, is delighted. With stars in her eyes, she says, "Stevonnie, listen to me. You are not two people, and you are not one person. You are an experience. Make sure you're a good experience. Now, go—have fun!" ("Alone Together" 1.37). These reactions are easy to read as responses toward people outside of the gender binary. Some find the very existence of non-binary people to be uncomfortable, stressful. Others may find it amusing. But some show respect and delight in its deep meaning. Garnet, herself a fusion of two Gems, understands the joy of the experience of their embodiment.

Stevonnie takes Garnet's advice and runs off to have a beautiful day. They run by the ocean, swim, and then pop into the donut shop to get some food. They are so striking that they are given donuts for free. They have a perplexing moment, wanting to share the two donuts they received but realizing they are one person. Still, they discuss it and choose to go on.

They end up going to a rave, where their day starts to sour. They become self-conscious, and a guy who wants to dance with them harasses them. As they become angry and overwhelmed, they miss being in each other's company and tumble apart. Unfused, Steven and Connie can again enjoy themselves and each other's company, laughing and jumping around as the DJ throws glowsticks into the crowd.

Like other happy, fun side adventures discussed in this chapter, Stevonnie's side trip brings Connie and Steven closer. It also reveals the benefits of not being fused, of being together separately. In their following adventures, the two sometimes choose to be separate and sometimes to be Stevonnie. This indicates the importance of maintaining and investing in the different aspects of the relationship and the self. As one critic writes, "and at no time is Steven's gender called into question. Not once is there any hint that a little boy becoming a woman is anything short of an experience to be celebrated. Stevonnie enjoys her day. She gets a donut. She dances. She just is. That's really all there is to say about her. You just have to experience her. As a viewer, you get to participate in a little boy's experience of womanhood and what's more awesome than that?" (Busnardo n.p.).

Finding Allies: Pet *(Novel)*

Of course, on the quest, a loving companion who provides endless support strengthens the hero. Allies are not always of the same species as the trans characters. The protagonist of the *Cute Mutants* series can talk with and understand the speech of objects, like a beloved baseball bat. In *A Psalm for the Wild-Built*, a human monk meets a robot who is searching for human civilization, and the two become friends. *Tess of the Road*,

Phoenix Extravagant, Return of the Dragon Guard, and many more feature dragon companions.

Some protagonists need new allies for more intricate reasons. The protagonist of Akwaeke Emezi's *Pet,* Jam, lives in a world where everyone believes all the monsters have been eliminated. In this world, the angels went to extraordinary lengths to banish them all—even as they symbolize child abuse, prejudice, secret crime, and all manner of injustice. "People started by believing the victims, and once this was apparent that it was safe to report the monsters now, more and more people did so. The monsters always tried to apologize when they were caught, using the same slippery words that had worked for them before" (79). However, by eliminating the monsters and creating a safe place, the evil still exists but goes unrecognized. While everyone insists everything is fine, monsters still surround them. Emezi comments:

> I grew up in Nigeria mostly under a military dictatorship, very different from being here. But one of the things that I liked about growing up back home is that everyone's very blatant about what's happening. Like when the government's trying to kill you, the government's trying to kill you. *Pet*, so far, is my most American book, it's set in America, it's about America. Here, people aren't really acknowledging what was happening around us, they're not really looking directly at things. So I wanted to tell a story where a young person is in the middle of that, being challenged to look directly at a problem without the support of the other people around her and as a young person, how do you deal with the problem if no one else will look at it [qtd. in Bergado n.p.].

This also works as a metaphor for society's ignoring the abuse of its most vulnerable citizens.

In such a world, the heroine calls up a new monster to fight the monsters around her. This creature emerges from her mother's painting, invoked by a touch of Jam's blood. This moment emphasizes their deep connection. Beyond this, Pet is Jam's sole non-binary friend and thus, in a way, a mentor. At first, Jam is afraid of the being, but quickly she realizes it is clumsy and tangled, and it asks her to help it step into the world. After, Jam finds it hard to be afraid. The creature, who calls itself Pet, can sense that someone is hurting a child. As it turns out, it is happening in the house where Jam's best friend, Redemption, lives. Here, Pet represents Jam's own awareness of wrongness and worry that she's unequipped to handle it. The best friend emerges from the subconscious as a partner to aid her with encouragement and intuition. This is common for children, who see the animals and objects around them as allies and enemies guiding them to understanding.

Pet insists, "The child they call Redemption is important to you, and you are important to the hunt for the monster and the house of

Redemption" (Emezi, *Pet* 72). Jam cannot let it go, even though her parents demand that she send the creature away. She can't ask her friend about it, in case it could hurt him. She wants to turn down its quest to track the evil—Jam insists that hunting is supposed to be Pet's job. However, Pet insists that they are a team. "I am not allowed to move so freely in this your world, it said with a trace of bitterness that pooled, oily, in the air between them. That is why you are important: there must be a hunter like me; There must be a hunter who is human, who could go where I cannot go, see what I cannot see" (73). It growls, filling her with terror, and insists it will do what she cannot do.

Throughout the story, friendship and allyship serve as a central theme. The characters in the story fiercely prioritize their loved ones, not only in big moments but also in little ones. For example, the story mentions in passing that Redemption speaks ASL (American Sign Language) with Jam without presenting it—through ableism—as an amazing, generous practice. As Jam and Pet investigate together, her friendship with Redemption explores the nuances of human relationships. Emezi comments:

> With Jam, what does it look like for a black trans girl to have this really wholesome, protective friendship with a black cis boy. And I'm only realizing that no one's ever asked me about their friendship before, and I just kind of put them together 'cause they felt right, but just looking around at what's happening in the world today, it's like, the main people who are killing black trans women are black cis men. I wasn't trying to make a statement with their friendship in that way, but just when you asked that question I'm looking back and I'm just like, oh, this is a wholesome future. This is the kind of future where she can be loved by someone who, perhaps, in a worse and different life, would have tried to hurt her [qtd. in Bergado n.p.].

Redemption's family is African American, and Jam's family is West African and West Indian, so the clash between immigrants and established Americans is also explored and modeled with idealistic kindness.

While Pet has different ideas than Jam's about violence and consent, Pet agrees to take Jam's lead time and again, as an ally should. In fiction, an animal sidekick is somewhere between a mentor and a surrogate child, teaching the hero to care for others. "Even Disney's submissive Cinderella sews coats for her tiny animal helpers. From caring for animals, loving, and being loved, Cinderella learns she has value. She discovers herself, while the stepsisters only polish their exteriors" (Frankel, *From Girl to Goddess* 37). While Pet and Jam sometimes debate values, Pet does not need this kind of physical care. It is its own person, and so is Jam. However, as pet allies often do, Pet has capabilities and symbolism beyond Jam's.

3. Safety with Others

Animals represent instinct and primitive understanding and have much to teach the questing hero; this is seen with Pet being upset when Jam lies to Redemption and Jam refusing to allow Pet to spy on Redemption's intimate conversation with his brother. Further, animals traditionally have gifts of perception. Pet tells Jam, "If you do not know that there are things you do not see ... then you will not see them because you do not expect them to be there. You think you see everything, so you think everything you see is all there is to be seen" (Emezi, *Pet* 71–72). Pet is between worlds, between Jam's and other places, a hybrid that symbolizes being many types of non-binary, beyond categorization:

> These creatures guard the border between land and sea, or life and death. Often dwelling in caves open to the air or deep in the forest, these creatures test the heroine: "Do not pass," they say. "Are your eyes or ears better than mine? Do you have a magic token or hidden talent? Only one who knows the secret of life, only one who is clever, or anointed in [mature] mysteries, may step into the shrine. For all others, death awaits." In this world, the heroine is weak, still a student beside the ageless power of the god-imbued immortals ... Thus the sphinx, half woman and half lion, defends her threshold, demanding a riddle of the nature of life itself. She is monster and woman, as chaotic and magical as the unconscious itself, a figure of nightmares [Frankel, *From Girl to Goddess* 66].

While gaining this added perception, Jam stands with Pet, learning and teaching with mutual respect. Redemption finally gets to confront his uncle Hibiscus about the abuse of his seven-year-old brother Moss. "Don't act like I'm the one anything's wrong with ... you're the one who is a lie, who's been a lie, hiding here for who knows how long. A false Angel. A traitor," he insists (Emezi, *Pet* 179). Hibiscus tries gaslighting, and he and Redemption fight. "Hibiscus had only a moment to look up before Pet was on him, and he didn't even have time to scream at the sight of the creature before Pet took hold of him by his ribcage and lifted him like he was a toy, a rag doll. Hibiscus let go of Redemption and Jam, both of them crumpling to the floor and gasping in pain. Pet opened its mouth and roared, thick smoke sheeting out. It threw Hibiscus against the concrete wall, and his body smacked into it with a dull thud before crashing to the ground" (182–183). This is the culmination of Pet's great hunt, and it doesn't want to stop, but Jam halts it by shouting voicelessly into its head. If Pet represents instinct, Jam represents reason and higher thought.

Pet protests that Jam's people will ignore the monster it has found, so Pet's particular outsider intervention is needed. "This is why hunters exist, to see the unseens, to track them down in the shadows they skulk in, to find them. To finish them. Let me do my job" (184).

Jam retorts that the town needs to learn better and find the chance to change. Thus, the monster needs to be revealed. Keeping Hibiscus as an example will help the town understand which red flags to look for. She is determined to stop the monsters before they become fully grown and prey on her community. Pet is a monster hunter in the shadows, but Jam protects the innocent more publicly. Both of their skills are needed to heal their society.

With this, Pet reveals its true self to Hibiscus with light and wings. It fills the room with glory, and Hibiscus screams and screams, devastated by Pet's light. As Jam thinks, "Screaming like that meant you had been broken, completely shattered and crushed, and there was no way you were a threat after that. There was no way you were even whoever you had been before, not after that. Not after seeing Pet's true face" (194–195). Pet leaves her with the reminder that in all aspects of life she mustn't be afraid and departs. As it wished, the monster has been exposed, and as Jam wished, he survives, repentant, as an example to the next generation. Emezi explains:

> There's this idea that angels are people wearing white with halos and white wings. Then if you read the Bible and the angels are described as having wings full of eyes and multiple heads on fire. They're really terrifying things to look at. They're not at all what humans have kind of made them out to be. So that was one of the themes of the book, so to speak, was what does an angel look like, what does a monster look like. And kind of turning those upside down and inside out [qtd. in Bergado n.p.].

4

Challenge and Growth

Partnering the Double: The Witch King *(Novel)*

Some protagonists find allies who have similar social parameters to theirs. Bells, of C. B. Lee's *Not Your Villain*, finds a group of friends who are mostly queer and have some relation to the superhero and supervillain battles that are central to their world. In *Sir Callie and the Champions of Helston*, Callie connects with a girl who is severely oppressed by the traditional gender roles her father uses to control and silence her. Callie also befriends an abused, gender-nonconforming child who loves horses, is gentle and kind, and turns out to be the prince. While the two are nobles, the three have much shared understanding of the wrongs of a binaristic and rigid gender system, as well as the social hierarchy of court and of knighthood. Danny of April Daniels's *Dreadnought* series has both. She welcomes other teenagers with superpowers, many of them queer. She also finds the help and support of an older superhero who is a robot and, like Danny, is not always perceived as being sufficiently human to matter.

When H. E. Edgmon's *The Witch King* begins, teenage Wyatt Croft has fled the fae world and a destiny of wedding the prince and producing babies to live as himself. He grew up in Faery, stigmatized and nearly killed because he was a witch—the unwanted and dangerous element of their society. Over and over, Wyatt's trans status and witch status are conflated in a metaphor for stigmatism.

Finding allies is no small task for transgender characters. As Malatino stresses, having a community of care is, for some, a question of survival. "Whatever being trans is about, it's decidedly characterized by upheaval and emergence into a social world with shifting and shifted parameters. For many of us, surviving this process means committing to forms of healing that are unthinkable, indeed impossible, without care webs" (*Trans Care* 3). Malatino describes a community supporting one another and relying on one another for survival. It should be noted, however, that such a system may not be enough. When a community is severely under-resourced, sympathy without societal change rarely leads to any solutions. Coauthor Dean Leetal's experience is that when one is in an abusive family situation, queer friends may realize they have no way to intervene and avoid the person out of discomfort, isolating them further.

In such a situation, with few friends or adults offering any protection, Wyatt fled. After three years, the prince, Emyr North, tracks Wyatt down in the human world. Wyatt is incredibly smitten. He also feels a deep connection beyond the attraction. On first seeing Emyr, Wyatt thinks, "The Fay are all monsters. But so am I" (Edgmon, *Witch King* 12). This meeting is a wake-up call, a reminder that Wyatt cannot go on passing for human but must return to his homeland to revitalize it. Further, Emyr insists he face judgment for the deaths his powers caused. However, Emyr ensures he will do so in a safe and protected space, with leniency and mercy.

One's allies, often friends and romantic partners, guide the protagonist to deeper insights and new ways of thinking, echoing the small voices within. Today, new commentators are moving beyond archetypes scholar Carl Jung's description of the animus or anima as the opposite-gendered guide to explore how homosexual relationships change the metaphor. Exploring this area, archetypes scholar Robert H. Hopcke observes: "Gay relationships are in fact a locus of individuation, even though, or, in fact, precisely because the so-called opposites of male and female are not at issue. As the incarnation of a union of opposites, all relationships, homosexual or heterosexual, serve to embody the self ... to affect the transformation of consciousness" (140–141).

Psychologist Mitch Walker proposes the term *the Double* as the same-sex best friend and possible lover (or rival) who offers new insights and skills through the relationship. "The Double is a soulmate of intense warmth and closeness. Love between men and love between women, as a cyclic experience, is often rooted in projection of the Double, just as Anima/us is projected in love between the different sexes" (Walker, "Double" 49). Achilles and Patroclus, Gilgamesh and Enkidu, Frodo and Sam—such love between opposites in areas other than gender offers "uncanny feelings of unity, strength, and reinforcement of personal identity" that incorporate profound familiarity, intuition, understanding, and joy (Walker, "Visionary" 224).

To Wyatt, Emyr offers the beloved memory of a childhood friend, protective and trustworthy. "The rest of the world can be bad sometimes, but I always feel safe with Emyr. When the Fay whisper awful things about me behind my back, when my parents yell at me for not wanting to act the way they tell me to, when my sister is cruel ... there's always Emyr" (Edgmon, *Witch King* 324). He's a nurturing force, as he's raised their beloved dog. He gave Wyatt the tarot cards that prove the key to his magic. As such, he's not just a comforter and protector but a guide to help Wyatt become his best self.

The epitome of a warrior king, Emyr is polite, generous, and unyielding in his interactions with others. He has healing magic, which symbolizes bringing self-healing to Wyatt. He also desperately loves Wyatt, emphasizing not just a source of support but also self-love. Emyr believes in their destiny together and regards him with perfect faith, affection, and trust, even in his worst moments. Moreover, Emyr, in this first scene and most others, stands out for genderfluid dress. At his entrance, he wears a pink suit with gold flowers, and later scenes show him in gauze and skirts. He models living as he wishes, though he also considers how to compromise. When he first finds Wyatt, he asks his pronouns, validating this part of his existence. He calls Wyatt beautiful, adding that beauty needn't be gender specific. Uncomfortably, Wyatt thinks that he resents this: "Because I don't want to be beautiful. Because I don't want any sliver of my value to be defined by you or anyone else finding me nice to look at. Because I'm a monster, and monsters aren't supposed to be beautiful" (Edgmon, *Witch King* 51). This gradually changes as he comes to see himself as Emyr does.

Reluctantly, Wyatt accompanies Emyr to the fae world to consider their shared destiny. Working with Emyr thus helps cultivate the duty and leadership Wyatt has avoided exploring in himself. Wyatt begins the story by deliberately acting like a bratty child. As he narrates, "I spent the first half of the flight bouncing the soles of my boots against the back of his chair just to annoy him and the second half writing profanities on my jeans with a sharpie" (50). Wyatt is terrible with people and terrible with diplomacy. He's known for breaking rules. Partnering with this disciplined near-adult, who's mastered public and private life, teaches him control.

Emyr also has more tangible offerings. He's made a hobby of blending technology and magic, with new tools for Wyatt to use and learn. Once they've returned, Emyr trains Wyatt in swordplay and works with him to plan new laws for protecting the witches. "The Double is facilitative of rapport. It creates an atmosphere between the friends of profound equality and deep familiarity, a mysterious, joyful sharing of feelings and needs, a dynamic, intuitive understanding. Such a pleasurable camaraderie easily extends to a sharing of purpose or goal through which difficult tasks are undertaken and fulfilled" (Walker, "Double" 50). This Wyatt finds in their closeness: the understanding friendship of the past combined with the growing same-sex romance in the present.

One's companions on the quest fill in what is missing in one's personality. Dorothy's companions teach her about brains, love, and courage, and most sidekicks play a similar role. The masculine side of the self, or double, evokes classically masculine traits: logic, rationality, intellect. This aids the questor in developing an understanding of the conscious world: business, rulership, and interpersonal interactions. At the most primitive level, the masculine aspect is a force of brute strength and power. This Wyatt has already encountered, in the constant bullying of his peers and his father, interactions so savage that he lashed out violently and fled the Faery world. As the questor matures, increasingly wise masculine figures step in to offer more developed stages: initiative and planning, rule of law, and wisdom (von Franz 194). These are offered mostly by Emyr, Wyatt's perfect match and companion.

> Freed from the power differential found in virtually all heterosexual relationships, romance between two individuals of the same sex can, at least in its ideal form, have a profound characteristic of mirroring equality, where both parties are appreciated as sacred individuals rather than objects to be conquered. Released from the biological imperative for literal reproduction, same-sex partners can focus their regard on the perceived inner and outer beauty of the beloved as a satisfying goal in its own right and may subsequently be thus so inspired, as Plato wrote, to produce "immortal" children of the mind in the form of intellectual and creative achievements. Fascination with the mysterious source of such ecstasy and ingenuity can lead an individual further inward in an effort to understand this powerful force of attraction, thereby encouraging the development of a psychological attitude and subsequent spiritual awakening [Kaufman 168–169].

In Faery, Derek is an evil double, the villainous cousin scheming for the crown. He persuades Wyatt to act out until no one wants him as king consort. Because Derek watched him grow up and knows him so well, his temptations are insidious. "Wouldn't you do anything to go back to your life out there? To take your human and return home? Do you really want to stay here in Asalin forever, constantly reminded of the horrific thing you did?" (Edgmon, *Witch King* 94). He adds that while Emyr plans to present Wyatt as a misguided child, Derek suspects Wyatt "would have more fun becoming the villain" (95). Under his influence, Wyatt tries joyriding and vandalism, taking glee in the teenage rebellion. Derek is an adversary, but also another type of double, using his deep perception of Wyatt's conflict and guiding him to lash out.

Comparing trans people's friendships with cis heterosexuals, cis queer people, and other trans people, the authors found unique benefits and barriers to friendship with each group. The quality of support can vary depending on these categories (Galupo et al. n.p.). For example, trans people appreciated that LGBTQ+ issues did not dominate conversations with straight cis friends but were frustrated that these friends rarely understood their "non-normative experiences" (Galupo et al. n.p.). Conversely, friendships with other LGBTQ+ people provided common understanding through shared experience, but LGBTQ+ issues dominated the conversation. Support via mentoring and shared resources was a unique benefit of friendship with other LGBTQ+ people (Kichler 2465). Accordingly, Wyatt has many friends, from the human foster sister who comes with him to Faery to the variety of allies who live there. All have different gender experiences and marginalizations to explore.

The expectation that being the prince's mate means having his babies torments Wyatt. However, the sequel reveals that this teaching has been twisted. The concept of perfect mates was never meant to mean biological compatibility. Instead, it is "this sacred fellowship exists between two people who are one another's perfect mirrors. A reflection of all they are and all they hope to be. These unions allow both parties to grow to their fullest potential" (Edgmon, *Fae Keeper* 315–316). Further, Wyatt is told that "to equate them to romantic unions or parental partnerships would be to diminish their value" (316). Armed with this knowledge, Wyatt finally takes a leadership role and creates a society where everyone is respected.

Emyr continues to fight beside him as a warrior, comforter, and lover. Wyatt thinks, "I don't know how it's possible for one person to be everything but he is. Masculine and feminine, strong and soft, a leader and a partner, darkness and light" (349). This complementary figure in its highest stage gives the questor "spiritual firmness, an invisible inner support that compensates for [their] outer softness" (von Franz 194). As the second novel ends, Emyr gives Wyatt a gift of completion: the business card of a changeling therapist who wants to work with them both. This, of course, suggests a new stage of healing and understanding. Their partnership has guided Wyatt through the growth stages and finally completed him.

One's love interest can also be a path toward learning one's own skills. The film *Boy Meets Girl* features a confident and capable transgender teen girl—a rarity in itself. Ricky (Michelle Hendley) has long since transitioned and is comfortable with who she is. (The actress was selected after her real-life transition videos went viral.) Her father, brother, and best friend, Robby, are comfortable and supportive as well. Her history is casually known around their small Kentucky town, and few worry about it. As the film begins, a pretty debutante named Francesca moves to town and shakes up the dynamic in traditional rom-com fashion. Ricky bonds with Francesca, sewing her pretty dresses like Ricky's own and enjoying the mirroring of being with a girl like herself. Ricky also has frank sex talks with Robby about what girls respond to and how to please them. She gradually finds herself losing interest in Francesca and falling for Robby, who offers more contrasting skills along with real understanding. Her crush on the double guides Ricky to true love for the one who's always been present.

Other doubles are more distant and idealized, though still a catalyst for growth. Joss Lake's *Future Feeling* offers a surreal trip through an allegory for the trans experience. The protagonist, Penfield Ruth Henderson, begins the novel obsessed with Aiden. Every weekday, he watches the man groom on holographic social media. "And each morning, I thought about killing him in a metaphorical way, the trans father whose shadow I wanted to step out of, even though the dude was younger than I was" (6). Having such love for a public figure, a social media image, is a projection—idealizing this figure from afar. Penfield knows his crush object is basically fictional, but that doesn't deter him:

> Tell us, you are wondering, *What kind of fool would take a gram seriously anyway?*
> Yes, that is where Aiden and I both erred. In our defense, grams are one of the few places to see trans folks; Blame it on the peculiar manifestations of late capitalism—*Saintly Secretions of Non-Solace!*—but only newer media contain any evidence at all that trans people are doing more than being murdered and getting kicked out of the familial abode. One could say my Aiden-rage reached hurricane-level swells because he was a trans dude—on the public Internet, with hologram status—and all he could offer my impoverished imagination was a life as sleek and empty as all architecture since 1991 [7].

He realizes what he's seeing is artificial, yet the perfection charms him, and he keeps comparing himself to the figure on-screen. "Each morning, I awoke, went to the backyard, and immediately scanned Aiden's bod on the Gram, asking, *Why can't I attain such delicate perfection?* A holey apple staring at a waxed, genetically modified one. I had no other trans role models, so who could really blame me for moving toward this trans-parent like a toddler swimming to open, tanned, and muscular arms?" (8). This figure is father, lover, best friend, role model—all the double has to offer, but also distant and unreal. Sometimes, stories show the two characters intertwining and completing one another on a more science-fictional level. In "Ports of Perceptions" by Izzy Wasserstein, Chase and Hunter "exchange":

> Hunter's arm-ports synched with the receivers on Chase's back and data flowed between them, which they agreed was worth the risk, despite Chase's cold and the v0x virus still being rooted out by antivi. Chase felt Hunter's concern turn to desire, and they explored each other and the PKD. Chase unclasped each of their right forearms, then swapped them. Hunter's arm, which was, or had been, or would be Chase's, moved over their bodies. They disconnected Hunter's not-quite-legal sensory enhancer and synched it with Chase's, and the rush was like data exchange but more immediate, more vivid. (73)

This communion represents a sharing and coming-together, augmented by the technology. It's a romance, but also a meeting of minds, a celebration of contrasting personality types merging to become something greater—a blended whole.

Following the Anim Guide: The Prince and the Dressmaker *(Graphic Novel)*

While Jung imagined the animus as the male voice within a woman and the anima as the *inspiratrice* (feminine inspiration) within a man, J. Hall writes that this can be more complex than a simple gender binary and either might be a same-sex figure or merged with the shadow. As he adds, "If there is identity confusion in the sex role of the ego, there may be a reflection of this confusion in the dream images of the shadow and anima or animus. It must be remembered, too, that these structural terms are to some degree generalizations; the actual dreams and dream images are more complex than the concepts" (75). In fact, though animus or anima is commonly the opposite gender of the protagonist and the mentor and shadow are the same, fiction and myth reveal many characters for which this is not the case. More fundamentally, these figures echo qualities that the conscious self cannot access, thus providing a path to discovering them.

Jung and Campbell said that the questing hero encounters the anima—mother, sister, or lover—that functions as a spiritual guide and leads the questor to explore the undeveloped feminine side of his nature. She can be a spirit of the natural world, like Tinkerbell, or a mother-protector, like a fairy godmother. The questing heroine learns from the animus—the masculine aspect of the self. At the same time, Jung warns that people misuse romance to express deep longings that are actually soul longings; people ask their partner to complete them when the seeker actually desires completion from their romantic inner voice. Identifying less with the body can help the questor discover the universal, mythic, and spiritual within the self.

Of course, the trans hero's journey is more complex. The hero, regardless of gender, might already have plenty of experience of "the other side." However, their guide should evoke a missing part of the self, as all friends and companions on the quest do. This friend may bring gender lessons by being the well-adjusted person whose gender the hero longs to actualize or by having fulfilled the quest in other ways. Hillman suggests that the "fantasy of opposites" discussed here contains much more than a simple gender binary: within it, there are "ceaseless pairings and couplings" of anima, animus, ego and shadow, persona, and self once people free themselves from being "walked into the contrasexual definition of anima and animus" (Hillman 140).

To rectify the heterosexist boundaries of Jung's concept, Walker has proposed the concept of the *anim* to take the place of the cross-sex inspiring figure. Walker opposes Jung's view of men (which Jung defaulted to heterosexual cisgender men) as having an erotic fixation on the anima. As he adds, "Jung's idea that the soul, the anima, is going to be reunited with you and that is symbolized through the work, the opus, of realizing yourself. That's what he called the *syzygy* of male and female. So how are we going to use this symbology for our gay experience?" (Group Interview 246–247). Hopcke observes, "Gay relationships incarnate a plurality of opposites that go far beyond the male-female duality that western gender ideology would have us believe is so central" (141). As many critics in this area add, the fundamental fiction is that the world must be divided into imagery of masculine and feminine, so much so that all opposites in life, which encourage us to strive, must be viewed through this metaphor. Whether these are built into the language or the early mythology, the separation of strength/weakness, light/dark, and so on into a gendered metaphor can be set aside to find a stronger image.

Jen Wang's *The Prince and the Dressmaker* is a delightful, sweet graphic novel that focuses on the triumph of finding one's perfect self through this sort of anim. A dressmaker, Frances, is obsessed with the beautiful costumes in the ballet *The Muse of Crystallia*. Inspired, she soon became a designer. When she's fired for making a young lady the off-putting, outrageous gown she desires, a mysterious client instantly hires her.

Frances quickly discovers that her veiled client is actually Crown Prince Sebastian of Belgium. He's been wearing his mother's gowns in private, but he seeks to dazzle in fantastical, dramatic gowns that make a stir and set the fashion. As he adds, "Some days I look at myself in the mirror and think, 'That's me, Prince Sebastian!' I wear boy clothes and look like my father. Other days it doesn't feel right at all. Those days I feel like I'm actually a princess" (44). As both Frances and Sebastian seek to stand out and show off each other, they've found a perfect partnership and soon a close friendship.

The anima, in Jungian psychology, represents the feminine side of the personality, for example, Frodo's inspiratrice Galadriel or Aragorn's beloved Arwen. The anima is also a best friend, providing endless support. This side of the self expresses unexplored emotions. "The anima is a personification of all feminine psychological tendencies ... such as vague feelings and moods, prophetic hunches, receptiveness to the irrational, capacity for personal love, feeling for nature and—last but not least—his relation to the unconscious" (von Franz 177). Frances takes this role for Sebastian, teaching him about his unexplored side. She accompanies Sebastian on his first outing, in which he enters the Miss Marmalade beauty pageant and, naming himself Lady Crystallia, instantly wins. Her glowing look of pleasure says everything. Of course, Crystallia is another anima figure for Sebastian. Even when straight men cross-dress for comedy or straight women to escape gender restrictions, it tends to evoke queer imagery. Mark Thompson observes that "the role of the drag queen, for instance, is based on a particular form of realizing the internal feminine as ally" (Group Interview 251). Crystallia isn't real, but to Sebastian, she's a force of gorgeousness and revelation. After, Frances gushes, "It was you, but you were more. Bigger. More amazing. You were like a goddess version of yourself. It was magic" (Wang 74).

"It's the first time I felt worthy of all this…. It's weird. I don't feel like Prince Sebastian could lead a nation into battle, but Lady Crystallia could" (Wang 75). As a persona, Lady Crystallia lets him show the world another self; as an anima, she reassures him. They continue, with the persona as a comforting retreat, even as Sebastian's pressure to marry continues. After one such dinner, he rushes for his costume, exclaiming, "I need to go out in that right now!" (86).

The two animas, Frances and Lady Crystallia, can both be seen helping his growth and self-assurance. When he shows up to meet Frances, she asks mildly, "No Crystallia tonight?" and he replies that he thought he'd try out the outfit she made for his prince side (130).

As dresser and model, the pair offer complementary talents, which is another essential aspect of the anima. Frances, famous as the gorgeous lady's seamstress, is getting offers and acclaim. However, when Sebastian bids her hide so people won't associate Crystallia with the prince, she quits. "I'd rather take my chances starting over than languish in your closet forever" (172). With this, she teaches him about the misery of hiding while also choosing to pursue her own goals. The best friend sometimes desires a plot of her own, and this too can teach self-reliance.

Frances's career takes off, even as the prince's secret is dramatically discovered and his bride dumps him on their wedding day. The prince runs off and hides at a monastery. Meanwhile, as she collects the dresses, Frances continues her role as mediator and protector. She speaks with the king, telling him they did nothing wrong. "All he ever wanted was to please you and your wife. This is the way he is" (228). She adds that Sebastian wasn't confused about himself, just afraid of his parents' judgment.

In a happy ending, Sebastian comes to Frances's big show, which she's allowed to become quite conservative. When he encourages her to be more daring, she has male models show off the gowns, all confident and powerful. Among them is the king in a stunning red robe, showing his support as he realizes how much Frances and Sebastian love each other. In a stunning butterfly gown, Lady Crystallia finishes the night, and Frances gets acclaim from everyone. The pair live happily ever after, each being whatever they desire.

Of course, the anim can be a literal voice from within in some stories. Emezi's *Freshwater* explores the inner life of Ada, a person with multiple personalities due to trauma. One of these personalities, Saint Vincent, allows Ada to explore crossing to the other gender. Taking her over and binding her chest are "in preparation for a shedding, the skin splitting in long seams" (188). The binder "felt like armor, like we were bulletproof, like Saint Vincent was being built up in layers of determined fiber" (188). The inner voices, including the narrator, insist that the mother loosen her hold and give Ada up to her new selves. She had "been an excellent guardian as far as she could, but what did she know of graces or beastselves or ugly, unwelcome embodiments or the sacrifices a snake must go through to continue its timeline, the necessity of molting, the graves built of skins?" (189). After this journey, Ada gets surgery and emerges more stable and secure.

The Norse god Loki is famous for transforming into gender-bending roles like a mare to distract a stallion for its mission and an old woman who refuses to weep for dead Baldur, both times to further his own schemes. Joanne Harris's *The Testament of Loki* takes this further, with Loki reborn inside the mind of a modern teen, Jumps (Josephine). She and Loki share her body as he lashes out against her drab clothes and eating disorder by enjoying the modern world's pleasures. He also chats up a lovely teen girl, Meg. As it turns out, Jumps likes her, and Meg admires Jumps's "real self" more than her Loki-inhabited wild girl. Jumps has been afraid to express this side of herself. "If it hadn't been sad, it might have been ridiculous. Much guilt and shame and fear in her mind. So many unnecessary feelings" (95). By the climax, her image of herself has changed. "Now she was a young woman: strong, not unbeautiful" who "seemed to glow with her own inner light" (230). She stands up for her friends and uses Loki's magic to save the day, showing her multifaceted growth.

One's art can be one's anim as well. In *And They Lived*, Chase shares with the readers a secret teenage sketchbook. "It was filled with self-portraits of me as both prince and princess, knight and witch, male and female, and sometimes a magical combination of both and neither all at once. I used to think I was a shape-shifter because some days I would feel more masculine, others more feminine, and sometimes in-between or something else entirely" (Salvatore 65). Chase's most frequent drawing is of a gender-ambiguous angel with mighty dragon wings and flowing robes. As Chase concludes, "Some days, I felt like that angel: ethereal, something beyond this binary world" (65).

4. Challenge and Growth

Loving the Anim: A Lady for a Duke *(Novel)*

One's love interest can also be a path toward learning one's own skills. The celebrated regency romance *A Lady for a Duke* gives Viola Carroll (self-named for the Shakespeare heroine) a difficult dilemma. Two years prior, at Waterloo, she was presumed dead and took the opportunity to maintain this fiction and live as herself. However, at the novel's beginning, her beloved sister-in-law insists that they go pay a call on her former best friend and fellow soldier, Justin De Vere, Duke of Gracewood, as he's been severely depressed. Viola explains, "When we were young, Gracewood and I were closer than—as close as two people can possibly be. To be aware of one another but kept apart by station and society and … all that goes with it" (Hall 18).

Viola discovers he's nearly mad with trauma and with mourning for her. She's also shocked at how differently he responds to her as a woman: flirtatious and polite, but also confiding in her about his emotions in a way he never did with any of his male companions. As such, she discovers that her identity becomes a path for them to relate differently.

As she tells him later, "I thought you proud and dashing and brave and all that you should be. But I did not understand how much I meant to you or how deeply you felt your father's hurts. I did not understand your thoughtfulness or your gentleness" (228). He protests that these are not admirable qualities in men, and she disagrees. Her new perspective lets her see the best qualities in him, not just display the best ones in herself.

They live in a world in which men and women live in different social spaces and fill wildly different roles, but crossing those lines lets them learn much more about the emotional spectrum. Viola comforts Gracewood and pulls him out of his depression with jokes, with unladylike swearing, with reminders of his responsibilities. At the same time, as he flirts with her, he awakens something new: "She just wasn't prepared to, well, to receive compliments from men, although she was, of course, aware in abstract that this was something that happened. In certain circumstances. From certain men. To certain women. Not her" (40). All at once, it's wonderful and horrible to be so noticed. His flirting makes her feel delicate and precious.

> And for the first time in her life she allowed herself to look at him, truly look at him, as she had never dared before because it would have entangled her with a different set of possibilities—possibilities she had somehow always known weren't the answer she was seeking. She looked at him now as a woman to a man, claiming all the freedom of it [45].

She's particularly touched when Gracewood finds her an ancient Tudor riding dress that will let her ride astride modestly. She admires how it feels "both soft and strong" (134). As she thinks, "The riding habit, though, with its corsetry and its heavy velvet skirts, felt like armor. Even looked a little bit like armor, with the decorated sleeves, and the zigzag pattern of exposed lacing down the bodice. And she loved it" (133–134).

While she keeps the secret for a few days, he's very drawn to her without realizing who he knew her as. When he finally discovers their history, he's overjoyed and wants to find a way to be together. "Damn the world. The world told you that you had to live the life it shaped for you and you defied it. The world told me that I had to be as my father was and I defied it or am trying to. We can make our own world, Viola, with our own rules" (269). While she refuses to compromise her reputation and be his mistress, she agrees to meet him in the library to talk late at night.

Viola's transcendent abilities before and after this revelation come from her double education: she can quote Latin scholars, fence, shoot, swear, cliff dive, and ride the fiercest horses. She can also embroider, simper, and flirt. She wields her two sides to comfort Gracewood, as she understands soldiering but also sentiment and the women's world of family life. When he hesitates to dance and fears putting too much weight on her, injured as he is, she points out, "We used to wrestle and fight with swords. You think because I'm a woman I'm suddenly weak?" (305). When fireworks trigger a moment of trauma, she covers for him, insisting loudly, "Please forgive me … but I have always been deathly afraid of fireworks. I…I think I feel a little faint" (323). As she mentions afterward, it is socially appropriate for a woman to be frightened, and she can use her status to protect him: "That the world expects weakness from women is an inequity that we can sometimes twist to our favor" (331). At the climax, she duels with Gracewood's sword, using her old skills to defend her new family.

When she hesitates to start a romantic relationship, Gracewood tells her, "I believe who I am resides in some element of me that is immaterial and immortal. Not my body" (338). Once again, he makes her feel beautiful beyond her outward self. At last he convinces her, and she decides, "I am done being afraid of myself…. I'm not going to apologize … or treat any part of me as though it is some kind of mistake…" (339). She removes her clothes piece by piece. "This body can fight. And ride. And sew. And play the pianoforte badly. It is mine. It deserves any carnal acts I want to indulge with it. And if you want to find it beautiful, Gracewood, I will let you. Because I don't see why it can't be" (339). After more adventures, she accepts his marriage proposal and his plan for a quiet life, adopted children, and constant love and support. Of course, they live happily ever after.

Finding love in another person represents validation from within. In her poem "Cinderella," Stephanie Burt explains that the prince loves his footman, a girl raised as a boy with her secret known only to the prince.

4. Challenge and Growth

They fear the kingdom won't accept them, but he doesn't want to marry anyone else. Since the prince has been commanded to choose a bride at the ball, he arranges for Cindy to show up in a beautiful gown, and he searches the town for her the next day. As the poem ends, this is the version that trans storytellers give cis people, but the true story is that the prince herself is the trans heroine, who spends a long time scouring the city in "her search for the one, the terrific, the just right shoe" (31). This story in particular emphasizes how much finding love with another means learning to love oneself.

> Love is the projection of an erotic aspect of Double or Anim onto another person. When love occurs, the projecting person sees in the other of the kosmic wonder, beauty and magick inherent in that spirit source. This is the cause of great happiness and sexual yearning and may lead to cosmic revelations seen in the sacred source of the projections [Walker, "Visionary" 223].

Such a love interest can be a force of strength and protection, with skills the hero lacks. Anna-Marie McLemore's "Roja" blends Red Riding Hood with the legend of outlaw Leonarda Emilia, who dressed as a man but flashed her breasts at the men she robbed. In this story, the wolf, El Lobo, was assigned a girl's name but redefined himself as Léon. Léon has been arrested for attacking soldiers and trying to stop their savagery. Roja, who loves him, dyes her poncho red, dons men's clothes, and invades the camp, spreading death with her bruja poison. She thinks that she and Léon will make love, whatever their bodies look like. She defiantly shows her breasts, teaching the outwitted men her identity. As Roja and Léon flee, the wolves arrive and kill the soldiers. "We left them with the salt-sting memory of us, a brazen girl and a boy with a heart so fearless wolves were his guardian saints" (28). They live to whisper their names to each other, even if they have no one else to tell.

World Running Down by Al Hess demonstrates the anim power of the non-binary ally. Osric is a cyborg who begins the story by passing out from lack of food and water because he didn't realize a mostly human body required such things. As such, he's incredibly innocent and attaches himself to Valentine Weis as a student of human behavior. Valentine rescues Osric, responding to "I'm not supposed to be in this body" with "Me neither, Hon" (22). As Osric reflects,

> people perceive Valentine as a woman, like the people in Salt Lake perceived Osric as an android.... Before Osric's time, this had been a common issue with the AI Stewards, to the point where programmers stopped assigning them arbitrary genders upon their creation and only asked for pronouns and identity once the Steward had sentience for several months. Sometimes it still took Stewards longer to decide, or they might choose a gender and then years down the road realize it wasn't correct [34–35].

Osric has chosen to identify as a man, but after encountering Valentine, he thinks, "He'd never realized how fortunate he was to be given a choice" (35). Throughout the story, Osric uses this upbringing to offer Valentine unlimited support. Osric has brought Valentine a fancy suit (as well as a dress that Valentine rejects). He is skilled at styling hair and does this for Valentine to make him look classier. With the new look, Valentine thinks, "The suit couldn't give him a sharper jawline or take away the softness of his eyes. It didn't change anything that was underneath. But he had been emulsified and poured into a man-shaped mold. He was staring into a mirror, and *Valentine* was finally staring back" (83). This new look is a pathway to self-expression and pride. This is the purpose of the anim: to make the hero more himself and reveal unexplored avenues and abilities. Likewise, Osric emphasizes how masculine Valentine is:

> When I look at you, I see a competent, selfless man.... I'm only attracted to masculinity, Valentine.... And I realize that my feelings can't negate what's going on inside you, but however you see yourself right now is not what I see. I hope you don't mind me saying so, but I like your size. You're scrappy and tough and your smaller stature makes a wonderful complement to your big personality [184].

As he goes over Valentine's attributes one by one, Valentine can take pride and pleasure in his appearance. Next, Osric guides him on a journey to the big city, where Valentine can get not only a visa, food, and supplies but also testosterone and access to doctors. They end the story as a romantic couple, with Osric quizzing Valentine to prepare him for his citizenship test. Over and over, Osric makes Valentine his best self.

Of course, expecting completion from another person can be a flawed goal. Episode one of *Pose* explores Angel's quest for a charming prince. When the client she picks up asks what she wants, she says that her greatest wish is for a home with someone to take care of who also takes care of her. In the next episode, he asks her to be his kept mistress because of her authenticity. She's touched by being seen. In his eyes, she feels validated. Of course, she's devastated when he spends Christmas with his family. She must slowly realize that her chosen family will always be there for her, but Prince Charming will not. "You're here with your family now. The men'll always come and go, but we're here for you," her house mother says. Still, she continues to struggle with this lesson. She approaches her wedding in season three to Papi, who adores all of her, celebrates who she is, and helps her embark on her dream career as a model, but Angel gets cold feet. She visits her father, who misgenders her and insists that she shouldn't get married and live an illusion. On the spot, Angel realizes he's never been reliable, but her fiancé is. They joyously wed in a beautiful ceremony celebrated by the entire community.

Mirroring: Hedwig and the Angry Inch *(Film)*

Older movies, in particular, often feature trans women sitting in front of a mirror, putting on or taking off makeup. In myth, a mirror symbolizes the inner soul and divine connection, a source of self-knowledge, identity, and revelation (Weston 139). However, in the case of trans people, Julia Serano discusses mirror-gazing as a transphobic trope, framing trans people as impostors, and focusing on their physical appearance rather than their personhood. As Serano explains, the focus on looks, often paired with changing those looks, is a way to claim their inauthenticity and frame trans people as lesser people compared with cis people.

Movies about people who are likely cis, such as *Mrs. Doubtfire* and *Tootsie*, portray mirror scenes in which protagonists face themselves in the mirror. In *Torch Song Trilogy*, the protagonist sits by one, chatting through it to the camera and the viewer. Presumably, as we see him, he sees us. He tells the story of a lost love who loves him, but not enough. As he does, he turns to the camera directly. He talks about life, romance, and independence, pouring his heart out as he supposedly watches the viewer watch him in the mirror. These "behind the scenes" moments may be intended to conflate the character's emotional openness with the "truth" of sharing the process of putting on his makeup. As Weston adds, "In coming-out narratives, seeking one's reflection often symbolizes an effort to affirm a coherent self in a situation that promises (or threatens) to transform identity" (139).

The movie *Priscilla, Queen of the Desert* (1996) shows Bernadette doing her makeup in front of a mirror time and again. One such scene does not show her face right away, as she tells a friend on the phone about mourning a partner who had an accident. Another such scene shows her potential new love for a person who respects and celebrates her. There is a moment of worry about his reaction when he sees her "behind the scenes"—both emotionally vulnerable and vulnerable to transphobia—reflected in the mirrors. However, when they stand face-to-face, he sees her as she is and celebrates her.

One may consider such scenes a moment of truth and self-inspection. However, in many cases, these scenes focus more on society's beliefs. For example, in S. T. Lynn's novella *Cinder Ella*, Ella doesn't like mirrors because they remind her of the way her transphobic stepmother understands her. Here, it serves as a reminder of society's critical gaze. Much like the mirror telling Snow White's mother she is not pretty enough, these mirrors are a "Big Brother" eye, a panopticon. Even in the closed intimacy of bedrooms and dressing rooms, the characters are exposed to transphobic eyes—to a gaze wishing to expose them as supposedly fake.

In other types of stories, like *Felix Ever After*, a self-directed gaze can bring personal revelations. Felix's teacher suggests Felix look deeper: "Self-portraits are empowering." Jill says, "They force you to see yourself in a way that's different than just looking in a mirror or snapping a picture on your phone. Painting a self-portrait makes you recognize and accept yourself, both on the outside and within—your beauty, your intricacies, even your flaws" (Callender 172). Before this, dysphoria had discouraged Felix from looking. Now Felix tries it out, starting with a selfie. He hesitates over confronting himself, searching for the beauty, admitting the flaws, but finds himself crafting a vibrant, dazzling self-portrait that celebrates all that he is.

A particularly thoughtful use of mirrors appears in the movie *Hedwig and the Angry Inch* (2001). This movie tells the story of Hedwig, an (arguably) trans/non-binary person from East Berlin. She's known for her rock performances full of glamour and color. As such, Hedwig is reflecting her audience and their gender assumptions in a funhouse mirror, emphasizing how much she surpasses the cultural assumptions surrounding her. At the same time, Hedwig uses these performances as an authentic confessional, sharing a quest for a higher spiritual truth. As such a transcendent figure, she is the audience's guide to seeking spiritual epiphany.

Hedwig is searching for success and her soulmate, who she believes is literally her other half, based on a story told by Aristophanes in Plato's *Symposium*. According to this story, humans once had four legs and arms and were whole. But as humans grew more powerful, Zeus decided to separate them. Ever since, both halves have tried to find each other and heal. As J. Hall observes, any quest for love often ends in disappointment because the lover cannot live up to one's romantic projection:

> The usual way in which the anima or animus is experienced is in projection upon a person of the opposite sex. Unlike the projection of the shadow, such projection of the anima or animus lends a quality of fascination to the person who "carries" them in projected form. "Falling in love" is a classic instance of mutual anima and animus projection between a man and a woman. During such a mutual projection one's sense of personal worth is enhanced in the presence of the person who represents the soul image in projected form, but a corresponding loss of soul and emptiness may result if the connection is not maintained. This projective phase, the unconscious identification of another person with the soul image in one's own psyche, is always limited in time; it inevitably ends, with varying degrees of animosity, because no actual person can live up to the fantastic expectations that accompany a projected soul image. And with the end of projection comes the task of establishing a genuine relationship with the reality of another person [16].

One-sided love will lead to even greater disappointment.

Still, Hedwig sets out on the spiritual and romantic journey toward finding her one true (monogamous) love, hoping to become complete. In the movie, which reacts to the modern toxically independent society, this quest is read as a story to overcome, to find that one is whole with no need of another person.

On this search, Hedwig falls in love with Tommy, the older brother of a child she babysits. They write music together, and she helps build his image as a music star. Throughout their relationship, Tommy remains uninterested in touching, kissing, or seeing Hedwig's body from the front. "I'm very much aware that we haven't kissed in all the months we've been together. In fact, he's maintained a near-perfect ignorance of the front of me," she reflects.

In one scene, it almost happens. Hedwig is doing Tommy's makeup as they talk about love. Tommy suggests that, in the same way Aristophanes told of breaking apart a whole person, the Bible tells of breaking Eve out of Adam.

> **TOMMY:** Oh, Hedwig.... When Eve was still inside Adam, they were in paradise.
> **HEDWIG:** That's right, honey.
> **TOMMY:** When she was separated from him, that's when paradise was lost. So when she enters him again, paradise will be regained.
> **HEDWIG:** However you want it, honey. Just kiss me while we do it [*Hedwig and the Angry Inch*].

With this, he suggests he wants to be penetrated by Hedwig. When this conversation starts, Hedwig holds up a mirror for Tommy to look at himself and see the makeup she gave him. It is a symbol she links with his stage name, Tommy Gnosis, meaning knowledge. It is also a cross. The way this imagery links the two narratives of the characters is telling.

Hedwig holds up the mirror, positioned so viewers see her face and Tommy's face come together as one whole person. Indeed, this is a moment of peak romance and love for the two. They finally have their first kiss, implying they will get to live happily ever after.

> In Tommy, Hedwig finds her Platonic match, something for which the many motifs of in-betweenness have been preparing us throughout the film. More than this, though, the song is an allegory for the sort of identity Hedwig has in being neither man nor woman yet existing in-between. Thematically and symbolically, the song speaks for itself as voicing the emotional core of the musical and the transitional state of a becoming-identity. However, the brilliant conceit of the film in presenting this song is to move away from the aesthetic of the rockumentary to occupy a sort of dream-space indicated by the artifice of animation. As an illustrative accompaniment to the song, animator Emily Hubley created a primitive-style sequence of line animations that seem both childlike and profound [Symonds 27].

In this way, the animation underscores Hedwig's spiritual ascent. However, the scene's dreamlike imagery cuts abruptly. Tommy looks at Hedwig's body and stutters—he's not the person she deserves or her other half after all.

Here, the mirror allows the illusion of finding love—of finding everything Hedwig ever wanted. It has nothing to do with gender, for a moment. It is a utopia of mutual celebration. However, the scene uses the trope that Serano explains: culture links trans people and mirrors with fakeness. Here, for Hedwig, the fakeness is not who she is; it is Tommy's fake love and support.

The mirror here symbolizes the perfect romantic love that Hedwig craves. Pearson and Pope explain, "When she removes the masks and shares her heroic vision through her actions and words, the hero is usually successful at finding or creating a sense of community with other people. Confident in herself, she is able to share her new understanding both of herself and of her world around her" (243). Hedwig has no such luck with Tommy. As the act of observing falls away and melts into a romantic and intimate moment, Tommy replaces looking with actions. Once he touches her, his transphobia and binarism take over, ruining the moment and hurting Hedwig. The two soon break up.

In the final scene, she stands before Tommy, who sings to her, begging for forgiveness. "At this point, she has the revelation that she has created him out of her other half" (Bell-Metreau 45). He is her anim figure, but she no longer desires him as an idealized mate. She appoints her new husband, Yitzhak, as her successor instead, and the animation shows the separated halves reuniting—through her quest, she has found wholeness within herself.

5

BATTLING SOCIETY

Misgendered: Sir Callie and the Champions of Helston *(Novel)*

One of the most ubiquitous forms of day-to-day transphobia is misgendering, intentional or not. When it's not deliberate, it is often a result of not bothering to change one's erroneous idea about gender. Some people are not invested in transphobia and binarism; they just don't bother to learn to stop weaponizing them.

Other people, of course, are indeed invested in harming trans people or asserting cisnormativity. When Theo comes out in *Chilling Adventures of Sabrina*, the local jocks repeatedly haze and insult him, especially for joining the all-boys' basketball team. The film *They/Them* likewise follows Ash having to live through being deadnamed and treated like a girl, even at home. At school, their teacher refuses to call them *Ash*, humiliating them before the entire class. Physical and verbal bullying follows, and students leak a video of them reciting a poem about their gender on YouTube.

In a school prank in *Parrotfish*, fellow student Danya plans to steal Grady's regular clothes and gym clothes while he is showering in the gym teacher's office. In their place, Danya plans to leave a sexy, revealing dress and pair of high heels. Grady thinks, "I could totally imagine walking out of the shower room wearing Danya's slutty clothes, and just how horrible I'd feel, and what people would say, and how they'd look at me. How they'd laugh. And I was perfectly able to imagine the grin on Danya's face. It nauseated me" (Wittlinger 180). As he adds, miserably, "Why couldn't people just leave me alone? Who was I hurting, anyway? Why did I have to defend my right to be the person I was?" (181).

Bobbi of Renee James's *Seven Suspects* is misgendered and called slurs often enough that she has turned this transphobia into somewhat of a wry game. When she gets called cruel words, she rates them on how gender-affirming they supposedly are. For example, *cunt* is rated highly for supposedly being femme related. Bobbi narrates, "I consider 'cunt' high praise when directed at me. It's such a nice break from 'prick'" (224).

Unfortunately, such abuse toward people simply existing is widespread. For example, at the time of writing, author J. K. Rowling has repeatedly spoken out against transgender people and promoted transphobic and dangerous policies. She directly compared trans women to harmful stereotypes, repeatedly disapproved of them, and used cruel language to mock and invalidate them (Uspenskiy n.p.; Quatrini n.p.). Rowling has also misgendered trans people to draw attention away from Black Lives Matter protests and issues (Tudor n.p.). At the time of writing, Rowling has been using her wealth and power to open an organization for survivors of domestic violence and sexual assault that only admits cis women. This is despite the high rates of assault of trans people (Harrison et al. n.p.), particularly women and those outside of the gender binary, especially multiply marginalized people. Jackson Bird wrote about finding strength to be his true gender by being a Harry Potter fan. A short time later, forced to face Rowling's transphobia, Bird published a piece in *The New York Times* titled "*Harry Potter* Helped Me Come Out as Trans, But J.K. Rowling Disappointed Me." In this essay, Bird suggests that while Rowling's devastating views may make it harder for him to associate with the official and financial side of this fandom, he still treasures the fans. However, as Rowling's statements have become more direct, more and more fans have been highlighting the impossibility of this disconnection. As Stephanie Huang explains, "death of the author" might be useful for literary critique, but it is not possible to disconnect art from an artist who is actively benefiting from attention and actively using that power to promote bigotry.

Likewise, in the essay "Tones of the Caparazón, or the Lizard Brain's Response to Misgendering by Folks Who Should Know Better," Ariel Estrella describes the pain of this callous treatment. Their tale begins with their initial hopefulness at a new job: "I loved my colleagues like cousins, and I thought I could help them confront their cis-normativity" (170). However, constant misgendering at meetings triggered panic deep down in the lizard brain, beneath rational thought. "In some primal lizard part of my amygdala, I do not frame intimate friendships and relationships as just that; this lizard brain, once spurned, redefines intimacy. Getting close to a friend or partner now also means opening myself up for more risks, more opportunities for greater violence and harm" (172).

In *Sir Callie and the Champions of Helston*, misgendering is a main part of Callie's journey. Callie, a teenager, grew up with their transphobic mother, insisting they were "not girl enough. Not good enough. Not trying enough" (Symes-Smith 1). When their father realized how harmed they were by it, he took them away. Now Callie lives in the forest with their two dads and a merry band of misfits. Their small haven is open minded, accountable, and even filled with love. After years of living in the forest as themselves, training to be a knight, Callie has an opportunity to visit the capital, Helston, and partake in a competition for potential knighthood training.

On the journey, Callie hears an insidious voice that encourages them to give up. "It doesn't matter how you dress and act.... People see what they want to see. And no one in Helston will ever see you as anything but a girl" (43). Such menacing words, echoing Callie's own subconscious, come from the witch who lives deep in the woods, banished for rebelling against the crown. As soon as Callie and their dad reach Helston, it is clear that things will not go smoothly. Callie is nearly shot on sight and is then dead-named repeatedly. As Callie sadly explains, "Other people calling me lady feels like being bashed in the shoulder because they don't see me. Calling myself lady feels like agreeing that I don't deserve to be seen, that I don't matter, that I don't exist" (192).

The worst of the offenders is Lord Peran, the chancellor and the voice of conformity. He insists on maintaining strict gender roles: Callie must live with the girls. Boys are forbidden magic, a law that affects both his son and the prince. Girls must stay indoors and learn women's skills. "There's no anger in his grip or on his face, just placid confidence that he has every right to do what he wants, like no one's ever suggested otherwise," Callie reflects (82).

Callie is repeatedly constrained to their quarters and told off for not behaving like a good young woman, despite their protests. Such moments always cause pain when one's entire identity is dismissed. One can be in the workplace, at school, spending time with peers and be shocked by the sudden lack of respect. Estrella describes the panic spiral that may emerge: "I tense up. I breathe in. I breathe out. I hope they notice my pain. I hope they will correct themselves. When they don't, I wish to correct them" (172). However, they are terrified they will grow angry and that protesting will only make things worse. Estrella adds that such disrespectful moments tend to come with gaslighting, emphasizing that the one being mistreated should put up with it and feel bad for insisting on ordinary respect. While it may seem small, such a constant responsibility of correcting people "is taxing, draining, unfair, and yet expected of me. Colleagues misgendering me is not okay" (175). As they conclude, "loved ones misgendering me, however, is its own kind of heartbreak" (175). They sadly describe how they had to grow a *caparazón*, or tortoiseshell, to survive daily cruelty.

Indeed, most painful for Callie is the fact that their dad does not entirely stand up for them but tries to be "diplomatic" at the time of the court's and the city's distress. As Callie narrates, "I hold my breath, waiting for Papa to argue that that's not how it works, to fight for me—but he deflates, nods, and my heart hits the bottom of my stomach" (62).

In such a controlling environment, the chancellor's daughter, Elowen, feels confined and forced to shrink down. Lord Peran abuses his son Edwyn and the prince Willow, teaching that only being brutal in combat can make them acceptable to society. "They have both been taught the only way they are acceptable is by being something other than themselves. They've heard it so often, it became true," Callie reflects (179–180). Edwyn is desperate for approval, but his father never grants it; he only insists that he do more and more impossible feats, having already buried the magic that makes him who he is. This, of course, has deeper symbolism:

> Gender and sexuality are inseparable from magic in children's fantasy fiction, since they all seem to emerge from the same organic drives, the same spaces of wonderment and confusion, and the same uncertain borderlands between body and mind, male and female, queer and straight. Magic is, after all, a queer force—a force that makes one "not normal" [Battis 324].

This magic can paradoxically help the child belong in the sheltered magical world, where companions are like them.

Callie befriends Willow and Elowen, encouraging them to do what they love. The three support each other with validation and comfort, ultimately leading to saving the prince's life. It's no coincidence that this is a fantasy space. Magic in young adult or children's novels explores "a very particular psychic landscape within queer life—the defiance of the queer youth against his or her unresponsive parents—but it is also the resistance of the exiled wizard, the magical subaltern who wants to make a claim for social rights in a world that rejects him, even if such a claim seems impossible" (Battis 325). Consequently, the children reach out to Edwyn, encouraging him to walk away from the toxic family that suppresses him in its own metaphor for misgendering. As the author observes,

> Edwyn's arc will always be precious to me, especially as it's very much the beginning of his story. Growing up, I feel like fiction always drove home that those who have suffered abuse have to forgive and let go and come out shiny in order to be worthy of a happy ending. As an angry, messy kid, that was really hard. Edwyn's journey is very winding in a "one step forward, two steps back" kind of way, but he is still as equally worthy of love as the others [qtd. in Koehler].

After the kingdom is restored to a better place, Callie gets a chance for revenge, facing the chancellor in single combat. He tells them it will be their shortest fight and calls them a girl, continuing to misgender them as he gloats. Callie stays cool as the aggressions continue. "You would never be happy here. Even if you get everything your little heart desires, surely you see the way people look at you? You're astute, not like that foolish prince. You know what people are whispering about you" (Symes-Smith 368). The words reflect the anxieties they keep within. Adding, "Little girls shouldn't play with swords," the chancellor even breaks Callie's beloved talisman (369).

Still, Callie refuses to give in. As they point out, the entire community can see the chancellor bullying a child, forcing conformity through bluster and intimidation: "You've already lost. You lost the moment I arrived in Helston. Do what you like to me, but they're looking at you now, and they can see you for what you are" (369). The queen banishes him along with his hateful rhetoric and works with Callie to create a better society.

Dumped for Being Trans: If I Was Your Girl *(Novel)*

Trans rejection appears as a plot point in *The Crying Game, Normal, Different for Girls*, and *Romeos*, among many other films and shows. Considering that it's been used as a defense for murder in the United States, revealing one's past to a romantic interest is devastatingly risky, both physically and emotionally. The pressure to reveal is cruel in itself. Actress and activist Jen Richards explains: "When you start watching trans clips back-to-back, you see how often all the people around the trans character feel betrayed or lied to. But frankly, I—I kind of hate the idea of disclosure ... [laughs] ... in the sense that it presupposes that there is something to disclose" (*Disclosure*). In *Hollyoaks*, Jason Costello, the show's first trans character, worries about his relationship but discovers his boyfriend, Bart McQueen, still wants to date him. Still, the message that the trans person needs to disclose is problematic. Richards adds, "It reinforces their assumption that there is a secret that is hidden and that I have a responsibility to tell others, and that presupposes that the other person might have some kind of issue or problem with what's to be disclosed" (*Disclosure*).

Many romantic partners stress, subtly or not, that they can't accept the other person. In the film *Gun Hill Road*, Vanessa recites poetry at the coffeehouse, where a guy picks her up. The boyfriend will only have sex with her in the dark, insisting, "I don't want to see that shit, aright?" She endures this but feels demeaned. He doesn't take her out where anyone will see them either. When they finally eat at a restaurant, he's uncomfortable and tells her after that she's not his girl. She's crushed. Likewise, on the show *Sort Of*, when Sabi's boyfriend professes his love at the supermarket, Sabi is skeptical. "Kiss me. Right here. Right now. In front of all these people. And I'll give you a second chance." He looks around the supermarket and can't do it. "You may love me, but you're ashamed of loving me. So that's not love" ("Sort of Stable" 1.04).

If I Was Your Girl by Meredith Russo explores the pain of trying to fit in. Amanda Hardy has moved from Atlanta to her father's small town, seeking a fresh start after a vicious assault at her own school. Her father reminds her over and over to be careful as she makes cisgender friends and goes with them to church. She starts dating Grant, who gradually reveals his own secret—he's the breadwinner for his family. Grant is very compelling as he tells her over and over that he's never felt the way he feels now: "Everybody's got a past ... that doesn't mean you can't have a future" (77). When she insists there are still many things he doesn't know about her, he tells her that she's beautiful and good, and she makes him happy. Further, he insists, "I want you and whatever it is about you that you think makes you so complicated couldn't make me want you less" (78).

Conflicted but hopeful, Amanda writes Grant a letter about who she is and how her life has been. She hands it to him and tells him, "Just, ahead of time, I wanted to let you know—if you're upset with me for letting things progress like they did, for being with you.... I'm sorry for that too and I understand" (183). Of course, this is a risky choice. Disclosure may and does lead to physical danger for trans people. As scholars such as Aeyal Gross explain, it is unethical to require disclosure from trans people for this and other reasons. Horrifyingly, a legal movement is pushing for mandatory disclosure, putting trans people at even greater risk. To Amanda's surprise, Grant burns the letter without reading it and tells her he'll never regret being with her.

There are other types of breakups explored in this book. A flashback shows how Amanda's friend reacted violently six years prior. Marcus found her journal and read it aloud to her: "Marcus is so gorgeous ... maybe one day I can finally be a girl like I'm supposed to, and then he'll see how I feel about him, and maybe he'll feel the same way" (173). Marcus punched her in the stomach. As Amanda heartbreakingly and unjustly apologized over and over, Marcus told her, "Whatever you are, never come near me again" (173). Further, Amanda is even led to feel she was the reason her parents got divorced: "I had a problem when I was a kid ... raising me was so hard that my parents were stressed out all the time, and they disagreed on basically everything about how to help me," she explains (118). Her father left. When Amanda attempted suicide, he didn't call or contact her in any way. Now they're trying to live together. He's worried that her spending time with fundamentalists and dating an athlete will end in her murder, but he does little to protect her other than victim-blame. Additionally, his threat, "One wrong move and I'm sending you back to your mother," shows his willingness to leave her rather than protect her no matter what (129).

5. Battling Society 105

In the present, Amanda is pronounced homecoming queen. As Amanda's heart pounds, Layla, one of her friends in the fashionable clique, crowns her and brings her to the middle of the room. "I just saw smiling faces pointed at me in every direction, Grant's the brightest of them, and I felt myself in my own body being loved and accepted, and it felt so good it was almost surreal" (221). However, this only lasts a moment. Bee, the one friend she told about being trans, arrives, terribly wasted. She snatches the microphone and calls out her friends one by one for pretending to be normal, as she puts it. She finishes by outing Amanda. Grant looks at her with "absolute confusion and horror" (223). Amanda panics and runs. Grant follows, but asks whether it's a prank, asks about her biology, and asks if this means he's gay. Amanda is revolted. She turns to face the staring crowd and hurls her tiara at Layla's feet. "I guess I'm disqualified" (226). At this moment, cruelly outed, she's uninterested in justifying her existence or body to the boyfriend who promised to support her through everything.

Parker, Grant's friend, comes after her as she walks home and menacingly insists on giving her a ride. She refuses, and he persists: "Like hell you want to be left alone. If you wanted to be left alone you'd have stayed a boy" (230). Like many frightening people in real life, he believes that who she is justifies his desire to attack her. Suddenly, Parker punches her and pushes her down to the ground. As he tells her, "You made me look like a dickhead for months, and now you don't got Grant to look out for you. You don't get to play hard to get anymore" (230–231). He pulls up her dress, and she fights him off. She runs into the woods. Just as he finds her and terrifyingly pushes her into the mud again, Amanda's girlfriends show up. They rescue her and explain that Grant sent them after Parker had called. "Said he sounded drunk, talking about helping Grant get revenge on you and putting you in your place" (233). They comfort her and tell her they still care. They value Amanda as she is and are determined to protect her as one of them.

When Amanda's father sees what happened, he goes to Grant's trailer and punches him, without pausing to hear that Grant was not the rapist, only transphobic. "You touch her again, or come near her, or talk to her, or so much as look at her, and I will put you in the goddamn ground" (239). Sticking up for his daughter is nice, but he ignores her protests the entire time. His pride and protective instincts are activated, but less so his ability to listen. Further, when they return home, he tells her, "I'm done.... I'm not watching you destroy yourself. When we get home, I want you to pack your things" (240). Amid Amanda's devastation, this is another brutal rejection.

She returns to her mother for Thanksgiving. As she narrates, since she's come out, "Mom and I had been informally exiled from all family functions" (251). This, of course, is another rebuff from the family who should love her. Mother and daughter prepare to spend a quiet day together, but Amanda's father shows up to make amends. He explains that he's always been afraid for his daughter since she was born: "but everything that made you happy, from the way you wanted to walk to the toys you wanted to the way you wanted to dress ... it put you in danger.... I ran away" (257). He asks for another chance to have Amanda move back and be his daughter. Touched, she is willing to grant that chance, though he has proven unreliable and even dangerous to her.

She returns to a loving greeting from her girlfriends, including the religious one, who points out that Jesus wants everyone to love one another without judgment. The one person Amanda cannot forgive is Bee: "No matter what she said, I knew I couldn't let her back into my life. What she did hurt me even more than Parker, even more than the assault in the bathroom, because I had trusted her. I knew now I would have to be careful with who I let myself get close to. But maybe that was a lesson everybody had to learn" (267). Forgiving everyone is not a requirement of life—some people never learn to stop wounding others, some are perpetually careless, and some have broken trust too deeply to be forgiven. This incident has taught Amanda discernment and shown her that she can persevere, even through what she imagined were the worst devastations.

Meanwhile, Grant is hesitant but tells her he still loves her and wants to try. He suggests that they get together and that she tell him everything, the way she had planned. She ends the story doing so, uncertain where it will lead. "Maybe this would be the last conversation I would ever have with Grant. Maybe not. Either way, I realized, I wasn't sorry I existed anymore. I deserve to live. I deserve to find love. I knew now—that I deserved to be loved" (273). More than whether she and Grant get back together, this is the vital lesson here.

Threatened: Supergirl *(Television)*

First introduced in *Supergirl*'s fourth season, Nia Nal (Nicole Maines) is television's first trans superheroine. Growing up, occasional intolerance shaped Nia into a determined defender of her community. Nia earned a degree in international relations and became a political speechwriter for the US president's press secretary. Nia joins the show as a CatCo reporter during the height of the anti-alien sentiment, a clear allegory for the persecution of minorities in the Trump era. The enemy in this season of *Supergirl* is the masses of people who loathe aliens and organize themselves into hate groups to attack the innocent.

The futuristic alien Brainiac Five meets Nia in line for pizza when his image inducer, which disguises him as a human, fails. The pizza store owner calls him a traitor and tries swinging a bat at him. Nia bravely places herself between them. "You need to back off. Did I stutter? I said back off." She threatens to write a news story about him and walks out with Brainy afterward. "I thought he was my friend," Brainy protests.

"A true friend will accept you for who you truly are," she replies ("Fallout" 4.02). Impressed by her kindness, courage, and wisdom, he asks her out. As the season progresses, she and Brainiac fall sweetly in love. Brainiac is the clueless alien, while Nia is the warm, lovable, emotionally vulnerable human.

Back at CatCo, Nia urges James Olson to denounce the violence and hatred. As she tells him quietly and passionately, "You have another chance to fight for justice now.... You may not know this about me, but I am a transgender woman. I know what it's like to be attacked and denied because of who I am" ("Fallout" 4.02). She defended the alien in danger and needs Olson, editor-in-chief of CatCo Worldwide Media, to tell the entire city that violence against aliens is not acceptable. At episode end, a reporter pulls a prank on an alien peer, and Olson shuts her down with, "We respect people here." He gives a speech on tolerance, even as he clearly realizes how cruel and insidious discrimination is. Sadly, this battle is not permanently won and comes up over and over. Actress Laverne Cox describes how common transphobia is in everyday life: "I can't even tell you how many times I've been in public space, particularly early in my transition in New York City, when I would walk into a subway car and people would just burst into laughter, as if my existence on that subway car was just a joke. And I think people have been trained to have that reaction" (*Disclosure*).

Nia is also marginalized as a half-human, half-Naltorian. She has a special once-per-generation gift from her mother to dream of future events. Nia's dreams—sometimes frightening premonitions—suggest knowledge of how dangerous the world can be, while energy whips show she's ready to defend herself and others. In "Blood Memory" (4.11), Nia goes to visit her family in the small town of Parthas. She tells her friend Kara Danvers that they always supported her being trans, especially her big sister Maeve, but she hasn't told them she inherited the dreams. This town is a special haven, as she notes,

> I always knew that I was a girl. My parents were amazing. They affirmed my authentic self and helped me transition young. I've always been able to be open about who I was in Parthas. I'm not saying it was easy. There were definitely people who didn't understand. But the town's ethos of inclusion is strong. And I think if I grew up anywhere else, it would've been a lot tougher.

As she adds, the town's name's meaning lies in the people's behavior—it's a paradise where aliens and humans have lived together in harmony for decades. It's a kind of haven, though it's vulnerable in a community of rising hatred.

The racists distribute drugs to teens, who, high and filled with rage, attack Nia's mother's funeral. Once again, racism endangers the fragile aliens living peacefully in the community. Nia reveals her gift to save her older sister, but Maeve is enraged that Nia inherited the gift she'd hoped for. She bursts out: "How did you, of all people, get the powers? They're supposed to be passed down from mother to daughter. So how did someone like you get them? You're not even a real woman."

At these personal attacks in her safe, precious family home, Nia is particularly crushed. "Maeve was always my biggest supporter. I can't believe she'd say something like that," she mourns afterward. This attack from within her family, a lashing out of grief and bitterness, is the cruelest. Kara, Supergirl, reveals her identity in response and offers all the hope she can. "I have faith that the love between two sisters will prevail in the end. I have to believe that. I just need you to know now that you are not alone. You have a family. You have me."

Amid more anti-alien sentiments, Dreamer steps forward as a spokesperson. Kara interviews her. To begin, Dreamer emphasizes that she was born in America, like so many of the marginalized. "The greatest gift we can give each other is our authentic selves and sharing that. Sharing our truth is what will make us strong." As she adds, "So, here I am. I am both human and alien. And I am a trans woman. S'mores are my favorite dessert.... I am an INFP. Uh, a Miranda. House Stark. I love Thursdays and April. And nerdy boys who think too much. And I am proud of all that I am." ("American Dreamer" 4.19). She humanizes herself, fighting society's hatred of aliens by sharing her geeky likability, hoping for acceptance.

The most visceral personal attack arrives a year later in "Reality Bytes" (5.15), when Nia's sassy roommate Yvette drags her out clubbing. Yvette's internet date lures her out to an alley and hits her. Yvette discovers that he was a predator who only asked her out to give a message to Dreamer. It reads, "The world doesn't want a trans superhero. So crawl back under the rock you came from ... or I'll keep attacking people like you." Of course, Nia is horrified as she confides in her friend afterward. Supergirl insists that they rely on the police to do their jobs, and Nia is stung:

> NIA: Kara, I love you, but do not tell me what I can and can't do right now. There is no catching this guy and redeeming him. There is no hope speech that can make this better.... Look, my community is vulnerable. This happens more than you could possibly know. And there are guys just

like this jerk out there who want to hurt us. They want us to hide and to be afraid to be who we are. They want us to disappear, and it happens ... every day.
SUPERGIRL: I know, and what this guy did is horrible....
NIA: He's not the first, and he won't be the last. And we haven't exactly been a priority for the cops. So, just trust me when I say that I am the one protecting this community. And now this bastard is going after my community, trying to erase me? No. No, this guy is over.

Giving up on the detectives, she joins the dating site as a target. Once the predator asks her out, Nia meets him and confronts the attacker as Dreamer, enduring his insults. She shoots back, "I get it. Your fragile ego was just shattered. Your sense of self is so shaky that anything outside your narrow world view threatens it." In a problematic moment, Supergirl swoops in to convince Nia to back down and stop attacking him. They finally turn him over to the police.

This storyline resonates with the transmisogynist notion of the transgender murderer. This harmful trope appears in culture in texts such as *Psycho* (1959) and *The Silence of the Lambs* (1991). It frames transgender people—particularly women—as dangerous to society and as likely killers, when statistically the opposite is unfortunately the truth. This trope doesn't only Other transgender people. It promotes the horrifying notion that killing trans people is acceptable and trans people defending themselves is not acceptable. In her thesis, Alexandra Chace discusses the way this trope depicts transgender women as monsters: "deviant, pathetic, reprehensible, and otherwise undeserving of empathetic feelings or positive identification.... Horror movies may seem over-the-top, but are they not analogous to the real-world over-the-top maltreatment of transgender women?" (9). Supergirl's talking Nia down likewise emphasizes the problematic message that Nia needs reining in.

In contrast with the Othered trans woman, the text centrally positions Kara, a cisgender, young, thin, white woman. Even as she performatively recognizes her privilege, she moves on to try to educate a transgender person about being trans. But, as Maier and colleagues explain, "Allyship is not an identity; it is praxis. Allyship means learning from those who live the life, not debating your theoretical knowledge. Allies must do the work of creating (and relinquishing!) trans, crip spaces. Performative allyship and virtue signaling merely affirm the privilege of those who have the least to lose" (11).

With this talk, Nia pulls back and takes the law-abiding approach, telling the assailant that he's going to prison. "And if you ever make a move against anyone in my community again, I will give you a nightmare you will never wake up from" ("Reality Bytes" 5.15).

Afterward, she collapses with Kara, frightened that her loved ones must always be in such danger. "I'm not okay.... When that bastard attacked my community, the one thing it felt like I had left.... I snapped. At least this was something I could control. I could find this guy and stop him. Permanently. I could do something to protect someone." While a season earlier, she gently shared her sweetest, most likable self in an interview, the repeated personal attacks have brought her to a helpless position of righteous anger and desperation to protect her community. Problematically, the text's framing it as "snapping" promotes the notion that marginalized people are eternally on the verge of becoming dangerous to people of privilege and that marginalized people's sweetness is more important than their safety and their ability to express a range of human emotions.

Kara consoles her and agrees that "sometimes being the good guy sucks, especially when you know how easy it would be to just get rid of someone so vile and full of hate. But, hey, not doing that ... that is what makes us different from them. That's what lets us keep protecting people, and your community needs you. They need Dreamer. And I'm so sorry. I didn't know how much pain you were in." Here, Kara lectures about morality and creates a false parallel between performing a serial hate crime and responding violently to a repeated hate crime in order to protect oneself and one's community. She demands nonviolence without providing a sufficient alternative. This position is incredibly privileged, if not worse. As Peter Gelderloos discusses, privileged white people often promote nonviolence and expect "oppressed people, many of whom are people of color, to suffer patiently under an inconceivably greater violence" (23). In other words, Kara's admonishment means that, in effect, continued violence toward transgender people is tolerable to her, but violence against transphobic cisgender people is not.

Indeed, choosing hope in the face of such endless brutality is not always possible, and fiction cannot lighten the pain of the constant struggle. Yvette ends the episode by deleting her social media profile, deciding the risk as a trans woman of color is too great.

Nia assures her, "You will find that kind of love, Yvette, but not if you shut down. They want us to be invisible ... because of their own fears. They want to erase us, so we need to shine even brighter. You are a beautiful woman. Big, beautiful life and sharing that life is what will change this world" ("Reality Bytes" 5.15). Of course, such a perky statement to a trans assault victim is terribly problematic too. Even this note of hope is tinged with suffering and injustice. Forcing a marginalized person to expend unreasonable amounts of work and put themselves in danger, hoping to decrease bigotry, cannot be a just solution. It's even more problematic in a world in which superheroes and law enforcement have that responsibility. Telling a marginalized assault survivor that this responsibility is theirs is victim blaming. Yvette's beautiful life should be hers and hers alone. She doesn't owe it to the world, let alone owe it to the world as a reward for harming her and enabling her to be harmed.

The 2004 film *Toilet Training* documents all the ways trans people are harassed and endangered. Fiction films tell similar stories: *A Fantastic Woman* tells the story of Marina Vidal in Santiago, Chile. When her lover dies, the film follows the discrimination and prejudice Marina experiences from Orlando's family and the larger community. Orlando's ex-wife forbids Marina from attending the funeral, and Orlando's son harasses her and takes her beloved dog. Thus, the titular expression emphasizes how much she must struggle against cruelty and transcend her situation—she is both fantastical and formidable. Likewise, the famous *Ma Vie en Rose* has the local parents sign a petition to get the young protagonist kicked out of school. As the entire neighborhood shuns them, the father loses his job, and they must all move away.

Many other stories pit the trans character against a terrifying society. In the *Nimona* graphic novel by Noelle Stevenson, Sir Ambrosius Goldenloin, an insider who works for the Institution of Law Enforcement and Heroics, explains in shock, "We assumed she was a girl disguised as a monster, but she's not. She's a monster disguised as a girl" (162). Indeed, the backstory she shared—that as a human girl she received shape-changing powers—was meant to cast her as less frightening. Those in charge lock her up, torture her, and call her an abomination. Echoing everyday myths about trans people, her tormentors demand to know who made her, and she replies, "No one made me. I was always like this" (196). She's seen afterward, shrunken into a tiny child. Her other half, a roaring monster, is ravaging the land. "The strong part stays and the rest disintegrates. That's how it works," her child side says directly (229). The two are contrasted: a tiny child whom society destroys, and a ravaging beast that frightens everyone by defending itself. It feels terribly abandoned and unlovable in this form. "You're not the first one who thought they could CARE about me until you found out how bad it really was," the flame-breathing monster tells her friend Blackheart (238). In the cartoon adaptation, she adds sorrowfully, "Kids. Little kids. They grow up believing that they can be a hero if they drive a sword into the heart of anything different. And I'm the monster? I don't know what's scarier. The fact that everyone in this kingdom wants to run a sword through my heart.... or that sometimes I just wanna let 'em" (*Nimona*).

Out of Salem by Hal Schrieve has the non-binary protagonist Z begin the novel dealing with life as a zombie. Of course, all the restrictions, microaggressions, and unjust laws (including the authority to kill them if they're found traveling without a custodian) are aimed at zombies but function as metaphors for other kinds of stigma (as do Z's Muslim werewolf best friend's response to the police). At the novel's start, callous Uncle Hugh describes Z as a criminal threat, adding, "I have worked all my adult life to ensure that monsters like zombies are dealt with cleanly, efficiently and present the minimum risk to the public" (16). To Z's relief, sympathetic family friend Mrs. Dunnigan takes them in. She's gradually revealed as not just a lesbian with a counterculture bookshop but also a selkie who understands prejudice and abuse of authority. Z has no chance to mourn their family as Z is put on trial for being alive, with the illegal magic used, their medical situation, psychology, and everything else weighed by judgmental outsiders. In school, a disgruntled teacher unable to do magic forces the students, especially Z, to read aloud about the history of zombies and their nonperson status. This teacher adds in slimy fashion that being a werewolf "is like any other mental illness. They are just sick, and in need of care" (240). This is an example of the way ableism and transphobia inform one another. Given that both are strongly stigmatized, a comparison between them might prompt transgender supporters to protest that trans people are "not crazy," especially since often transgender people are denied care based on ableism. However, this notion excludes neurodivergent people and harms them—particularly within trans communities. Ableism within transgender communities harms some of their most marginalized members. This is perhaps even more severe since the trauma of marginalization makes it likely for trans people to be neurodivergent. A different reply to such a statement is that transgender people and neurodivergent people are marginalized and share that similarity.

Forced to Suppress Legitimate Anger: Seven Suspects *(Novel)*

In the celebrated trans-written episode "Elliot," on the show *Two Sentence Horror Stories*, Elliot's teachers and principal bully and misgender him. The students are cruel as well. In the basement, he meets a janitor who offers to grant his wishes with a magic ocarina. As she explains, "It's just like any old instrument. Y'know, you pour your heartache into your music; people hear that, right? You pour your pain into this bad boy, and they feel it. Imagine—people *feel* the way that you feel." Hoping the bullies will leave him alone, Elliot trades his beloved songbook for it. After harassment, he plays it, and a sharp whistle emerges. The girls cringe in anguish and instantly apologize. Back in the basement, the janitor offers a permanent trade. The next bully lays hands on Elliot, and then, thanks to the ocarina, his own hands yank him away. The principal comes after him, and frightening growths burst from the man's skin. Back in the basement, the janitor gloats about her harvest, which will live in the ocarina dolorosa forever. Elliot is horrified: "Essence of suffering? I'm more than just my pain! My body isn't yours to take!"

"Play one more song for the bad man, and your pain will be living in the ocarina forever!" the janitor coaxes.

Elliot protests, "I never wanted to hurt anybody! I just wanted them to know what I was going through!" The principal tries to kill him, and Elliot blows again, destroying him. However, Elliot smashes the ocarina, relinquishing the power. He gets a happy ending and new friends. As emphasized in this story, few trans and non-binary characters are allowed to feel, let alone express, rage. This suppression continues, despite many of them experiencing severe transphobia and binarism, as well as other forms of bigotry such as racism and ableism.

Even overly polite and gentle communication with cisgender people is often framed as violent. As Earle discusses, nondisabled and cis people often consider such words aggressive and even "slurs." Earle goes on to explain that this is partially because making a socially invisible group visible puts into question its position of power. It may also bring a bit of the discomfort hegemonic groups create in marginalized groups by Othering them. As scholars such as Ashley discuss, this is also a very common racist stereotype of Black women. Naoko Shibusawa discusses the burden often placed on Black women to insist on "diversity [even] on diversity committees" (261), making this even less fair.

The notion that trans rage is simply taboo is reflected both in and out of narratives. In *Wizards*, a war occurs between King Arthur's court and the Arcane Order, demigod siblings outside the gender binary. The three, Nari, Bellroc and Skrael, once built the universe and are dedicated to balancing the fields of magic and humanity. Bellroc and Skrael despair of humanity and decide to wage war against it all. They are killed remorselessly and dramatically. Nari decides to join and possibly assimilate with the human side. The narrative provides no alternative that is respectful of the balance, let alone of the trio's needs. The healer Nari's quiet gentleness and rejection of rage are the reasons Nari is permitted to survive. Nari is only allowed to be less demure to better serve cis people against her trans kin—a titanic battle in which Nari kills Skrael. Bellroc is killed by Jim, the story's (white, thin, cis) hero.

Susan Stryker discusses trans rage in her queer reading of Mary Shelley's Frankenstein's Monster, describing how she matches the monster's cadence and pleas:

> I have asked the Miltonic questions Shelley poses in the epigraph of her novel: "Did I request thee, Maker, from my clay to mould me man? Did I solicit thee from darkness to promote me?" With one voice, her monster and I answer "no" without debasing ourselves, for we have done the hard work of constituting ourselves on our own terms, against the natural order. Though we forego the privilege of naturalness, we are not deterred, for we ally ourselves instead with the chaos and blackness from which Nature itself spills forth ["Frankenstein" 257].

As Stryker discusses, society in general, as well as parts of even queer cultures, not only oppress and endanger transgender people, but then blame them for it by pushing transgender people into the role of monster. Stryker points out the story of a trans woman treated horribly by the queer community who committed suicide: "Not only did the angry villagers hound their monster to the edge of town, they reproached her for being vulnerable to the torches. Did Filisa Vistima commit suicide, or did the queer community of Seattle kill her?" (246). Danter finds, "The continued fascination audiences around the world have with disasters, monsters, and zombies belies an awareness of problems that overstep accustomed boundaries and our uneasiness about our lack of power to deal with them" (200).

The heroine of Renee James's *Seven Suspects*, Bobbi, holds back her rage and tries to appease cisgender people in many ways. The novel opens with a woman at Bobbi's beauty salon who is offended that it serves trans people. She has a tantrum, and Bobbi must soothe her for putting up with the existence of people like her. "It would be nice to suggest it's none of her damn business who our other clients are," Bobbi thinks, but she remains nonconfrontational to keep the business (6). It's a disturbing look at how much trans people must be polite to those who are brutally insulting them and insisting they shouldn't exist. Her mentor, Cecelia, reminds her over and over to stay gracious. As Bobbi narrates,

> "walking through them" means walking through the clouds of bullshit spewed out by the ignorant and intolerant. Cecilia told me once, it's just walking through a shitstorm. You have to hold your breath for a few minutes, and take a shower when you get to the other side, she said, but it's just an inconvenience compared to letting people like that run your life [130].

This, in itself, is, of course, a privilege compared with the amount of harm other trans people have to deal with, which is not actually possible to brush off. Bobbi often finds empathy and absolution for violent, hateful cis men, even when they do not make a single attempt to seek accountability. For example, she forgives a cis man who calls her a cunt to coerce her into sleeping with him. After she confronts him, he tells her a sob story about his recent divorce and about how women keep rejecting him, so he's miserable. The book frames him as mostly a good person, with no requirements

5. Battling Society

to act decently. Next, the man she sleeps with and walks away from comes and bangs at her door, terrifying her and insisting that she had no right to come back to his place and possibly reveal that they had a relationship. Both cis men protest that they have been victimized here. Then, as they ignore the selfish side of their own behavior, they demand she bend over backward for them while offering slurs and casual cruelty. Bobbi feels guilty for their anger, thinking to herself, "A lot of men have a hard time expressing their feelings about women in an appropriate way, but sometimes they mean well" (115).

Some of the time, Bobbi allows herself rage, but it is not always directed at the people who are actually oppressing her. She is, unfortunately, comfortable saying bigoted things about most marginalized groups, a practice that serves the hegemonic society harming Bobbi, in a painful example about how the system turns many into oppressors. Some of her rage serves existing structures, and her kindness is granted to hegemony instead of those marginalized. For example, her employee calls another employee a string of slurs regarding her race, status as an ex-sex worker, and being a trans woman. The protagonist accepts the employee's apology easily, tries to appease her, and muses about how pretty she is. For another example, the protagonist evicts an admittedly unpleasant tenant when he can't pay rent, claiming her support of individualist neoliberal capitalism. She fires an employee who seems to have depression for being late and not "positive" enough—again, promoting capitalism over disability rights. In a less clear-cut act, she beats up the violent ex of an employee she cares for. However, in doing this, she also stresses that the man is an addict, as if that is a partial justification. Uncomfortably, she feels that her willingness and ability to fight make her "not a real woman," both physically and emotionally. Still, she refuses to back down. These beliefs of otherness and inhumanity resonate with Stryker's view of trans people as monstrous in transphobic societies. These instances of rage are meaningful but may bring less social change for the better and less danger to the protagonist, because they serve many hegemonic agendas.

In previous novels, Bobbi was beat up and raped by men, with the story and society punishing her after she defended a friend—a classic hero moment in many narratives. As the provocative prologue explains,

> the major turning point in most transsexuals' lives is their gender transition. But for me, that moment came when I decided to track down the monster who beat my friend to death and got away with it. That's what led me to John Strand. He was rich and powerful and admired by everyone except the transgender women he brutalized and sometimes killed. The police wouldn't dream of investigating him, so I did. The consequences of that decision keep sprouting up in my life, like dandelions in a suburban lawn. The repercussions won't stop until I die. I just hope to God there's no afterlife [James n.p.].

In response, he had two of his goons corner Bobbi in an alley and rape her. She, in turn, hired someone to mug and beat up the rapist she could identify. She later promised herself that if anyone ever did that again, she would take from them as many parts as she could, even if she could not stop them. However, she feels guilty for her rage, her desire to defend herself, her feelings of relief when she finds out her assailant is dying.

Since the rape, Bobbi has spoken to people aggressively. Her friend Cecilia scolds her for threatening to rip out a man's eyeballs if he doesn't stop touching her. Disturbingly, she adds, "Women resist advances without threatening bodily harm, and they reject men with a lot more consideration about the guy's feelings" (50), as if women mustn't protect themselves as they can, or they will give up the right to call themselves women. Even when the man bursts out with transphobic slurs, Bobbi is still expected to be polite and give way. Her surrogate daughter Roberta suggests that she dress more modestly to protect herself from vicious men. In response, Bobbi asserts that she has the right to choose how she wants to look and that aggressors have no right to attack people, whatever they are wearing.

In the previous novel, *A Kind of Justice*, Bobbi is investigated for taking revenge that the police won't. As the investigator narrows in, Bobbi worries that she will be convicted only because she's trans or that even being on trial will create enough bad publicity and unmanageable costs to ruin her business. Indeed, Cecilia tells her that her being innocent won't save her from the investigating cop: "He doesn't need much to indict and he doesn't need much to get a conviction. You're a trans woman. Most jurors are retired people who think trans people are perverts. You could get convicted without a shred of physical evidence" (111). In fact, the cop investigating her is terribly prejudiced and makes a deal with her rapist. The system is clearly against her.

As the climax of *Seven Suspects* approaches, Bobbi is assaulted again. The assailant pretends to be her friend and insists on spending time with her, even when Bobbi tries to set boundaries. She tells herself the man is like a homeless dog on the verge of freezing to death. But unlike this dog, the man may be specifically dangerous and have extreme privileges. The stray dog she imagines does not. Seeing how sad he appears, she feels obliged to take care of him and unlocks her door. The man enters her apartment, drugs her drink, and kidnaps her.

She finds herself tied up on a concrete floor in the man's basement. There, he rapes her again. As she reasons with him, she pretends to be the hateful trans stereotype he sees her as, begging to use the bathroom. There, actualizing cisgender dark fantasies of what transgender people might do if allowed access to a bathroom, Bobbi defends herself. She manages to find a small pair of nail scissors and an electric cord. She saws at the cord,

5. Battling Society

hoping it can be used as a weapon. As she continues to soften him, she thinks, "I hate this phony bimbo act, but he must see me as a defenseless wretch who has no threat to fight back. Whatever slim chance I have of surviving depends on him underestimating me" (284). Even in such terrible circumstances, she must pacify her attacker. When the rapist tries to beat her to death, she stabs him with the scissors and electric cable, managing to kill him and save her own life.

Cis, white, nondisabled, affluent men in action movies regularly and easily kill antagonists of all sorts. When Bobbi, a trans woman, does it, the text must stress that it is in self-defense that she would have died had she not, repeating, "He's coming to kill me and he still can … he might still kill me if I give him a chance … I have to lie on the floor. The tunnel vision is starting again. I think this will be the last of it. The last of everything. But at least I went down fighting" (293). She also clarifies that she will likely have to carry the emotions for life regarding killing someone.

The heroic detective pays a heavy price for saving herself. But she is not left alone. She has her loving found family and her ex-lover turned lover: "Phil knows about killing and dealing with the aftermath, and he's taken it upon himself to help me come to grips with the horror" (309). The two become closer through this shared experience.

In "My words to Victor Frankenstein," Stryker encourages trans people to embrace the role of monster, to put it on, and to harness their rage for trans benefit. She concludes, "If this is your path, as it is mine, let me offer whatever solace you may find in this monstrous benediction: May you discover the enlivening power of darkness within yourself. May it nourish your rage. May your rage inform your actions, and your actions transform you as you struggle to transform your world" (251).

Punished for Rage: Orange Is the New Black *(Television)*

The celebrated Netflix show *Orange Is the New Black* likewise considers how badly society treats trans people, especially those who stick up for themselves. Laverne Cox's Sophia Burset stands out in the series as a transwoman of color, whose credit card fraud for her surgery got her imprisoned. Christina A. DiEdoardo, a trans activist and lawyer for trans clients, considers Sophia's crime and sentence. As she concludes, Sophia's is "arguably the most victimless crime of any prisoner in Litchfield" since "credit card companies can mitigate much, if not all, of their risk of garden-variety fraud" (32). The show's protagonist, Piper Chapman, has a sentence half Sophia's length for smuggling deadly heroin across international borders for organized crime. "Some might argue this evident sentencing disparity has nothing to do with the fact that Burset is a working class trans woman of color and Chapman is an upper-class, bright-faced white cisgender ... woman. However, I will not insult your intelligence by attempting to do so" (DiEdoardo 32).

Through the series, Sophia finds the positive in prison life, working in the salon and beautifying her fellow prisoners while participating in the fashion show and offering the other women a hilarious anatomy lesson. "Burset is patient, calm and eschews violence as a means to pursue her goals. From a macro level, this makes her one of the most courageous prisoners in Litchfield" (DiEdoardo 35). She's campy, self-affirming, and delightful. Moreover, before and during her sentence, Sophia is married, monogamous, and striving to be a good parent to her one child. She's not involved in sex work or prison contraband and was a firefighter in a respectable, lower middle-class household. She's never a seductress or scheming villain.

While Sophia's attempts to better her life (and others' lives) are dismissed, she is generally accepted—not as anyone's best friend or in any of the cliquey groups, but as their mostly impersonal hairdresser and gal pal. In her perfection in home and prison life (which demands she fulfill the parent role to her child, the big sister/confidant role to the inmates, and the supportive partner role to her wife), as well as her stoicism in the face of enduring transphobic slurs without losing her temper, Sophia must always be controlled. She is the quintessential Black superwoman—which Michele Wallace theorized as a "fundamental image" from the "intricate web of mythology that surrounds the Black woman" (154). In stereotypical popular culture, Black women are shown to possess "inordinate strength, with an ability for tolerating an unusual amount of misery and heavy, distasteful work. This woman does not have the same fears, weaknesses, and insecurities as other women, but believes herself to be and is, in fact, stronger emotionally than most men" (154). Of course, her stoicism and optimism are central to her depiction.

Dean Spade, Alexander Lee, and Morgan Bassichis, in "Building an Abolitionist Trans & Queer Movement with Everything We've Got," describe how much "queer and trans people are disproportionately policed, arrested, and imprisoned, and face high rates of violence in state custody from officials as well as other imprisoned or detained people" (19). The maldistribution of chances in life includes "high rates of unemployment, homelessness, and imprisonment," as well as "trans vulnerability to premature death" thanks to poverty, transphobic violence, inadequate or inaccessible healthcare, as well as discrimination, harassment, and neglect by medical professionals (Spade et al. 37). After release from prison, ongoing discrimination continues to follow them "in employment, interpersonal relationships, and through interface with state agencies" (Malatino, "Sophia" 107).

A transgender woman protests, "Let me re-capitulate what I can personally articulate through transgender: misogyny, homophobia, racism, lookism, disability, medical colonization, coercive psychiatrisation, undocumented labor, border control, state surveillance, population profiling, the prison-industrial complex, employment discrimination, housing discrimination, lack of health care, denial of access to social services, and violent hate crimes" (qtd. in Stryker, *Transgender History* 66). While Sophia is less abused in prison than many trans inmates, because she's imprisoned among women, her story calls attention to the injustices in the prison system for trans people in particular:

> Circumstances are shaped by inadequate medical care, placement in facilities that are not gender-confirming, solitary confinement, sexual assault, and harassment. This ensemble of oppressive relations amounts to what Orlando Patterson has termed social death (1982)—a state of being characterized by systemic violence, routine humiliation, and alienation from communities of support, exacerbating what legal scholar and trans activist Dean Spade (2011) has called the "maldistribution of life chances" (126) that already structure the conditions of existence for many trans folk, particularly trans people of color [Malatino, "Sophia" 95].

Sophia has some setbacks, as, in one of countless cases of prison abuse, her hormone supply is cut. Sophia tries getting them back through rational and logical arguments to the prison and less legitimate channels but fails. She continues working politely within both systems, to no avail. Later, in "WAC Pack" (1.06), she campaigns for prison leadership to bring her fellow inmates healthcare. She gives a variant of the "All we have to lose are our chains" speech but is ignored once more. Piper, the privileged white lady, is appointed instead. After this, Sophia's mostly a supporting character in others' stories. The show features over thirty highly individualized inmates and has been widely praised for exploring the backstories of so many marginalized women. Of course, any show with a single trans character places all the representation responsibility on them and risks stereotyping.

In season three, matters escalate. Gloria Mendoza and Sophia are fighting, both frustrated at how much they're kept away from their sons. At last, this reaches a peak as Gloria shoves Sophia. Gloria insists, "I am mothering. And I'm a ferocious, pissed-off, real mother, but you wouldn't know nothing about that, would you? Nah. 'Cause you ain't nothing real" ("A Tittin' and A Hairin" 3.10). Stung, Sophia shoves her into the wall. As Gloria crumples and cries, Sophia is instantly contrite, begging her forgiveness.

However, the violence against Sophia escalates disproportionally. Three women (all not the main characters for whom the audience most cares) surround Sophia in her salon, asking what she has between her legs. Sophia tries to deescalate, but they all attack her. The guard Sikowitz, first on the scene, panics and runs off for help instead of intervening.

Later in the episode, Sophia realizes, "You start to feel like one of the girls. But then something turns, and you realize you're still a freak and you'll never be one of them." Malatino observes, "Sophia goes on to articulate her rage, her desire for revenge, but Sister Ingalls encourages her to model non-violent resistance, to not give the fellow inmates the satisfaction of seeing her unravel" ("Sophia" 98). Sophia is disappointed, and they cry together over Sophia's suffering. This episode is one of the first moments in which visceral, brutal transphobic violence occurs, one of the first moments in which Sophia's prison experience approaches the accounts offered by imprisoned trans people of color, "who report consistent harassment, high incidences of segregation, sexual and physical violence, and fear of reprisal if they avail themselves of legal assistance to address these issues," Malatino reveals ("Sophia" 98). Sister Ingalls's advice, of course, is painfully reminiscent of that offered to minorities throughout history—suffer through abuse because there's no other path.

Afterward, bruised and clutching her ribs, Sophia speaks to the prison warden, Joe Caputo, who agrees that this wasn't her fault—less than the bare minimum of his job. MCC, the newly privatized corporate system of season three—charged with maximizing profit and armed with teams of lawyers—has made it less likely her demands will be heard. Sophia demands that Sikowitz be removed for being improperly trained due to MCC's institutionalized negligence. She also demands crisis and sensitivity training for all the guards. Once more, this is certainly a requirement of their profession. When Caputo tells her she needs to be "realistic," Sophia despairs and then fights back with the only weapon she has—her story.

> **SOPHIA:** Here's what I got. A *Post* headline "She-Male Jail Fail. Balls to the Wall in Tranny Prison Brawl." That shit sells like hotcakes. And everyone will be reading about it, and everyone will be talking about it, including the ladies of *The View*. You think MCC wants that kind of attention?
> **CAPUTO:** Jesus, Burset. Why you do you have to make everything so hard?
> **SOPHIA:** No offense, but fuck you sir ["Don't Make Me Come Back There" 3.12].

Sophia realizes how precarious her position is but keeps arguing for fairness, willing to use media fascination with people like her if that's what it takes. Skyler explains: "In a predominantly androcentric society where manhood is considered quintessential and womanhood is considered either secondary or inconsequential the act of abandoning or denouncing manhood in favor of womanhood elicits a far stronger sense of offense than the reverse" (qtd. in Scott and Kirkpatrick n.p.).

Sophia's attempt only makes things worse. At episode end, as Sophia curls up on her bunk, bruised, the guards come to drag her off to solitary confinement. They tell her someone higher up has insisted she be locked away for her own protection. This is described as being "for her own good"—some time alone to calm down in the aftermath of her beating, while acknowledging that those in charge have no way of preventing transphobia among the prison population. They fear bad publicity but aren't prepared to spend money on proper guards. Because Sophia has demanded her constitutional rights, she must disappear. The show makes it clear that by protesting, she has lost to the prison-industrial complex and her wealthy tormentors.

With no choices left, Sophia insists on walking out with some dignity, but she passes a judgmental and sheepish Gloria. The episode leaves viewers clear that a trans prisoner of color will lose in every way against the system and those with wealth and power. "This is a double segregation, a double isolation: her entrance into Litchfield has already severed her, significantly, from communities of support and care located beyond the prison walls; now, she is excised from the minimal support and care she was able to experience from her fellow inmates" (Malatino, "Sophia" 106). This is an illustration of social death.

In her cell, Sophia is symbolically trapped in the underworld, the unconscious side of the self. Silvia Brinton Perera explains in her Jungian guide, *Descent to the Goddess*, "It feels monstrous and ugly and even petrifying to the non-initiate. For it sheers us of our collective understandings and of the hopes and expectations of looking good and safely belonging. It is crude, chaotic, surprising, giving a view of the ground below ethics and aesthetics and the opposites themselves" (33). The hero does not always choose this condemnation into the symbolic underworld, the small, dark cell of despair. Sometimes, they are violently kidnapped or killed there, as with Eurydice or Persephone, or hurled there by an unjust authority.

This descent to the unconscious occurs when "we are reduced to the depths of numb pain and depression, to timelessness, proverbial chaos and emotionality—all that we call awful or infantile and associate with the archaic dimensions of consciousness" (Perera 29). This is a place where one sinks to their lowest state but also finds new strength to fight the system and rally once more. Ostensibly, this story moment allows for soul-searching—a time to not only pull back and regain control but also face the raging shadow and incorporate it. This belly of the whale, as Campbell called it, is a common step in many heroes' journeys, after which the hero tries another approach. However, in this and many minority situations, this show's hero has been locked up unjustly, and the only lesson is how there will be no justice. No alternate path will fix this system or allow Sophia to win. As such, this step is flipped into a brutal lesson in hopelessness.

The next season, Sophia is still in lockup, looking vulnerable without her wig. All her defenses and coping strategies have been stripped away. Her wife, Crystal, tries persuading Caputo to release her but is unsuccessful. Despairing, Sophia tries flooding her cell and finally lights it on fire with a broken lightbulb and toilet paper. When her cell is next seen, it's empty and bloody, suggesting suicide. She finally appears with heavily bandaged wrists as her last friend, Sister Ingalls, smuggles her a letter.

In "The Animals" (4.12), Sophia returns from solitary to find her old salon is now a center for the drug distribution business, with transphobic abuse scrawled on the sign. However, in a healing scene in the next episode, Gloria orders the drug gang out. Sophia comes in, and Gloria brushes her wig for her and replaces it on her head. The system is brutal and unfair, but those within it can still find compassion and sisterhood. Eventually, Sophia is one of the few seen released from prison and thriving, making her a rare success story of the brutal system shown here.

6

UNDERWORLD DESCENT

Descent Within and Without: The Watch *(Television)*

The beloved fantasy parody series Discworld features bearded dwarves who all identify as men. In several books, rural dwarves encounter big city life and see women enjoying gowns and glitter. Some relate to these presentations and decide to adopt them. In one famous adventure, Night Watch officer Cheery Littlebottom goes to the dwarf capital determinedly dressed as a woman and faces many slurs. The fundamentalist dwarves call her "dangerously different" and treat her with contempt (Pratchett 301). At the end, however, the Dwarf King publicly acknowledges Cheery and adds, "Do be sure to let me know the name of your dressmaker.... I may have some custom for her in the fullness of time" (440). The king likewise may be coming out in gender and dress.

The series was modernized for the television adaptation, *The Watch* (2021). In it, non-binary actor Jo Eaton-Kent plays Cheery, who determinedly uses she/her pronouns in a skeptical population and works as the smart scientist on the team. After several adventures, Cheery faces a personal challenge in season one, episode six, "The Dark in the Dark."

The questing hero often shows great agency and courage as they choose to enter the underworld, "a well-known symbol of the unconscious with its unknown possibilities" (von Franz 170). It represents the realm of inner dreams and visions one hasn't yet explored. For the child hero, this is often the villain's stronghold, like the Wicked Witch's castle or the Death Star. The trans hero may go to any of these places, but the most traumatic descent is the personal one. Some heroes thus enter the dark heart of their birth community, flooded with censure and judgment.

In the larger series' crime-solving caper, they're questing for an ancient crown hidden in the dwarves' realm. As Cheery insists, she's the only one who can guide them, though she's scared. "Down there is not like anywhere else ... there's a dark that hunts ... it hunted down my mother" ("The Dark in the Dark"). As Perera explains of the young questor, "She does not flee from her fate, nor does she denigrate the goddess of fate.... She volunteers. And in this courageous, conscious acquiescing, she ends the pattern of scapegoating by choosing to confront the underworld herself" (91).

Indeed, Cheery has been getting by in a land far from her underground birthplace, burying her impulses, and being a friendly and useful member of society. It's not enough. The darkness she left behind has been calling her back. One makes such a descent in the service of life "to scoop up more of what has been held unconscious by the self in the underworld" (Perera 50).

"Promised myself there'd never be any going back," she mutters ("The Dark in the Dark"). Preparing to go nonetheless, Cheery removes her earrings and nose ring. She turns to show her friends that she's wearing a full fake beard. "This is what my mother used to wear. It's how we keep the dark away. You can't be yourself down there. You have to be the same. No man or woman. Everyone has to be the same." Angua (a werewolf woman) and Carrot (a human adopted by dwarves) don their own fake beards. In the novels, both struggle with people's assumptions as they present themselves as humans. By venturing into the underworld, they too are opening themselves to absorbing the elements of themselves they've been keeping concealed. "It is an even greater need to seek it to discover it, to learn its vital lessons. Those who suppress their dark side are vulnerable to its impulses and desires, yet unable to accept them" (Frankel, *From Girl to Goddess* 129).

Cheery, Angua, and Carrot venture to the Mines of Tak. (On the way, Cheery's misfit friends exaggerate their masculinity, humming, grunting, and walking with huge strides until Cheery must tell them to stop.) There, Spike, the king and Cheery's old flame, has inherited the throne, taking Cheery's birthright. Spike confronts her in dwarfish. Cheery protests, "Hey stop. You know I don't use that name. Not just because it takes six minutes to say."

SPIKE (smirking): He needs my help.
ANGUA: She.
CHEERY: Angua!
SPIKE: There is no she.
ANGUA: There are two in front of you.
SPIKE: There is no she! ["The Dark in the Dark"].

In response, Cheery insists, "You will heed the authority of my name," and fiercely spends a comedic six minutes reciting it. This does not get them in, but Cheery's newer status as an officer of the Night Watch does. Cheery's willingness to use the deadname and pronouns emphasizes the conformity of the forced birth home. Here, "she" is a slur, and as Cheery says, "the worst thing you can be around here."

Cheery left this place, but she's surprised that Spike doesn't seem angry. "There was only time to save one of us when your father found out we wanted to shave our beards," Spike says with a forgiving intensity. However, Spike finally admits his resentment. Aiding the villain, he pulls off everyone's fake beards and abandons Cheery and Angua together in the dark.

As they kneel there, chained, Cheery's horror is greater because she knows the spirit of conformity that's coming for them. Cheery tells Angua that losing their concealing beards will trigger reprisals. Her mother removed her own beard, and the dark stole her. Cheery fled when she started questioning their practices, since "the dark, it's summoned by different." Bravely, Cheery defies the dark, insisting it keep away from Angua. "Yeah, that's right, you know me," she challenges. It swallows her.

Initiation requires a descent into hell to overcome the dark side of one's nature and reconcile with it before resurrection and illumination. This can involve fear and guilt, as well as the damage that holds one back from greatness. Cheery finds herself in a surreal, swirling pink and blue realm, dressed in a suit, then a poofy prom dress, then a tight tank top and miniskirt. Haunting singing surrounds her. This is the primordial shadow mother. "She is the energy banishing itself into the underworld, too awesome to behold—like primal childhood experiences and the darkness of the moon, places of oblivion that are the perilous grounds on which daylight consciousness treads, the primal matrix" (Perera 23).

"It's you, Cheery. It's all you," says her mother, emerging from the mist to hug her. She's glamorous, with long, curled hair like Cheery's and a rainbow streak.

Cheery looks elegant with her returned jewelry and makeup, but she also looks vulnerable in the skimpy outfit. "I thought the dark took you," she protests ("The Dark in the Dark").

Her mother looks calm and wise as she laughs gently. "The dark doesn't seek those who are different and punish them. It's time to leave that cruel lie behind. Here in the dark lie endless possibilities. Multiverses...." Of course, the mother here is the protective spirit, embodying the blessings of the feminine. She embraces her child, inspiring her to persevere. As Cheery's mother adds, "The summoning dark is your ally. It will follow, protect you. You can wield its power." With some inspiring words, her mother calls her "my sweet girl" and vanishes.

Returned to her body, Cheery discovers her chains are gone. She breaks Angua's chains and extinguishes the lanterns with a thought. "Now we have help." Later, Cheery explains, "It's a kind of magic. It's an infinity of all that I can be. And there's no shame. There's no right or wrong. In there, you can be anything. Everything." The most transcendent heroes don't just survive the death journey but claim it, incorporating the powers of the underworld to become deeper and wiser, wielding the magic of death as well as life. As Perera adds, "Until the demonic powers of the dark Goddess are claimed, there is not strength in the woman to grow from daughter to an adult who can stand against the force of patriarchy" (42). Taking down society will be the next task.

Upstairs, the villains, Carrot, and Spike see the mine entrances glow deep blue and close. As Cheery threatens them with the summoning dark, the villains flee. Cheery turns to her old flame, her voice compassionate. "The dark's our friend, Spike. It helps us be anything we want to be" ("The Dark in the Dark"). She turns on the lights with a gesture. Gently, she adds that the dwarves need to embrace it—Spike must go tell the fundamentalist dwarves they're wrong to deny all the sides of themselves. The dark is not a hall monitor enforcing conformity; it's power that supports individual choice. Many, like young Cheery, have always feared the tremors of the unconscious. Spike is stunned at the newer, more confident Cheery and her assertion that they need a revolution.

Up above, assassins have captured more members of their team. With new confidence, Cheery springs to action. "I got this…. I got a friend who can help us." After incorporating the darkness, the questors are no longer obedient and submissive but assertive and strong. They can wield the fury and majesty of the underworld that they've banished from their everyday selves and tear the system apart.

Cheery strides in with curled pink hair, a nose ring, a beard, a red low-cut tank top, silver sparkling boots, shorts, and a ruffled open skirt in a joyful gender presentation hybrid. Using the summoning dark, she snaps to summon music and angel backup dancers (of different presentations) and performs a campy glam rock dance that suggests *Rocky Horror* to "You Make Me Paranoid." Cheery sings that their weapon is hate, but hers is not. Bursts of dark energy she flings make the villains disappear. With this, she wields the power she has found in the darkness to celebrate all she is.

Belly of the Whale: Look Past *(Novel)*

As Penfield narrates in the satirical *Future Feeling*, "It wasn't terribly long ago that I was off in my own shadow lands, getting my wagon wheels stuck in the same ruts, hating myself, like hating myself beyond the level of hatred that any transphobic person would care to reach, imagining a thousand lost futures, experiencing moment to moment reality as a constant plunge into humiliation, a receptacle of the underside of an entire culture's

6. Underworld Descent

anxieties about trans people.... I mean, not to discourage you, but every day I have to drag myself away from its magnetic pull" (Lake 120–121).

Mirroring this symbolism, Campbell's belly of the whale is a journey into the darkest place of all—the villain's stronghold or another place of torture and despair. "The hero, instead of conquering or conciliating the power of the threshold, is swallowed into the unknown, and would appear to have died" (*Hero* 74). Traditionally, the hero may descend many times into the abyss throughout the story, with each descent growing increasingly hazardous. Luke Skywalker enters the Death Star, then reaches the emperor's chamber within it, and then succumbs to moments of fury that hearken to the dark side. This reflects going deeper and deeper into one's subconscious, facing one's most terrible shadows in order to overcome them and grow.

At the climax of April Daniels's *Sovereign*, the supervillains catch teenage Danielle and throw her into an unlit cell. Her powers have been blocked, so their blows hurt particularly badly when they land. Even as she thinks things can't get worse, goons come and drag her into a medical experimentation chamber. The villains strip away her clothes and paint mystical symbols on her. Even as all this torment continues, they misgender her, adding to the cruelty. Garrison, the main villain, tries to persuade her to give up her powers and, with them, possibly her physical transition. This is a test in which she discovers what she's made of. In the worst place of all, at the height of her torment, she insists, "You don't deserve my powers and I will die screaming before I let you have them" (138).

"Don't Press Charges and I Won't Sue" by Charlie Jane Anders offers a body horror story thanks to the clinic ironically called Love and Dignity for Everyone. Its mission is "to repair the world's most broken people" (257). As the narration adds, "Everyone agrees on the goal—returning healthy, well-adjusted individuals to society without any trace of dysphoria, dysmorphia, dystonia, or any other dys words—but nobody can agree on the fine details or how exactly to measure ideal outcomes beyond those statutory benchmarks" (258–259). Rachel is wheeled in and lectured about how she is selfish to think everyone in the world must respect her gender. They bring in a man's corpse and connect her to it so that her voice comes out of the corpse's mouth. It even rewrites her words: "She tries again to say, this is not medicine. This is a human rights violation. And it comes out of the dead man's mouth as, I don't mean to be a jerk. I just have things to do, you know. Sorry if I'm causing any trouble" (262). The nurse calls her Mr. Billings and tells her she'll be released into the community soon, where everyone will be so happy to see her. As Rachel is transformed, she feels herself slip away bit by bit. Rachel makes her escape, dragging the man's corpse that is connected to her in a painful metaphor for society's expectations as well as its brutal facilities.

Thrillers put the protagonists in deadly danger, emphasizing the testing that comes with facing death and harnessing one's dark side. *Look Past* by Eric Devine has teenage Avery solving a murder mystery in their small town—the murder of his beloved, who fully accepted him. How symbolic and personal this murder is to the hero emphasizes the novel's mythic nature. In fact, the murderer cuts off body parts and leaves them to be found, wrapped in Bible verses. Mary's lips appear just after Avery speaks on her behalf, voicing what she no longer can.

The first descent occurs when he visits the place in the woods where her body was found. This is a horror for him as he hears how the body was maimed and catches a glimpse of her "lying in the open, unprotected and so vulnerable" (39). His horror at the sight is compounded when the police arrest him for trespassing at a crime scene and one adds, "You are that freak, aren't you? Girl who's a boy or whatever. Tom's niece, right?" (41). This personal attack, while Avery is mourning the loss of his beloved, adds pain and trauma to the encounter.

As Avery investigates, the killer sends him text messages, taunting him. They reveal that Mary was murdered to push Avery to repent and punish Mary for their relationship. Amid Bible verses, the killer harasses Avery, mocking and horrifying him. "You need to ask Him for forgiveness, and if you do, then maybe I will show you some mercy" (221). As such, the murderer offers the bigoted voice of the community, but also the judgmental voice Avery hears within. Further, the killer echoes Avery's fears of persecution, observing, "This town cares about Mary and it took one week to find her. How long do you think they would take to find you?" (51). The killer texts him a picture from childhood, looking like a little girl in pigtails. "This! This is who you are! Until I see you as you should be, this is possible…" (102). A picture of Mary's murdered body follows.

The funeral is yet another descent, with organized religion battering at him, the reverend righteously preaching, and everyone whispering and judging. The police also push him further into personal revelations, as Avery must confess that he and Mary were in love, and that's why she was killed. Many of the police are against him, and his friends Beth and Charlie are taken away: first because their parents insist that they distance themselves from Avery because he has a target on his back, and then after the killer targets and hospitalizes each of them.

Another descent comes when Avery enters the town hall meeting where the police report on how the investigation is going. As Avery walks in, he hears his name a few times, along with slurs and sexual threats. Without his friends, the comments hit harder. Further, he suspects the murderer is in the room. In fact, battered by everyone's cruelty and judgment, as the crowd shouts insults and the police captain suggests he may be

6. Underworld Descent

responsible, Avery lashes out. He reveals confidential details of the investigation and criticizes the police for not investigating all the leads. As Avery reveals, Mary's father, the Reverend Mathison, used to hit Mary. "When she talked back about the church and about its hatred, he used a belt. That's not religion, that's hypocrisy" (187). In response, the reverend leads the crowd in prayers condemning Avery for existing. At this moment, it feels to Avery as if the whole town is against him. Over and over, the descents take place in public among people he grew up with, emphasizing their daily hostility. His ordinary world has become a crucible. Afterward, his father tells him he must "be smarter" about how he fights and pick his battles more carefully, even among the cruel and judgmental neighbors (190).

High school is its own descent into the belly of the whale, as Eva mocks Avery from her prayer group. She insists that if he accepted God, he wouldn't be so confused. Later, in an attempt to catch the killer, Avery appears to capitulate. He returns to school in a dress and pigtails, once again abandoned by his best friends. All the teens at the school, even the teachers, stare and make brutal comments. They snatch selfies and post YouTube videos. Eva misgenders him and calls him adorable. In response, Avery thinks, "I feel like one of her prized animals, not even close to human anymore" (211–212). As he adds, "They all get to behave as they truly see me without fear of getting in trouble. To them, I'm a joke" (214). Any civility they once showed is abandoned. As all the students whisper, misgendering him and making lewd remarks, Avery thinks, "I am going to be everywhere online, and I realized just how much of this is precisely what the killer wants. Repentance by humiliation. The price had better be worth it" (216). He finally punches one of the rudest teens, but this exercise in mortification has done its work. It has not even revealed the killer.

In another tormenting test, the killer challenges Avery to repent at church. A temple is actually a traditional womb of the world, as Campbell notes: this is where the hero goes "to be quickened by the recollection of who and what he is, namely dust and ashes unless immortal" (*Hero* 77). Avery goes there, hoping to draw out his enemy. His uncle the cop tells him, "You just need to speak from the heart. That's what he wants. Some piece of you. This is a game, and you are the ultimate chip ... it's not going to be easy, but do what needs to be done" (Devine 244). Avery walks toward the altar where the reverend gave Mary's eulogy a week before. Obediently, Avery prays aloud, admitting that he has sinned and seeking repentance. This is self-mortification, as Campbell and the murderer suggest, but one ironically rooted in lies and performance. As Avery thinks, "Every word of this lie burns like a candle being snubbed on my tongue. But I continue" (245). As he leaves, he feels ashamed that he gave in to the murderer here and at high school. It's a personal wrench, betraying who he is to stop his enemy and save his own life. After each of these moments, the killer continues to taunt him.

When Avery finally figures out the killer's identity, he goes to her house in a vicious descent into the final, deepest belly. The sweet-faced teen churchgoer is eager to dress him like a girl. "Peel off those clothes, sweetie. Just us girls, no shame in that." One final time, Avery puts on an act for the killer. As Avery stalls, she helps him undress, cutting off the binder with a frightening knife. "This is what Mary must have seen. I draw on this and I find strength" (265). Symbolically, he's undergoing what Mary did—the stripping and disassembling that ended with her murder. Alone with the killer, Avery prays to Mary for protection. The killer, meanwhile, dresses Avery in her clothes and then does his hair, and he succumbs to the humiliation.

He toys with the murderer and finally extracts a confession. This moment of facing judgmental society in the form of a wicked peer who voices the fears within Avery is the challenge. Even as he resists her words, some part of him fears that she is correct, that society is right, and that he caused the death of his beloved. Therefore, this becomes a challenge not just for survival but for the heart. Avery triumphs, emerging stronger after this testing that shakes him to his core.

The journey into the belly can be more positive—even a triumph. Alex Myers's *Continental Divide* sees its young hero losing his parents' support and thus his place at Harvard. He goes to Wyoming to find himself and live as a man for a year—Ron, not Veronica. Among ranch hands, he hopes to discover quintessential manliness. When he goes to fight a fire, he enters Campbell's Belly of the Beast.

> It felt like I was in some alternate reality—like somewhere between the station and the clearing, I'd stepped through a portal. Nothing like Narnia, of course. But otherworldly, nonetheless. Maybe it was the smooth wood of the shovel handle. Maybe it was the anonymity and uniformity of our shit-brown pants and red brain buckets. Maybe it was the rigor of the task at hand—but I felt pared down to my core in a good way. Simple Necessary. Just digging. Just right here. Even though I had no idea where "here" was. I thought of the note I would write: I've gone off the map again. Look for the large plume of smoke. Head up the crummy dirt road. Wander into the woods some distance. Listen for chainsaws. I'm somewhere in there, looking like everyone else [260].

He's alone with himself, fighting the fire with his own strength. He also saves a teammate's life and feels new respect from others. Emerging from this experience, he thinks that he's found his place: "My whole life, whatever I'd really wanted, I'd been able to get. It had always been the case that when I thought about what came next, I saw success, excitement, fulfilment. Even greatness. But recently, I looked ahead, and it made me flinch.

It felt a lot like walking into a sandstorm. I was inclined to turn my back on it. Now, though, maybe things would work out" (247).

Supreme Ordeal: No Man of Woman Born (Short Stories)

The ordeal one faces in the underworld is the initiation ceremony. This descent allows the character to free themselves from the entanglement of personal relations and find individuality with a deeper consciousness. Metaphorically, one descends as a child and returns as an adult. This is heightened in fairytales like Sleeping Beauty or Snow White, in which the shock of sexuality or original sin plunges the heroine into a death sleep, from which she only emerges when she's ready to absorb the new understanding. "During puberty, sleep is the refuge in which an adolescent girl can absorb the new sense of herself that she gains from the prick of the spindle, and changes from girl to woman: a transformation more radical than from boy to man" (Gould 108). Of course, more radical yet is the transformation in societal position, pronouns, name, and so much more if a hero claims a new public identity. Such an ordeal of descent, initiation, and return can also symbolize other stages as the young questor returns as a hero, certain in purpose and affirmed by the community.

This journey is an essential step in parting with the youthful self to become more mature: "The child, whether seven or seventy, can only break that unconscious bond with the mother world when it realizes it has a soul of its own, which has been born onto this earth through the body of the mother but does not belong to her (or to anyone else)" (Woodman, *Pregnant* 118–119). Certainly, while facing death, the hero must use their unique powers to endure the challenge and come through it wiser, with new powers. In some stories, this power involves flexibility and nonconformity.

Ana Mardoll's short story collection *No Man of Woman Born* plays with the concept of prophecy. In *Macbeth* and *The Lord of the Rings* (inspired by older traditions like Western fairytales and Hindu legends of the goddess Durga), a villain insists that he's invulnerable to any man born, only for the heroes to find loopholes in the phrasing. In Mardoll's first story, "Tangled Nets," the local village requests an annual volunteer to be sacrificed to a dragon in return for food for the person's family. Armed only with a fishing net and scaling knife, Wren goes.

In fact, Wren volunteers to save xer sick mother, Eirlys, but more because xie can't stand to lose another person. "If I'm going to die, I'd rather die trying.... Better to die doing something worthwhile than live off the dead" (15). This selfless protection of the community shows a desire to be a leader and a hero.

Beyond this, several encounters with a witch give Wren hints of destiny. While xer sister Swynwen was declared "a girl but an ill-fated one" before her birth and then sacrificed to the dragon, the witch Halwen said nothing at all about Wren before birth, an unlucky omen. Halwen, further, always calls Wren "child." As Wren thinks, "The word in the witch's mouth wasn't condescending; it simply filled a space nothing else could fill" (9). Halwen considers Wren odd and different but adds that everyone's strange—she is a witch after all. Further, she wasn't born one but made one.

In fact, Halwen got her powers when she was sacrificed to the dragon. After a seer touched her, her eyes changed, and she watched in her mind as an army battled the dragon and lost. As she adds, "We could hear its boasts all the way down to the village, crowing that no man nor woman would ever kill it, nor beast, nor fish nor fellow dragon" (14). Wren is struck by the wording and pleads, "There are people—there *must* be people who aren't—" (14). As Wren thinks,

> soldiers and seers had been helpless before the dragon, but they had been men and women. Wren was neither, yet the knowledge did not make xer feel special. Xie was simply xerself, in the same way Halwen was a witch. Xie had resolved to face death so Eirlys might live, but now xie could not help but wonder if there might be another way [15].

At the final sacrifice, xie nets the dragon and guts it with the knife to avenge Swynwen. "Wren's hands were not free of blood, but no one else would ever die in xer place" (20). The dragon is the shadow—all the primordial rage that polite society has banished to its outskirts. By sending the young hero there, xie has the chance to absorb its wisdom. The dragon is penned savagery, like a primordial goddess: "Here there is a quality of primal rage about her. She is full of fury, greed, the fear of loss, and even of self-spite. She symbolizes raw instinctually split off from consciousness—need and aggression in the underworld" (Perera 23). After the triumph, Halwen arrives to observe that Wren's eyes have turned black from the dragon's blood. "There are easier ways to become a witch, you know," she concludes with humor (21).

"Artists know instinctively that there are times in life where we must be unreachable, times when we must insist that those around us, especially those nearest and dearest, remain at a distance if anything significant is to develop inside us," explains Gould (98). The journey is about achieving greatness and finding purpose together. This is a rite of passage from ordinary child to supernatural one, accomplished through the mentor and the heroic deed, as well as Wren's being non-binary and thus fulfilling the prophecy. Through the monster slaying, Wren has found xer true inner power.

"No one can go through an experience at the edge of death without being changed in some way," warns Vogler (30). Even for ordinary humans, after a near-death experience, "colors seem sharper, family and friends are more important, and time is more precious. The nearness of death makes life more real" (164). Now that xie has come through the challenge, xie is prepared for adulthood and its power.

Tyrant Parent: Funky Dan and the Pixie Dream Girl (Novel)

Funky Dan and the Pixie Dream Girl by Courtney Lanning introduces Selene, the dream pixie, who offers Roxie, "a pure hearted maiden," the opportunity to deliver good dreams in her place. Roxie is feeling impostor syndrome, insisting, "Three years of puberty blockers, hormones, speech therapy, and it wasn't enough, Selene! Then I had that surgery because I thought that would make me feel real, like I wasn't some impostor. But weeks have come and gone, and even this hasn't solved my problem. I still feel like I'm just pretending to be a woman instead of actually being one like I desperately want" (23).

As Pearson observes, such uncertainty is common: "No matter how old, wise, or mature we become, each of us has within us a vulnerable little child who still bears the scars—whether great or few—of our formative years" (30). Of course, trans lives are more complicated and nuanced than such a fictionalized divide. As Fisher and colleagues explain, it is uncommon for trans people to experience a clear "before and after" the way media describe it: "As we listen to trans stories, autobiographies, poems, prose and narratives outside the clinic we notice that they are irreducible to the presupposed chronological progression from a 'terrible-present-in-the-wrong-body' to a 'better-future-in-the-right-body'" (2).

Indeed, Selene knows she has not made a mistake. The job involves banishing people's nightmares, healing the vulnerable across the world. This functions as aiding weaker substitutes for herself, as she cures all those in pain. However, her own nightmares express how much she too is wounded and needs healing.

Later, Roxie comments that she worries her father will die without them making up. "I just want to believe that someday he's going to come around, you know? Like, I'll just wake up one morning and my father will be downstairs with a bouquet and a thousand apologies for the way he treated me. But with every text he sends, and every deadname he drops, it just gets easier to hate him. And I don't want to hate him, Mom. I want to love my dad, but he just makes it impossible, and I don't know" (54). Her mother agrees that she felt the same way before divorcing him.

As folklorist Marion Woodman notes, "We see the frozen gods we can no longer worship. We thaw these frozen images with our tears, restore the stone gods to life by enacting them in our own flesh. We endow them with the blood of our own suffering" (*Ravaged Bridegroom* 126). This cruelty can function as a wake-up call that destroys the young protagonist's father worship. Accordingly, at the climax, Roxie's father kidnaps her and insists that an angel is guiding him on how to fix Roxie. He snatches away the magic bracelet that makes her a pixie dream girl. However, he's not in control—an ancient evil is using her father. This is Hiawatha, the Queen of Tears, who has plunged their town into a nightmare.

Hiawatha drags Roxie into a dysphoric dream with her surgery undone, forcing her to conform to her old family role. The spirit tells her, "Here's how this works, Johnny. You're going to live your new life in this nightmare until it breaks you, and you finally accept who you used to be. Once that's done, no matter how long it takes, I'll release you. Your father can take you back to Kansas, and I don't ever have to worry about the pixie dream girl ever again" (Lanning 223). Defiance is met with electric shocks.

> The father represents the parent or authority figure, but a reader must remember that each fairytale character represents a part of the self. The father, in fact, is the guardian, the intellect and system of rules meant to protect the self. Usually, in fairytales, the father fails to protect the daughter, or foolishly bargains her away (as in Beauty and the Beast). He rarely understands the connection between the conscious and unconscious world—that things are not always as they appear. This lack of guidance reveals the young woman's innocence at the beginning of her journey. At the end, she returns as a goddess or teacher, powerful beyond the dreams of the once authoritative father. This leap in power represents the growth in soul and knowledge that the heroine has achieved [Frankel, *From Girl to Goddess* 92].

In the dream, Roxie's future self, at age fifty, intervenes to comfort her and confirm who she is. She reminds Roxie that she's not alone. This inner guide exists to protect the self, especially from the dark, frightening figures of childhood. This is Pearson's Orphan archetype, which, as she describes, is "the part of us that learns to recognize and thus avoid situations that are likely to hurt us" (33). To do so, it acts on knowledge that the everyday self cannot even acknowledge having. Thus, it functions as a secret, hidden sidekick. With the aid of this inner voice, Roxie finds the strength to defy her father and claim herself.

In myth and epic, the questing hero encounters an adversary who is all they have rejected in their everyday existence: Luke and Darth Vader,

6. Underworld Descent

Alice and the Red Queen, Dorothy and the Wicked Witch. In each of these stories, the gentle adolescent faces the evil ruler—parental monstrosity, antilife, and evil. The hero is repulsed but also drawn to all these abilities they've chosen not to explore.

> The negative face of the Shadow in stories is projected onto characters called villains, antagonists, or enemies. Villains and enemies are usually dedicated to the death, destruction, or defeat of the hero. Antagonists may not be quite so hostile—they may be Allies who are after the same goal but who disagree with the hero's tactics. Antagonists and heroes in conflict are like horses in a team pulling in different directions, while villains and heroes in conflict are like trains on a head-on collision course [Vogler 71].

The highest spiritual encounter here shows the hero absorbing some of the adversary's abilities and gaining unexplored powers—all the heroes gain maturity and a touch of authority through these conflicts. By the third film, Luke has faced Vader and developed mature confidence. He speaks with cool authority and dresses in black. Further, by risking his life to save his father, connecting with him, and sensing the good within him, he acknowledges the nuanced darkness within himself and matures.

Of course, symbolic father-tyrants can be as menacing as family members. In a subplot, a neighbor attacks Roxie in a bathroom, terrifying her. After, she asks, "When's it going to be enough, Mom? How many times do I have to get hurt before they finally see I'm not a threat to them? … Do I have to let them kill me, Mom? Is that what it's going to take for people like Mr. Parker to realize I'm not a bunch of perverts out to hurt their families?" (Lanning 128). She adds, "I wish for just one second they could feel the absolute terror of knowing there are people there that want to kill you for no other reason than the fact that you exist. I wish they could feel the unending shame of having people point and laugh at them. I wish they could cry and pray that the floor swallowed them up when they realized no one is coming to help" (128).

Sometimes these bullies can be confronted and deflated. Roxie invades Mr. Parker's dreams and finds him desperate to save his son from a fire. In fact, the son died. As he pleads with her for help, Roxie tells him, "There! That's what I wanted from you. Do you feel that hopelessness? That absolute pit you've sunk into, realizing someone else holds all the power? I've spent the last two days screaming and crying because of what you did to me, you monster" (138). However, when she remembers how much others have faith in her, she puts out the fire. She explains to Mr. Parker how he bullied his sons to make them strong, but he turned them into bullies who preyed on others. He promises to teach them better, and they each apologize. This lesser adversary reflects her father along with the cruel side of society. Mr. Parker thus serves as a threshold guardian, training her to stand up to bullies before facing her greatest one. By passing this test, she is better equipped for greater fights. Here and with her birth father, she discovers they are weak puppets of society who can be defeated by her inner fortitude.

> On the heroine's journey, the young questor comes to realize that she is mightier than the tyrant: Dorothy cowers before the "Great and Powerful Oz" when she reaches his Emerald City. But after facing the far more terrifying Wicked Witch of the West, she grows into someone strong enough to kick over the Wizard's pasteboard head and confront the fraud cowering behind it [Frankel, Chosen One 85].

This is the classic confrontation with the cruel father—facing him only to find that he's a puppet, broken, or defeated. He cannot continue dominating the protagonist's inner life but will crumble away if confronted.

In a literalizing of this trope in Hugo and Nebula finalist K. M. Szpara's "You Can Make a Dinosaur, but You Can't Help Me," Emerick flies out to visit his dad, literally an evil mad scientist, to discuss his upcoming surgery. His dad deadnames him and dismisses him as usual. Emerick narrates, "And it's not that my dad doesn't believe trans people are real. He believes that dinosaurs and portals are real—that Noelle is basically magic, for fuck's sake. He just doesn't believe that his son is no longer his daughter" (n.p.). When his dad's assistant Noelle gives Emerick and Leo a tour of the dinosaur pens, she mentions that some dinosaurs have been having "spontaneous sex changes" and are scheduled to be destroyed. Emerick tries breaking them out, thinking, "You wouldn't mind if your father's creations took control of the island and ran everyone here through the damn portal" (n.p.). The entire compound exists to control nature and destroy it when it defies the mad scientist's plans. The story ends with Noelle helping Emerick change as the dinosaurs change. Emerick learns to ignore his father's callousness and accept that they'll never be family. "He doesn't matter. You found the support you needed—on his own island, at that" (n.p.).

Felix Ever After emphasizes the difficulty of this personal conflict. Felix describes how much he feels like an awful son but is terribly frustrated that his dad won't just accept who he is. As Felix adds, "Maybe this is fucked-up, I don't know ... but somehow, it's his approval I need most, even more than anyone else's. I need his validation. His understanding, not just acceptance, that he has a son. I'm not sure that's something he'll ever give me" (Callender 69). The difficulty is that Felix's vulnerable side is still so desperate, still acknowledging the father's inner voice as a source of judgment he's determined to live up to. This struggle sometimes has a happy ending, but in other stories, it never does. It is this judgmental voice the hero has incorporated more than the father himself, who must be faced and defeated.

In the film *Gun Hill Road*, the father insists that by coming out, his daughter stole having a son from him. "That's my life. That's my boy, understand?" he tells his friend. "He took that from me." In a savage scene, he wrestles his daughter into the bathroom and brutally cuts her hair short. When he hears she's using the girl's bathroom, he's obsessed with how that makes him look as a father. He even hauls her to a prostitute to teach her how to be a man. This is all suggested to reflect his issues after returning from three years in prison and finding that the family has been surviving without him. His days are spent pacifying cruel bosses and parole officers. However, he finally softens toward his daughter as he accepts that he wants to stay in her life.

Leaving the powerful father is essential in order to carve out one's place in the world, free from the stifling patriarchal force. Kai Cheng Thom's "I Shall Remain" follows a sacred intersex person, Medusa-like with "scales and head-tails ... bare breasts and phallus" (99). Once the narrator dwelled in the shining city: "I was Best Beloved, Daddy's Delight, preferred child of the Shining Father by whose Divinity we are all called into Being" (99). The highest duty is singing the Shining Father the songs of creation. However, Shining Daddy strips the narrator of voice when banishing them from the city—he can provide all and take all. Still, the narrator desires "a freedom of my own making" and "a Divinity that is mine and mine alone" more than protection and luxury (104). The narrator brings a glimmer of power—transformation and healing—to the world below. At a turning point, a warlord comes to the shrine and begs for healing, which the protagonist grants in a sensual encounter. It is impossible to heal all of humanity's corruption, but a few glimpses of the divine are still possible. The fallen ones still answer prayers, even if Shining Daddy does not.

Shadow as Otherself: Loki *(Television)*

The mythological god Loki is gender fluid, and his Marvel adaptation acknowledges this, especially in the comics. On his own Marvel Cinematic Universe show, his genderfluid identity is only mentioned in a document the camera focuses on, but his interactions with a spectrum of variants emphasize his multitudes (Johnston). "Breadth and range of identity contained in the character has been emphasized and is something I was always aware of when I was first cast 10 years ago," his actor Tom Hiddleston says. "I know it was important to [showrunners] Kate Herron and Michael Waldron and to the whole team. And we were very aware, this is something we felt responsible for" (qtd. in Johnston).

In episode three, Loki is unwillingly teamed up with Sylvie, a femme-presenting "variant" of himself from another universe. This alternate self is a mirror who also guides him to deeper understanding. The pair squabble over and over, even as Sylvie discerns harsh truths.

To begin, Loki accidentally whisks them to a doomed apocalypse—a high-pressure belly of the whale, like being trapped in a frying pan. The planet will soon be destroyed. Asteroids are pummeling the moon where they stand, and there's even a ticking clock until doomsday. This is the unconscious realm, a place of stark truth with nowhere to hide. Compounding the pressure, Sylvie continues to interrogate him, pushing him to reveal the dark truths of his makeup.

> **Sylvie:** Yeah? What exactly makes a Loki a Loki?
> **Loki:** Independence, authority, style.
> **Sylvie:** So, naturally you went to work for the boring, oppressive time police.
> **Loki:** I don't work for them. I'm a consultant.
> **Sylvie:** You don't know what you want ["Lamentis" 1.03].

This is the job of the shadow—and an even more intimate shadow than the parent is the self who might have been. The Hugo finalist "Unknown Number" by Blue Neustifter is a short story made of Twitter screenshots. In it, the protagonist Gabby (labeled *You* in the texts) receives messages from an alt-self who never transitioned (called *Them* in the story, with a deadname occasionally blacked out). They text, "I don't even know how to say this. I needed to know if there was a universe where I figured it out. I'm in my mid-forties. I'm alone. I'm in prime midlife crisis stage. And for years, for decades, I have felt this hole in me. A void" (n.p.). This other self is surprised to find how assertive Gabby is. Gabby replies, "Well, it turns out when you're not being crushed under a mountain of dysphoria you find a lot of energy" (n.p.) As she adds, "You broke the laws of physics to find out if you could be a girl. I'm gonna say yeah that's dysphoria" (n.p.). She advises the alt-self on her own life and what she's discovered. At last, she sends them off to consider, adding, "I know that when you stop running from this shit, you'll find out you're a lot stronger than you think" (n.p.).

> **Them:** I'll.... I'll make some calls
> **Them:** talk to my doctor or something
> **You:** and a therapist?
> **Them:** yeah and a therapist
> **Them:** didn't realize when I finally talked to myself I'd be so ruthless
> **You:** yeah well, you're in a rut and someone needed to help you break out of it

6. Underworld Descent

This is the power of the shadow—to tell insightful truths no one else can. The graphic memoir *Welcome to St. Hell* takes a similar angle, with the post-transition narrator showing up to confront his past self and comment on events.

In the dystopian *Annex* by Rich Larson, Violet finds herself tortured by a world in which her parents accept her. On being thrust into the world of what could have been, she's mesmerized. Her other mother calls her Violet, as has never happened in the past. In the mirror, she's "more her than she'd ever been," with "higher brows, higher cheekbones. Thinner jaw. She was fucking beautiful" (118). This is an idealized world, one that draws her in. "She had never called her Violet. Not once. Violet didn't reply, half because she wanted to hear it again, half because she wanted to stand in front of the mirror forever" (118). To break out of this illusion world, she must turn her back on this alternate happy self. This is the shadow—the self that never got to emerge.

> The archetype known as the Shadow represents the energy of the dark side, the unexpressed, unrealized, or rejected aspects of something. Often it's the home of the suppressed monsters of our inner world. Shadows can be all the things we don't like about ourselves, all the dark secrets we can't admit, even to ourselves. The qualities we have renounced and tried to root out still lurk within, operating in the Shadow world of the unconscious. The Shadow can also shelter positive qualities that are in hiding or that we have rejected for some reason [Vogler 71].

Sylvie's questioning why her counterpart works for the forces of order emphasizes how much these questions are coming from within Loki himself. By not addressing or facing them, he's left the conflict to bubble within until it bursts out to take form as Sylvie. "The shadow personifies everything that the subject refuses to acknowledge about himself and yet is always thrusting itself upon him directly or indirectly—for instance, inferior traits of character and other incompatible tendencies" (Jung, "Conscience, Unconscious, and Individuation" 285). Notably, she has the name of the Roman trickster forest gods, once again suggesting a different understanding than his own. Her name also suggests a mystical understanding of the forest. After they wrangle about their goals and allegiances, they work their way to romance:

> **SYLVIE:** You're a prince. Must've been would-be-princesses, or perhaps another prince.
> **LOKI:** A bit of both. I suspect the same as you. But nothing ever ... real.
> **SYLVIE:** Mmm.... Love is mischief, then.
> **LOKI:** No. Love is ... uh, something I might have to have another drink to think about ["Lamentis" 1.03].

Once again, she pressures him to explore the truths of his life and what it lacks.

Loki continues to insist they work together and takes her traveling TemPad hostage to ensure it. He's compelled by this alternate self and her discernment about him. He's always had low self-esteem from growing up in Thor's shadow (a conflict that directs all their films), and he still feels he must prove his worth. The shadow reveals qualities the hero can see in other people but not in himself—"such things as egotism, mental laziness, and sloppiness; unreal fantasies, schemes, and plots; carelessness and cowardice; inordinate love of money and possessions"—all the little sins one might have ignored in the self (von Franz 174). Sylvie, a more successful Loki, emphasizes through her example how much he still needs to grow. She has greater knowledge of the timestream, greater nihilism, greater magic, stronger planning skills. Loki's technical skills, illusion, and charm keep failing, symbolizing that he's being broken down into his essential components.

> For the individual, one of the major tasks in the process of psychological development is to recognize, acknowledge, and accept those rejected aspects of the self (the shadow). The process of integration through acknowledging and accepting the shadow aspects of our personalities gives us depth and access to a greater range of expression. Oftentimes the shadow will hold hitherto unknown powers and capabilities [von Franz 170–171].

The stronger Sylvie is the one to get them on the only evacuation train with stronger magic. As always happens on shadow journeys, Loki must learn from her and absorb some of her skills. On the train, she's still critical, telling him his plans are simplistic. She's voicing the worries of his subconscious, stressing that his cleverness needs work.

When she goes to sleep, he finds the bar and sings a boisterous song, which is actually about loneliness and waiting for one's love. Even as the song suggests the feelings he rarely acknowledges, his lively performance with glass-hurling channels Thor, his more favored brother, and thus another shadow. Every choice Loki has made has been to be unlike Thor, leaving the pair eternally connected. Honest through his drunkenness, he also tells Sylvie his real feelings about love: "Love is a dagger. It's a weapon to be wielded far away or up close. You can see yourself in it. It's beautiful. Until it makes you bleed. But ultimately, when you reach for it.... It isn't real." This moment of public honesty blows their cover and sends the guards chasing them. In the process, Loki loses his disguise and jacket while ruining the TemPad, shedding all the layers of defense that surround him. Sylvie berates him for his clumsiness.

SYLVIE: You're a clown. You got drunk on the train.
LOKI: I'm hedonistic. That's what I do.

6. Underworld Descent

SYLVIE: I'm hedonistic. A lot more than you, I assure you, but never at the expense of the mission.

"When the conscious personality is asked to confront such affects, it blocks, feels embarrassed, fears being shattered by superior strength, often retreats into anxiety or detachment, suspended out of life" (Perera 24). Such startling, powerful energy can be a source of strength if welcomed into the self. As they wander through the empty wilderness, Loki makes what amends he can. They work together and realize that the Time-Keepers have mind-wiped and manipulated their employees. This mutual self-exploration becomes a path to insight and success, peeling away Loki's layers and finally pooling their talents in a picture of self-love.

A fascinating variation on this story is seen in *Doctor Who* with the Master (John Simm) and Missy (Michelle Gomez). While past and future copies of the time-traveling Doctor get along well (and sometimes help one another through catharsis with pithy observations), the Master and his future self are much angrier. Disturbingly, they flirt:

MISSY: Hold me.
MASTER: Kiss me.
MISSY: Make me.
DOCTOR: Do you two want to be alone? Which, in your case, would mean more than it usually does ["The Doctor Falls" 10.12].

The Master is cruel, but after a year as the Doctor's prisoner, the more evolved Missy has learned compassion and kindness. To aid the Doctor, Missy actually stabs her former self in the back, and he in turn shoots her. "You see, Missy, this is where we've always been going. This is our perfect ending. We shoot ourselves in the back." The greatest betrayal comes from the self.

Friends and family reflect these buried qualities and thus evoke the shadow. On *Pose*, Candy's ghost appears after her death to confront her judge and mentor, Pray Tell. When she asks why he was cruel and didn't give her the breaks he gave others, he responds, "Maybe.... Maybe I didn't want to look at you. You are unapologetic, loud, Black, femme. All the things I try to hide about myself when I go out into the real world. You are all of them.... I was jealous of that bravery" (2.04). This is the shadow in others—reflecting all one finds uncomfortable and has denied in the self. However, speaking with this reflection can create transformation and growth.

Loki's episode five throws him in with many more alt-versions of himself. Kid Loki killed Thor and became the next king. Boastful Loki killed Iron Man and Captain America and claimed the six Infinity Stones. Alligator Loki is a menace all on his own. Classic Loki escaped Thanos with his illusion powers. Next to all of them, our world's Loki feels inept. With the wisdom of age, Classic Loki explains the insights Loki has yet to learn:

> I cast a projection of myself so real even the Mad Titan believed it. Then hid as inanimate debris. After I faked my death, I simply drifted in space. Away from Thor, away from everything. Thought about the universe and my place in it, and it occurred to me that everywhere I went, only pain followed. So I removed myself from the equation, landed on a remote planet, and stayed there in isolation, in solitude, for a long, long time ["Journey into Mystery" 1.05].

As he concludes, "Because we, my friends, have but one part to play, the God of Outcasts." One Loki betrays them and lets in an army of other Lokis. They all double-cross one another and fight, of course. Ours sneaks away with the sad survivors—Classic, Kid, and Alligator. Classic mourns what they've become: "We lie and we cheat; we cut the throat of every person who trusts us, and for what? Power. Glorious power. Glorious purpose! We cannot change. We're broken—every version of us. Forever."

"And whenever one of us dares try to fix themselves, they're sent here to die," Kid Loki observes. These are the voices from within Loki—who's finally facing the consequences of the constant treachery. He's learning that it not only isolates him but keeps him from success.

> Like the other archetypes, Shadows can express positive as well as negative aspects. The Shadow in a person's psyche may be anything that has been suppressed, neglected, or forgotten. The Shadow shelters the healthy, natural feelings we believe we're not supposed to show. But healthy anger or grief, if suppressed in the territory of the Shadow, can turn to harmful energy that strikes out and undermines us in unexpected ways. The Shadow may also be unexplored potential, such as affection, creativity, or psychic ability, that goes unexpressed. "The roads not taken," the possibilities of life that we eliminate by making choices at various stages, may collect in the Shadow, biding their time until brought into the light of consciousness [Vogler 74–75].

Sylvie arrives with Loki's affable partner Mobius and shakes up their plan entirely: They need to reach the architect of all this, beyond the void at the end of time. Before battle, Loki and Sylvie share a quiet moment of understanding, symbolizing the warring sides of their personalities coming together. She asks whether he will betray her, and he responds, "Listen, Sylvie, I...I betrayed everyone who ever loved me. I betrayed my father, my brother ... my home. I know what I did. And I know why I did it. And that's not who I am anymore. Okay? I won't let you down" ("Journey into Mystery" 1.05). As they sit there together, uncertain where the future will leave them, he suggests they might figure it out together. Through their adventures, he's found a new loyalty and unity toward the disparate parts of himself.

The others leave them, and the pair go into battle side by side. Then, as Loki prepares to sacrifice himself as a distraction, Classic Loki joins the battle with his magic. "I think we're stronger than we realize," Loki decides. As his mismatched pieces come together, he realizes how to fight through the illusions surrounding him. All these components symbolize unity of purpose. Accordingly, Campbell describes facing this shadow as the "destruction of the world that we have built and in which we live, and of ourselves within it; but then a wonderful reconstruction, of the bolder, cleaner, more spacious, and fully human life" (*Hero* 8).

Sacrifice: Sandman *(Graphic Novel)*

The hero's journey traditionally resurrects characters with new wisdom from their death journey. This, seen from Gandalf to Jesus to Buffy, symbolizes the death of the old self and a new, more powerful and divine self, claiming power and wisdom, along with metaphorical adulthood. Sometimes, however, the character achieves transcendence by literally dying, as seen in Andersen's original "The Little Mermaid" and "The Little Match Girl," as well as films like *Pan's Labyrinth*. This journey appears in Neil Gaiman's *Sandman* graphic novel series, featuring an early trans comics character. *Sandman: A Game of You* sends a maiden, mother, and crone into the world of dreams to rescue a princess, Barbie, who's the dreamworld's chosen one. Considering her name and her talking animal friends, the comic plays with tropes and fairytale clichés in a self-aware fashion. Stuck at home guarding Barbie's sleeping body is Wanda Mann, a transwoman. Wanda, Barbie's friend, is seen earlier encouraging Barbie to shop and have fun looking fabulous, even as Wanda cares for her and calls herself "Auntie Wanda."

Wanda wants to enter the dream world and help. However, Thessaly, the crone (symbolizing trans-exclusionary radical feminism's [TERF] appropriation of this symbol), tells her she can't join in their drawing down the moon and invoking her magic. "This isn't your route. It can't be. I'm sorry, what you're doing's every bit as important. Guard Barbie. Don't let anything happen to her" (n.p.)

Wanda sits. "You know what's really spooky? Hazel and Foxglove. I mean, they just fell into it. Like it was all natural as anything. I, on the other hand, squeal and toss my cookies. Maybe I'm not the woman I thought I was" (n.p.). This self-doubt, inflicted by Wanda's transphobic rejection by her community as well as the dictates of religion, is devastating.

With this, they're gone. Wanda guards the immaculate, beautiful princess, a reflection of the beautiful body she's made herself. Wanda and Barbie are actually splitting the journey through deathlike sleep and resurrection. The younger innocent is off in the magical world, while the more experienced "auntie" is guarding her. Here, Wanda's journey is the more traditionally menacing path for the fairytale heroine:

> Heroes wield their gifts in a more straightforward world, where their powerful swords kill antagonists and defend the helpless. Heroines, however, live in a more treacherous, shifting world, where even their mentor can seek their death. Just as the outdoor world threatens the hero, the interior world of the home offers shocking treachery for the heroine, which she must defeat in order to rule. Only through valor and ingenuity, not swordplay, can the heroine survive this surrounding threat to one day preside over her own household [Frankel, *From Girl to Goddess* 52].

Left behind, Wanda spars with George, a sliced-off man's face on the wall. The face calls her a man and suggests that's why she was left behind. Critic Mey Rude observes, "I was raised Catholic, and so the scene where Wanda is told 'it's like gender isn't something you can pick and choose as far as gods are concerned' really shook me. Even though Wanda tells the gods to go and shove their opinion of her, she's still not allowed to go with her friends because the Moon doesn't consider her a woman" (qtd. in Scott and Kirkpatrick n.p.). Indeed, Wanda insists, "Inside, I'm a woman." When she's told that the gods (a metaphor for society) still consider her a man and are obsessed with her chromosomes, she retorts, "Well, that's something the gods can take and stuff up their sacred recta. I know who I am." Commenting on this comic, J. Skyler notes that while it's useful to combat the biological essentialism view rather than ignore its widespread discussion, Gaiman should have done more to acknowledge that such a perspective is very Western. "Considering the diversity of supernatural elements present in *Sandman*, it's odd Wanda would find no affirmation of her gender among the numerous deities present in that storyline" (qtd. in Scott and Kirkpatrick n.p.). Indeed, considering that the gender binary is intrinsically baked in with colonialism and is not part of many cultures, this argument fits badly into an ancient god's voice.

For Wanda, it's a prophetic and deeply symbolic journey. Estés adds, "While the metaphor of sleep can denote unconsciousness, here it symbolizes creation and renewal. Sleep is the symbol of rebirth" (151). Wanda dreams of beautiful dresses, of her school friends' envy. However, soon the demonic "weirdzos" arrive, and one calls her by her deadname. Her long hair vanishes. Another insists, "Us must operate immediately to make you imperfect."

Earlier in the series, Wanda describes her love of *Hyperman* comic books, specifically the weirdzos—a reimagining of the Bizarro Superman clones. They, too, mimic judgmental American society. As the dream

6. Underworld Descent 145

continues, Wanda appears naked, shaking with terror, and insists surgery is too terrifying. The nightmare is of being transformed without choice, and of society dictating the new body, of the fears that keep her in the body she has. "Innocence am no excuse. Him will thank us one day," the weirdzo babbles.

In a closer connection with divinity, Wanda also sees a "crazy old lady" talking to herself on the curb outside—Maise Hill, the wise crone she wishes to someday become. Wanda invites the woman upstairs to get out of the storm. However, Thessaly's bringing down the moon while oblivious to the damage she's inflicting on her allies (in another painful TERF metaphor) causes a hurricane that destroys the apartment, killing all three. Continuing the cruelty of the metaphor, only the questors chosen by the gods are spared, as they're in the dream world. The princess survives, with the old woman's body covering hers. Less-privileged Wanda dies. This moment calls attention to society's unequal privilege—or would if the characters addressed it, which they don't.

Her transphobic family cuts her hair, dresses her in a suit, and buries her under her deadname. Barbie attends and is told not to upset the family. She defiantly writes Wanda's name on the headstone in flamingo lipstick as a tribute to her friend. The hero "may either be a mere witness of the divine drama or take part in it or be moved by it" (Jung, "Concerning Rebirth" 117). As such, this is an adulthood quest for Barbie as well, surviving and carrying on the memory of her friend. This is an unfortunate use of a rare trans representation. The text frames Wanda's death as unfortunate, but it is also clear the reason she was left behind to be killed is her being trans. Or rather, the reason is transphobia. This is depicted but not addressed. Instead, the text focuses on Barbie being sad to have lost Wanda and making a small gesture against her misgendering. Barbie is sad, yes—but she hadn't insisted on including her from the start. At the time of writing, the television series inspired by *Sandman* is in the process of being created. Perhaps some of these issues will be fixed and addressed there.

Hero's journey stories, including this one, feature death as a pathway to enlightenment, armed with knowledge from the otherworld. The mature hero has learned adulthood and consequences from the dark realm. Her death can lead to new opportunities for those living, while Wanda herself can achieve transcendence as a guiding spirit.

This occurs with Angel in *Rent*, who dies halfway through but doesn't leave the story—a motif aided by the fourth wall breaking of theater. As they mourn Angel's death, the others reference their friend constantly, protesting that they would die for the same kind of romance Angel had. The funeral brings everyone together, even while emphasizing that they need to live as fully as they can in the moment. After this, Angel's unsubtle presence continues. Mark insists that his friend Roger not leave and break up their family, letting Angel's death be in vain. Collins rewires an ATM Robin Hood style to give anyone money who has the code: ANGEL. Symbolically, Angel still represents love and is still dispensing hope and money to the people of New York. At the musical's climax—Mimi's sinking into death herself—she awakens and insists Angel has saved her, demanding that she return to life and hear Roger's song of love: "I was in a tunnel, headed for this warm white light. And I swear, Angel was there—and she looked *good*. And she said, turn around, girlfriend, and listen to that boy's song." This intervention is a miracle and blessing, emphasizing Angel's continued presence in their lives. In this scene, Angel is indeed her guardian angel and guide. Symbolically, Angel has gained the enlightenment of the underworld to become a spiritual protector.

Barbie likewise dreams of Wanda, beautiful with long hair and a Lolita dress, pink with bows and ruffles; she's with Death, a sweet young woman. Both wave goodbye and go off together, to the afterlife of Wanda's choice. Barbie narrates, "I dream of Wanda, only she's perfect. She reminds me of Glinda in the Oz movie, something I'm sure she'd get a huge kick out of hearing. And when I say perfect, I mean perfect, drop-dead gorgeous. There's nothing camp about her, nothing artificial and she looks happy." In contrast with her return to Kansas, the real Wanda has made it back to Oz.

It should be noted that Barbie's equating Wanda's existence in life with imperfection, which she links with being camp or artificial, is deeply problematic. It frames cisgender "natural" womanhood and the non-camp performance of womanhood as superior. It frames cisgender womanhood as trans women's dreams. Later works address this perception. For example, when the heroine of *Dreadnought* receives an opportunity to get her ideal body, she chooses a pretty transgender body. The heroine of *Fierce Femmes and Notorious Liars* also becomes enraged by the idea that she must strive to be a white trans rich woman in order to be accepted.

Critic Rachel Stevens notes that Wanda was one of the first trans women she ever saw in comics and adds, "I did remember Gaiman talking about her being based on trans women he knew and how he was trying to make her a sympathetic character. She was reassuring for me at the time, even if I didn't relate to her entirely." Mey Rude agrees that *Sandman* "was also my first experience with trans characters in 'superhero' comics" but adds,

> I think it's important to mention the trans women that are shown as murder victims in the "Serial Convention" storyline in those same comics. Those were the ones I read first, and they frightened me. One of the serial killers at this convention is talking about how he only kills "preoperative transexuals"

because something about them made him "uncomfortable." So this is how I was introduced to trans women [qtd. in Scott and Kirkpatrick n.p.].

In their work about media coverage of the murder of transgender women of color, Wood and colleagues found that reports focused on the murders' effect on loved ones rather than the transgender person herself. They also found that "emergent themes revealed that media focused on the brutality of these deaths but failed to describe such murders as hate crimes or gender-based violence. Misgendering individuals was common in our sample of media covering trans deaths ... the message was clear—their lives are disposable" (380). As more fiction arrives and is adapted, creators' growing knowledge of problematic tropes helps to write more inclusive stories.

Rebirth: Birdverse *(Series)*

The journey into death, literal or metaphorical, often helps the questor find wisdom and understanding. Thus enlightened, the hero returns to the daylight world with this new knowledge to pass along.

In R. B. Lemberg's celebrated Birdverse world of short stories and novellas, Bashri-nai-Tammah (who shared a family name with her two co-wives in their trade group) begins the ceremonial transformation denied for decades out in the sands, surrounded by the winds and birds of bright fire. In their world, magic is available to everyone who desires it:

> grandmother's body cleared, with arms still raised up, singing for the first time the dawnsong—that sacred melody that scholars sent out every morning in supplication to the men's god, Bird's brother, Kimrí, that song the women were forbidden to sing.
>
> With the last grains of sand pouring down to the ground, grandmother—grandfather?—walked over to us. He—he—looked glowing, radiant with light and newly made. His arms spread to us in a blessing, in a wave of great and unfeigned happiness ["Grandmother Nai-Leylit's" 63–64].

The non-binary grandchild Kimi responds with joyous song. As well as being the inspiration and hope for the future, Kimi is like a benevolent spirit, blessing the elder's change and welcoming the grandfather into the community. Kimi's celebratory dance and magic evoke the most vulnerable part of the self from within.

For the unnamed hero, who has not chosen a name since petitioning the Bird Goddess to transform his body, carpet weaving has been intrinsic. The transition was inspired by Kimi's first weaving made of wind, "of joy and glowing weft-threads, gentle" with tiny lights floating all around—the carpet of change ("Grandmother Nai-Leylit's" 57). Another is the cloth of winds that the wisewoman Benesret once made but that the protagonist's lover didn't want him to use. "*When you're ready, tell me, give it back to me, I said. Accept me as I am, from north to south and back, a man, a woman, I will always love you, I will never leave you*" ("Grandmother Nai-Leylit's" 48). However, by the time the gift was given, they were both set in their unhappy ways and had failed to challenge the status quo. Further, the grandfather worries about how his choices have affected his descendants, gifted carpet weavers. In the sequel, *The Four Profound Weaves* (nominated for the Ignyte, Nebula, World Fantasy, and Locus Awards), other carpet types are revealed—sand is the magic of wanderlust, song makes the carpet of hope, and bones are the carpet of death.

In *The Four Profound Weaves*, Little Kimi's first weaving, made of joy, wind, and butterflies, is sold to their enemy, the selfish Collector. The grandfather protests, "What joy is there in trading the cloth of change to a man who will never change? The Collector will lock this cloth in his coffers, away from all eyes but his, away from the people who would use it, who need it, themselves, to change" (13). He is like Hades, the god of death, who maintains a silent, imprisoning realm, denying growth and change. Further, the grandfather once traded the Collector a precious carpet of song to save his wife Bashri-nai-Divrah. "The crime was that of showing her face unveiled beyond the walls of the Khana quarter, her magic plain for all to see" in a stagnant land where women are not allowed to go unveiled or possess magic ("Grandmother Nai-Leylit's" 25). Her two spouses went to plead for her "for her veil had been torn away by tormentors, and through no ill will had she defied the law" ("Grandmother Nai-Leylit's" 25). However, she had already died in his captivity. Now the Collector is seeking to possess even more in his greed.

The protagonist quests as the nameless man, only called *nen-sasaïr*, son of sandbirds; he comes from a society so gender-segregated that he never knew his father and has no model for fitting in. The desert people are freer, but he does not fit among them either, trained in a woman's skills but living as a man. He and Uiziya, Benesret's niece, quest to the Collector to recover the glorious carpets he has taken. Uiziya, meanwhile, reveals that she spun a cloth of wind and transformed when she was a child. She understands nen-sasaïr's struggle and tries to help. On his quest, he hears the whispers of "Kimrí, Bird's hidden brother, the God of my people's men" (*Four Profound Weaves* 97). This god, with a name so similar to Kimi's, suggests that his two guides are the same. In the scene, it brings him hope.

At the climax, the Collector on his birdcage-shaped throne of bones (another image of static, rigid sameness), kidnaps Uiziya and demands a carpet of death. The Collector is rigid in his outdated gender beliefs as well, insisting that civilized women serve their husbands. He has murdered defiant women and hoarded their bones, keeping them from the life cycle. He misgenders his prisoner and adds, "Change is not a thing I embrace. Changing my body to that of a woman would never occur to me" (*Four Profound Weaves* 131). All this brutal enforcement of the gender binary emphasizes his lack of fluidity on all levels.

This prison is a place of torment for both questors, in which even hope is a possession of the Collector. It is the crucible that breaks them down but leads to their emerging as more powerful. In this stronghold, Uiziya learns to listen to the dead and thus weaves their bones into a carpet. Among the cries of her dead sisters, she feels their commonality and chooses not to abandon them. She rescues them from their stagnant existence and weaves them into beauty and power. As she discovers, love is required. "To weave from death, you had to listen to the dead. To know them deeply, to attend to what had been silenced, to care enough to help the dead speak again" (*Four Profound Weaves* 136). With storytelling, sacrifice, and hope, she weaves the carpet of death, the fourth profound weave. Estés writes, "This is our meditation practice as women, calling back the dead and dismembered aspects of ourselves, calling back the dead and dismembered aspects of life itself. The one who re-creates from that which has died is always a double-sided archetype. The Creation Mother is always the Death Mother and vice versa" (33).

In this dark prison, nen-sasaïr faces the ghost of Bashri-nai-Divrah, who asks about the third of their marriage, Bashri-nai-Leylit, and pushes nen-sasaïr to unburden. He finally confesses to this optimistic lost mirror of himself how much their third had stifled his life and forbidden him to change: "We were not happy. My secret burdened her and bent her, until she could hold it no more" (*Four Profound Weaves* 153). At last, nen-sasaïr faces his pain. Now he discovers the carpet of death and considers surrendering to it. This is a catharsis, a moment of communing with those who have gone on and then reaffirming one's commitment to life. After their testing, the two heroes present the carpet to the Collector. With its power, the souls of those the Collector killed devour him.

Afterward, they return to the desert, a place of emptiness, but for them, also freedom and spiritual enlightenment. They offer the Carpet of Death to Bird, and the goddess comes to them, carrying all the bones of the dead away to return to nature. They have been freed from their captivity to rejoin the life cycle. Symbolically, the same is true for the questors.

With nen-sasaïr's lover returning to nature, he names himself Kaveh-nen-Kimrí, a man who has hope. This moment also confirms his connection to the land and the larger world, as well as to his hidden male god and the child who inspires his anticipation of the future. As he ends the story, he predicts grimly, "A new ruler will rise in Iyar, to do this and worse, unspeakable things until the world overflows with them, and the scream of bones chokes the land" (*Four Profound Weaves* 172). Still, when this happens, new weavers will rise, even ones with the death magic of bone. "And these new makers will weave and be woven, from hope and death, to bring the Collector down. Over and over will we rise" (*Four Profound Weaves* 172).

He returns the carpet of wind to Kimi and tells the story of everything he learned. Here, he acknowledges his role as a teacher of the next generation, who must guide Kimi as the hope of the future. "This too is a powerful metaphor for the idea of saving the childSelf, the soul-self, from being lost again in the unconscious, forgetting who we are and what our work is," Estés explains of this tenuous inner voice (449–450). The quest has brought hope and identity to the questor, his partner, his perished lover, and his grandchild in a loving renewal.

Other characters work through a more literal death to find a similar transcendence. Rusalka, homeless and taken into custody, kills herself in "In Her Mind's Eye" by Selene dePackh. However, things are more complex, because she does it for revenge, but only after uploading herself to a sympathetic computer system that has already taken in a disabled Puerto Rican teen, likewise innocent and preyed on by the system. When Sergeant Lynch, her protector who routinely turns on her, enters Russalka's prison cell, Rusalka asks him, "How would it be if you were found alone in here with a dead brown trans kid?" As she adds, "I got no life out there, Lynch. That's the point. The order that *la gente privilegianda* never gives out loud is that we've offended them by daring to exist, and we are going to suffer for it. You too, now, with proof of your nastiness smeared on my freak body" (173–174). She dies but triumphantly discovers nine of them are in the artificial intelligence together, a new community that can influence the world.

> These stories all emphasize the connection between birth and death. Within the Great Goddess both concepts link, showing the deep understanding ancient people had for the duality of life. The heroine completes her journey by mastering this knowledge, incorporating the death-energies of the underworld into herself and acknowledging their glory. Only thus can she merge with the cycle of life, growing gracefully into mother and wisewoman without fearing death. For it is not an ending but a regenerative spiral. As one life ends, another begins, and on, and on [Frankel, *From Girl to Goddess* 172].

"Lady Marmalade's Special Place in Hell" by David Sklar follows a drag queen who sasses demons in hell and, as she dominates them, gets a promotion. She starts looking for her beloved Princess Buttercup, who committed suicide. In fact, she finds Buttercup's father and tortures him. "And oh! How I relished the fear in his shoulders and back. I rose with newfound clarity. If the halls of hell were filled with men like Princess Buttercup's dad, then torturing them would be no dilemma for me. An old man stared in terror as I strode across the rock, and I slashed him across the throat with the tip of the lash, cold comfort for whatever child he had failed to love" (193). Lady Marmalade finds her own parents and discovers that she can forgive them. "The next few days were all about contrition. I apologized in person to everyone I'd whipped in my rage. I knew the risks, but flipping out like I did, that wasn't cool. I had a face to face with each of them about what they were in for, how long they've been damned, and what they hope to accomplish well in hell" (194). Their scars fade, except for Buttercup's father, who is made up only of hate and anger. Lady Marmalade gathers her people and helps them all work through their issues and atone for the people they wronged. After years of group therapy, no one remains but the lady and her parents. Lady Marmalade tries many things as both parents give confusing advice on which gender to be. At last, Lady Marmalade realizes that it's about willpower and imagines herself as she desires. "And I was me. I was finally, finally me" (199). Sassily, she walks out, with self-acceptance and truth as the keys to opening the gates. She arises as a woman with her wings healed as beautiful rainbow feathers and a plan to rethink her wardrobe.

Transcendent Treasure: Peter Darling *(Novel)*

The cis man of traditional stories often gets prizes at the end of his adventure, such as a crown or magical artifact with which to save the land. This prize often comes on top of living happily ever after. Of course, such a talisman reflects the real prize: the deep inner healing of the world, which reflects the self. "In myths one finds that the magic or talisman that can cure the misfortune of the king or his country always proves to be something very special ... whatever it is, the thing that can drive away the evil is always unique and hard to find" (von Franz 170).

Trans heroes may receive their happily ever after or not, but few receive a physical trophy. Tam of *Mooncakes* finds love and a better understanding of themselves. Rinn of *The Tea Dragon* series also finds a meaningful new relationship and learns that it is fine to do what they like rather than what's seen as ambitious. Jebi of *Phoenix Extravagant* leaves with their loved ones at the end of the novel. Jam of *Pet* quests to save a child and restore her community, which she does with aid from her animal friend.

In this tradition, some have meaningful achievements at the story's end, but those are largely symbolic. For example, in *The Heartbreak*

Bakery, Syd is given a shirt that celebrates Syd's agender identity. While this encourages Syd to celebrate being agender, it is not the focus or goal in itself. Many seek physical treasures on the quest, but these will not solve the hero's problems; the spiritual treasures are much more important.

Peter Darling merges monetary and emotional treasures in an adaptation in which Peter grew up as Wendy and left that identity behind to journey to Neverland. Many critics have already observed how open *Peter Pan* is to a queer reading, with the pirates' theatricality and the Lost Boys' found family, even as Hook invites the boys to join his campy masculine paradise. Both groups have fled rigid Victorian England for Neverland, where they can live by a new set of rules. Peter Pan's being played by a woman on stage adds feminine coding. The 1953 Disney cartoon keeps Hook's suggestiveness:

> Many read Captain Hook in *Peter Pan* as a queer-coded homosexual man. Hook comically exaggerates Father's more feminine tendencies. Father stumbles about without a confident masculine gait, while Hook glides girlishly across the floor. Father worries a little too much about his cufflinks, while Hook dresses with impeccable style. Hook's costume also reflects femininity, complete with loose long hair, a flowing cape, a pink shirt, and a bushy feather in his hat [A. Brown n.p.].

Peter Darling leans into these tropes and considers the personalities behind them. Peter explains, "No one would let me do what I wanted or be who I wanted before … in Neverland they can't stop me" (Chant 33). Having returned to Neverland, Peter finds he's bored with the Lost Boys: "Peter knew all the games the Lost Boys played, all the places they visited, all the beasts they battled. They still had fun, but it was the same fun. They had no real fears, no want for anything new. Peter had no explanation for why, unlike the rest of them, he had been struggling to sleep—no explanation for the anxious buzzing in his head" (63). Material success and winning bore him.

Hook too agrees, commenting, "It's been a long time since anyone managed to take me by surprise. It's been a long time since anyone did anything interesting around here" (69). Their loyalties to their tribes disintegrate as Hook reveals that they are all illusionary—dreamed into being by Hook and Pan. Seeking truth in a world of distractions is a symbolic part of the quest. Mark Thompson observes: "The keyword here is experiential; that is, the actual living out of unconscious impulses—literally grounding ourselves in a shared, created reality and not just an ideological or intellectual abstraction" (Group Interview 252). Engaging with dreams and fantasies liberates the questor and helps them explore their hidden depths on a multifaceted soul journey.

Having discovered they are nearly the only real people in the story,

Peter and Hook feel drawn together. Next, they spend a significant story arc looking for treasure together. At last, they find the pirate Red Dog's hoard with thousands of sapphires. But this is only worldly wealth. In Neverland, there is no way to spend it, emphasizing its uselessness as anything but a source of pride. The treasures decorating Hook's ship and cabin are equally showy and useless. Indeed, physical treasures are rarely the point of the quest.

Beneath the hoard, they find a small painted chest containing Poseidon's crown, symbolizing rulership over the magical realm. This, of course, is a more symbolically powerful reward. Peter snatches it and crowns himself King of Neverland. This gives Hook a moment of epiphany: "*It suits you*, he wanted to say, against all his better instincts. The crown made Pan look like a lazy young god, his curly hair spilling out under and over the golden rim. His eyes matched the jewels and their gleaming. *Prince of Runaways*, Hook thought, and caught his breath and looked away" (Chant 186).

Meanwhile, Hook is delighted by Red Dog's gleaming merskin boots and spidersilk coat, which he calls "the most beautiful thing you've ever seen" (186). These, he decides, complete him: "Clothes, adventure, and a worthy opponent," Hook says. "Who could ask for more?" (187). This moment stresses his showmanship and delight in appearances, qualities commonly observed by Barrie scholars. As Peter thinks in this adaptation, "His hat was trimmed with peacock feathers. Peter cocked his head, wondering who Hook had to impress with that outfit. Everything about Hook seemed a little frivolous, yet perhaps that was the point of it. He was such a dastardly villain that he could stand to do everything in twice as many ruffles as the next man" (68–69).

However frivolous, the clothes are part of the persona, embellishing how Hook presents himself to others and crafts his appearance. Even as a hobby, they are a treasure to be savored. As a reflection of one's desire, they are far more. His role as the most glorious of pirates is confirmed here, as is Peter's as king of the magic land. As with many quest stories, the hoard symbolizes what they truly desire. Scholar Chris Kilbourne adds, "I would say that the treasure is not just inside of you, but it's here, now, with you now. That's what it's all about, creating ways of being for yourself that will encourage and develop and let that treasure in yourself grow and be" (Group Interview 253). While they believed they were questing for jewels, finding each other was the triumph. Estés observes that recognizing this moment, however earned or unearned, is vital:

> For the naive and wounded, the miracle of the psyche's ways is that even if you are halfhearted, irreverent, didn't mean to, didn't really hope to, don't want to, feel unworthy to, aren't ready for it, you will accidentally stumble upon

treasure anyway. Then it is your soul's work to not overlook what has been brought up, to recognize treasure as treasure no matter how unusual its form, and to consider carefully what to do next [135].

The pair are forced to leave the coat and crown behind. However, their true prize is each other's moment of displaying themselves and their revelation in the beauty of each other. This has given them a turning point, and they soon start a romance. As Peter thinks, "He had never felt that way before about anyone or anything. But it had been happening all along with Hook, he realized, from the very first moment they had reunited in Neverland. Something in him came to life when they faced each other, when they fought, when they made war" (Chant 200–201).

After fully accepting Peter, despite the baggage that caused them each to flee to Neverland, Hook proposes they live happily ever after together in his secluded cottage back in England. Here, another surprise awaits as Hook reveals his secret life as a painter:

> Much like the captain's cabin, the cottage had treasure piled everywhere, waiting to be unearthed—except instead of gold and jewels, it was paintings. There were landscapes and nudes, dreamy abstracts and vivid sunsets. James painted in exquisite detail and piercing color. On the wall, dulled by the dust motes floating through the air, there was an enormous canvas depicting the Jolly Roger at anchor. The ship was bathed in the glittering of the sun on the water, and Peter felt sure that he had seen it look just like this. He traced his fingers carefully along with black rigging, feeling the ridges and waves of dry paint [287–288].

Symbolically, Neverland awaits here, with colors, beauty, and Hook's beloved ship. What Peter actually finds is inspiration, imagination, and Hook's vivid inner life. Even as Peter is stunned by the beauty of the art, Hook offers him a typewriter, which will allow him to create his own stories and share his truth about the world. This is the final boon, empowering Peter to express himself. They have moved past material jewels, crowns, and costumes to find love and acceptance, and then soared higher together toward a new level of spiritual creation.

Other stories likewise focus on spiritual growth, transformed into enlightenment. With artist Ted McKeever, Rachel Pollack explored the transformation of early trans character Coagula, Kate Godwin, in DC's *Doom Patrol* arc "The Teiresias Wars" (#75–79). When Cliff challenges her gender as a woman, she points out that both he and their leader, Niles, have been remade without changing who they are within. She and Cliff are beginning a romance, complicated by his human brain in a robot body. When he doubts he's human, she replies, "I've had to deal with questions like that all my life. Please, let me help you" (#76). Meanwhile, Niles tells the team the legend of the Teiresiae, ancient shape-shifting magicians who maintain the world's knowledge and consciousness. Ages ago, one tried sorting the world into categories, "a fixed place for every object and creature. A forced separation for every moment" (#77). This created gender, as the new species gave birth to "an army dedicated to ending all transformation" (#77). As with *The Four Profound Weaves*, this works as a metaphor for gender inflexibility and stigmatizing. At the climax, Kate and Cliff oppose these spirits by merging. Kate finally convinces the slaves of the Babel force that they can still transform. She tells them, "Look at me. I changed my body to match my vision, my desire. You can change easier than I can blink. But so what? I did it. I made it happen." She also describes the dismembered and remade Doom Patrol team. With Elliot, the last Teiresiae, convincing them, they break the tower and let the Builders fall into slumber once more. Though Elliot is cut off from the timeless world, the earth is saved (#79).

In some texts, often older ones or ones written by cis people, the treasure at the end of trans people's adventure must be "the operation." The term is put here in quotes because it is erroneous, as Julia Serano explains: "Most people believe that all trans women are on a quest to make ourselves as pretty, pink and passive as possible" (35). First, the assumption that all trans people want or can have any medical transition is false. Second, there are a variety of social, medical, and other elements to transitioning. Still, some creators focus on one possible element as if it means far more and as if it is for them to discuss. One text that frames "the operation" as a goal is the movie *Transamerica*. Here, the protagonist, Bree, hopes to receive a letter from her therapist that will allow her to medically transition. The therapist oddly requires that she reestablish a relationship with her estranged son as an arbitrary condition. After an emotional family journey, Bree reconnects with her son and ends the film with the operation and a family bond, but associating the operation with the happy ending is awkwardly simplistic.

The boon is likewise complicated when one is given what one does not desire. *The Story of Silence* by Alex Myers adapts the medieval tale of an earl's daughter, raised as a boy, who trains at arms and becomes a knight. When accused of seducing the queen, Silence must reveal the truth. All at once, the king condemns his treacherous queen to death and proposes marriage to Silence. As the servants bustle Silence away and find him a gown, Silence is horrified. As Silence insists, "I cannot" and "I'll die," Silence reveals how much the reward that would delight many young ladies represents a life of denial and misgendering, because the king does not understand (438). Returning to the king, Silence uses clever language to claim that he has already pledged to another because a friend made him swear he would be true to himself. Being the queen would deny that. Instead, he surrenders his knighthood, queenhood, earldom, and land. The king warns that he will be no one, but Silence insists, "I would be myself" (443). Giving up one's worldly trappings for freedom is the true reward here, chosen by the questor.

7

RETURN AND ACCEPTANCE

Escape with Allies' Aid: Sense8 *(Television)*

Lana and Lilly Wachowski (who wrote *The Matrix* and *V for Vendetta*) created the 2015 Netflix original series *Sense8* with J. Michael Straczynski. It introduces a cluster of eight people across the world who were born at the same moment. They, like others, are a separate species, *Homo sensorium*. The characters must learn to unite as a single entity to evade the Biologic Preservation Organization (BPO), a eugenicist group that lobotomizes clusters to use as remote weapons. This, of course, is a metaphor for conservative groups stomping out empathy and uniqueness in favor of conformity.

The cluster begins telepathically connecting and sharing their skills and knowledge to defend one another. "The series probes beneath descriptive accounts of identity, exploring trans as an intra/intersubjective experience of entangled sensories—a constant navigation between what is internally sensed and what is externally perceived" (Keegan, *Wachowski* 110). The characters all gain additional bodies and learn to experience the world through them even while facing the world's judgment, "achieving a unique televisual language that aestheticizes the trans sensorium as both a narrative and pedagogic form" (Keegan, *Wachowski* 110). The show's message is one of empathy for those who are different and who come from wildly disparate backgrounds. The cluster also represents the voices from within and the abilities a person has only begun to tap. As Campbell notes,

> the unconscious sends all sorts of vapors, odd beings, terrors and deluding images up into the mind—whether in dream, broad daylight, or insanity; for the human kingdom, beneath the floor of the comparatively neat little dwelling that we call our consciousness, goes down into unexpected Aladdin caves. There not only jewels but also dangerous jinn abide: the inconvenient or resisted psychological powers that we have not thought or dared to integrate into our lives [*Hero* 8].

Transwoman Nomi Marks is the first one placed in serious danger. Nomi is arguably the center of the story. Nomi's name comes from gnosis, the knowledge for which they all quest. Further, "in becoming sensate, Nomi and her cluster will become a 'we'—in other words, a 'no me'" (Keegan, *Wachowski* 113). Her home in San Francisco, a well-known queer space that shows the "Gay Beach" of Delores Park and the Pride festival, is first and last in the world-spanning credits. In season one, episode two, "I Am Also a We," Nomi blogs about growing up: "I was taught by my parents that there's something wrong with me. Something that you could never love." She describes how LGBTQ+ people often must leave their families of origin and find loving found families, symbolized by their cluster.

She rushes off to the San Francisco Pride Parade, but when she falls off her girlfriend Amanita Caplan's motorcycle, she's rushed to the hospital unconscious. This is a descent, not by choice, but still a quest into the underworld. Her symptoms include the growing shared senses with her cluster. Misinterpreting this fragile magic, Dr. Metzger tells Nomi she has an abnormal brain and needs a lobotomy. "Without the surgery, the tissue will continue to metastasize. Patients will begin to experience a deterioration of mental faculties," the doctor insists. "It's common for them to experience very intense, very real hallucinations and synesthesia that precedes a loss of memory and a complete occlusion of identity." The doctor's lack of understanding and refusal to listen to his patient quickly become a deadly threat, as well as a clear metaphor for treatment in trans lives. Susan Stryker notes in *Transgender History*:

> Medical science has always been a two-edged sword—its representatives' willingness to intervene has gone hand in hand with their power to define and judge. Far too often, access to medical services for transgender people has depended on constructing transgender phenomena as symptoms of a mental illness or physical malady, partly because "sickness" is the condition that typically legitimizes medical intervention [52].

To Nomi's horror, her parents are working with the doctor, forcing the surgery on her and calling her by her deadname. "Don't touch me! You are not my family!" Nomi protests (1.02). She fears that her fragile, precious connection with the friends in her cluster will be destroyed. In trans stories, the evil doctor is often a terrifying antagonist who wields all the power. This sadly comes from a long history of abuse: "In historic Gothic tales as well as in real life, trans people were often thought to be criminally insane; it was not unusual for trans and queer people to undergo shock treatments and partial lobotomies at the hands of men of science attempting to normalize them" (Haefele-Thomas 389–390). Here, the Wachowskis place viewers in Nomi's quivering shoes to show how endangered she is from society's callous, judgmental transphobia.

7. Return and Acceptance

Since the end of the eighteenth century, science has gradually come to replace religion as the highest social authority, and since the middle of the nineteenth century medical science has played an increasingly central role in defining everyday life. It has often been used for very conservative social purposes—"proving" that black people are inferior to white people, or that females are inferior to males. Medical practitioners and institutions have the social power to determine what is considered sick or healthy, normal or pathological, sane or insane—and thus, often, to transform potentially neutral forms of human difference into unjust and oppressive social hierarchies. This particular operation of medicine's social power has been especially important in transgender history [Stryker, *Transgender History* 51].

Nomi tells the nurse, "You can't keep me here against my will." The nurse replies, "I'm afraid we can. Dr. Metzger and your family have signed the papers." Nomi protests, "I cannot believe that this is happening to me in the twenty-first century." Worse yet, Nomi doubts herself and wonders whether they're right.

Amanita, a loving cisgender African American woman, manages to borrow a phone at the nurse's station and call her room. Heartily, she tells Nomi, "I will burn this building down before I let anyone touch that beautiful brain." Amanita's love and assurance are as vital as the medical intervention. At this point in the story, with the cluster only beginning to connect, she is Nomi's staunchest ally, like a voice from within that reassures and affirms. She and Nomi are voices of counterculture—hackers and activists trained to defy the system through different forms of stealth and cleverness. (Nomi reveals in season two that she makes fake IDs because sometimes the government makes it too hard for trans people to get them, for example.)

> Note that the Wachowskis redistribute the power to those people whom the Victorian scientists would have seen as less than human. Amanita is African American, and so is her friend who works at the hospital who sneaks her into a private staff room so that she can use the hospital phone to call Nomi. As women of color, and more specifically as queer women of color, Amanita and her friend work together against Western white medical systems of power that have historically (and sometimes still do) dictate who is fully human and deserving of human dignity and who is not [Haefele-Thomas 390].

In episode three, Nomi lies strapped in the operating room, being prepared for anesthesia. Terrified, she struggles and argues to no avail in a classic scene of body horror. Suddenly, the fire alarms go off, and the surgery is paused. Drugged, Nomi hears the nurse say, "Some lunatic set fire to the visitors' lounge." Nomi knows her lover is saving her. However, the two women need more help to defy the overpowering institution.

In the fourth episode, Will, a police officer in Chicago, reaches through their cluster and occupies Nomi's body as Dr. Metzger is putting

Nomi under anesthesia again. Nomi escapes and falls into the arms of Amanita, who, in an easily overlooked nurse uniform, puts her in a wheelchair and rushes her out of the hospital doors and into a cab. "Nomi's escape with the help of the other sensaters and her lover, Amanita, serves as the Wachowskis' antidote and answer to Hitchcock's and Demme's portrayals of monstrous trans women" (Haefele-Thomas 390). They are the protagonist couple fighting the brutal patriarchal system and making a sympathetic and joyful hospital break. Without her lover and the rational, skilled, wise man, Will, this would not be possible—only their bolstering Nomi from within and without helps her escape. In real life, one finds external allies but also internal ones—the voice of confidence and support that speaks from the soul. Amanita and the cluster represent both types of voices.

This scene emphasizes how much Nomi has only escaped through mastering the sensate powers—connecting with Will and using his abilities to break out. Meanwhile, Amanita is not only a wise helper but one who connects with the hospital, understanding its ins and outs enough to save her lover. Such imagery has its roots in the most ancient tales:

> The escape with tools like comb and mirror is a popular pattern throughout the world, known as Motif D672: The Obstacle Flight. While the tools vary, they are women's symbols—food and drink, circles and cups. Like Athena with helm and aegis, the heroine must prove she has mastered the tools of the goddess and their shapechanging magic in order to snatch power from her enemy [Frankel, *From Girl to Goddess* 152].

Nomi and Amanita go on the run, using their hacker skills to help the rest of the cluster in continued allyship. The eight grow closer, learning how to reach for one another and share skills. As a distant observer, Nomi becomes a wise adviser, using her perspective to protect her growing team.

Another pattern common to the escape is the reluctance to return. Once characters have found power and acceptance in the magic world, the real world seems hostile and unpleasant. Lito Rodriguez, a cluster member in Mexico City, struggles as a closeted action star. "My whole life, all I wanted to be was an actor. But you can't be an actor and get the parts I want and be gay," he protests (1.09). After being outed beyond his control, he finds his community.

Episode six was actually filmed at the massive Brazilian Pride Festival. Lito is shocked to be asked to speak as Grand Marshal and finally does it. "Thank you, São Paulo! Thank you. I wanted to say that I am very honored to be here. That isn't the truth. To be honest with you, I ... I have never been as scared as I am right now. All of my life, I've had to pretend to be something I wasn't. And to become what I wanted to become, I couldn't be what I am." For the first time, he utters the words, "I am a gay man."

7. Return and Acceptance 161

Next, he introduces his boyfriend Hernando to the crowd, adding, "He is the love of my life. I am a better and braver person because of him. And whatever it costs for me to be able to do this, I know in my heart that it is worth it." (2.06). The third member of their household, Dani, celebrates alongside them. "Back Where I Belong" plays triumphantly as they kiss in front of the enormous crowd. Surrounded by rainbow balloons and cheers, Lito feels celebrated. Nomi and the cluster dance and smile along.

> Pride is not the aggrandizement of self, but just the opposite: it is humble service to a higher ideal, intended to elevate everyone, and a dedication to become a good ancestor and smooth the way for those who come after us. It is the creation of sacred space—queer space—that not only says "You are safe here," but goes beyond to say: "You are special. You are loved and celebrated here." Pride is having a sense of worth that not satisfied with mere "acceptance." This Mystery says, "I'm better than that. We deserve better than that, and I'm going to help make it happen" [Kenson 259].

After this joyous scene, the trio return home decked in rainbow decorations, dancing and chanting, "We're here; we're queer; get used to it." To their shock, Dani's abusive ex, Joaquin, is waiting. He emphasizes that even after a happy interval, the threats the protagonists have fled will still be waiting. He exhibits toxic masculinity straight from Lito's action films and has even brought Dani's parents to help drag her back into her prior life. Campbell notes that the protagonist often finds the otherworld so joyous "the world may have to come and get him. For the bliss of the deep abode is not lightly abandoned in favor of the self-scattering of the wakened state" (*Hero* 178).

However, leaving the haven of the cluster would mean returning to torture. Dani refuses. With aid from the cluster, Lito and Dani stand up to them all. Meanwhile, Lito discovers that his agency has dropped him for coming out. Their return from rainbowland is a series of brutal shocks, though first Dani and later Lito learn that they are strong enough to thrive without the old patterns of their lives. Soon Lito gets a film role thanks to his speech, and the trio embark on a new, happier life.

This episode has other cluster members explore how much they've been living in a fantasy and need to awaken—a subtler metaphoric departure from the magic land. In her own story, Kala confronts her husband about profiting off selling expired drugs. They must abandon their fantasy of privilege to discover empathy and stop exploiting the poor. As Sun, whose brother betrayed their family, stands by her father's grave, the entire cluster visits her to offer advice. Wolfgang compares his abusive father and her brother for their use of power to control and manipulate and to perpetuate gender expectations. Each member of the cluster considers their own baggage and releases it as they prepare to confront the tyrannical BPO.

At season two's end, with Wolfgang captured and tortured, the cluster all meet in person to save him. This is Campbell's rescue from without, when a protagonist cannot pull themselves from the abyss and someone must come rescue them. As Halberstam discusses, failure itself can be queer, as it falls outside of heteronormative norms (n.p.). Several of the cluster partners (platonic or romantic) come along, emphasizing allyship. These partners are often confused or left out of conversations, and they certainly aren't at risk like the cluster, but they insist on fighting beside those they love. They model real-life partners and friends who do not fully understand their beloved's struggle but want to help them however they can. With their imperfect but full support, the team's fighting strength grows, and they save Wolfgang and one another. Their superhuman ability emphasizes an ability to transcend the fear of return, with otherworldly protection from the allies who have preserved them through the journey. However, as Campbell observes, "the myths of failure touch us with the tragedy of life, but those of success only with their own incredibility. And yet, if the monomyth is to fulfill its promise, not human failure or superhuman success but human success is what we shall have to be shown. That is the problem of the crisis of the threshold of the return" (*Hero* 178).

The mythic cycle is meant to show the heroes, having learned enough from their adventure to share their new insights with the ordinary world, bringing a new empathy and beauty to its dreariness and rejuvenating it. As Campbell adds, this hero must "confront society with his ego-shattering, life-redeeming elixir, and take the return blow of reasonable queries, hard resentment, and good people at a loss to comprehend" (*Hero* 186). In this case, the elixir is empathy and closeness, learned by the cluster and offered to their wider community.

In the joyous finale, Amanita and Nomi are married in a show of light and color in the Eiffel Tower. In their vows, they mention the cluster, acknowledging that their marriage is not isolated but shared with many loving friends. All of their cluster attends, as do all their families and friends, emphasizing the larger circle of allyship. A French government official performs the ceremony and tells them:

> The improbable unfolding of recent events have led me to consider that no one thing is one thing only. How people endow what is familiar with new, ever-evolving meaning and, by doing so, release us from the expected, the familiar into something unforeseeable. It is in this unfamiliar realm we find new possibilities. It is in the unknown, we find hope. Here we stand in the Eiffel Tower, which was conceived in gratitude for the French Revolution. It has been a zeppelin lookout, a transmitter tower, and, for generations of Parisians, an aspiration for a better, a brighter future. Similarly plural in meaning is a wedding. A wedding is a celebration which can also be understood as a

7. Return and Acceptance

union of two families, and in this case, this union takes on an even deeper significance. And for me, this wedding is proof. Proof that for all the differences between us and all the forces that try to divide us, they will never exceed the power of love to unite us [2.12].

They have reached this moment because they have saved one another whenever they needed it. After the ceremony, fireworks burst: "A gift from Paris and the new BPO in honor of the accord and this celebration." Thus, all of Paris joins their celebration, honoring it with more color and light. All the unconventional families and pairings dance happily. The show ends in a celebration of love for all the characters together. The sacred marriage in alchemy symbolizes unity—a merging of opposites into a greater whole. This is the perfect symbol for *Sense8*, a show about coming together and finding support from without and within.

The Tyrant Crumbles: Sort Of *(Television)*

Parents need to be faced as the youth grows into adulthood. Still, even understanding parents can make it awkward, if not worse. In Lee Lai's "This Far," a mother complains, "I wonder if you'd be feeling that way if your flesh and blood told you they wanted to leave home and become a tree" (176). As she adds, "It just feels like you're going so far. It's not possible to just, change a little less?" (178). Her mother finally admits that being older doesn't give her all the answers. She accompanies her daughter to the place of transformation, worried but supporting her choice.

Sort of is notable for starring non-binary protagonist Sabi Mehboob (played by Bilal Baig, also a show creator) struggling to find their place as a Pakistani Canadian millennial. At the show's start, Sabi lives as non-binary while working at an LGBTQ+ bar and as a nanny, but hides this life from both parents. Episode one sees Sabi being discovered when their mother, Raffo, arrives unannounced to drop off chicken. Sabi slowly turns to face her, in makeup and styled hair.

> **RAFFO:** Your face. You're crying.
> **SABI:** Wait. That's all you want to say?
> **RAFFO:** I can't remember the last time I saw you cry ... Are these my bangles?
> **SABI:** Yes.
> **RAFFO:** (stunned) I'm going to go home now, maybe.
> **SABI:** (tearful) Ma? Can I have the chicken?

The scene cuts to Sabi getting home with the chicken and telling their sister, "Mom just saw me in makeup.... Mom and I are never gonna talk again, are we?" ("Sort of Gone" 1.01). Sabi is terrified at the shattering of their mother-child relationship. Culture writer Amil Niazi observes: "I think that that scene is one of the most powerful in the entire series. The very real tension but also the very real love that exists between Sabi and their mom is so ever present. It's a third character. It's just sort of living there between them" (Weldon et al. n.p.). As she adds of the South Asian community, "You know, it's such a matriarchal community. And the love and acceptance of your mother—and I can say this as the daughter of a Pakistani woman—it's something that you're always reaching for and always striving to understand" (Weldon et al. n.p.).

After this, Sabi gradually ceases to hide the dresses, the pronouns, the workplace, the nannying job. (Sabi's mom reacts to each of these with mild shock and silence, except for the "servant" job that she feels is beneath her American-born electrician child.) A notable switch comes when their mother embraces being a free spirit and literally tears down a wall in her house, also phoning both her children and telling them, "Live your life" (1.06). Like all the other characters, Raffo is torn between society's expectations and her own desires. "Almost everybody [on the show] feels that they're not seen for who they really are but are forced into rigid identities that don't really contain them. If *Sort Of* has a governing idea, it's hinted at in its title, which suggests that nobody is wholly one thing" (Weldon et al. n.p.). They all straddle multiple identities even as they exist in transition on their way to growth.

Taking Sabi over to investigate after their mother's provocative phone call, Sabi's sister and even the Lyft driver suggest they "de-femme" in "Sort of a Miracle" (1.07). Sabi defiantly goes to their mother's house in a sparkling gold dress after a late-night party. Raffo freezes for a moment at the ensemble, then just offers, "Food!"

"Yes," says Sabi.

"Take the napkin if you don't want to dirty your, uh, outfit," Raffo adds carefully. She's clearly trying to show support for her child. However, there are complications. As the episode continues, Sabi's mom asks Sabi to dress down to hide the truth from their cousin and uncle, who will report to their father in Pakistan. When Sabi does not, their cousin calls their father home.

"When the Orphan is dominant in our lives, the world seems a pretty hopeless place. We have been abandoned by whatever paternal figure might rescue us…. Finally, the child stops crying, but the pain and loneliness inside do not go away. Sometimes orphans feel like exiles," Pearson explains (84). Sabi ends season one panicking and running to a trans friend, where they roleplay asking their mother for acceptance. Sabi continues to stress about where the relationship will go. When they emerge, Raffo is waiting in their workplace. "When you're as important as you are, you can't leave people for that long," she insists. "Don't go away from me."

7. Return and Acceptance

Sabi agrees. "I won't. If you don't go away from me" ("Sort of Back Again" 1.08). Sabi ends the season by eating Raffo's chicken, symbolically accepting the love that their mom is offering.

Their dad is harsher, returning from Pakistan to warmly greet the rest of his family without a word for his non-binary child. "Why does everyone keep things from me?" he protests.

"Is that a serious question? 'Cause we're like afraid of you," Sabi answers ("Sort of Who She Is" 2.04). Raffo is also spiraling between living for herself and seeking his approval. She finds she's hesitating to go about her routine with her husband in town and expecting attention. She's uncertain whether to make a fuss or conform. Of course, this struggle, which mirrors Sabi's, is a traditional adversary test on the journey: the patriarch will crumble if confronted, but the protagonists often cringe at their perception of him.

Further, the patriarch is not only the head of the family but often has a position in the community that pressures the young hero. In the aptly named "Sort of Love," their dad hauls Sabi to the imam. To both their surprise, the imam defends Sabi: "We have to let go of control. We can't control our child's mind or future. We have to let go, Imran bhai. The only thing we can do in this case is to try and understand each other. And why is that, you ask? Because to love someone, you need to understand them" ("Sort of I Love You" 2.06).

After, Sabi protests, "Feels like you wanted to fix me. What you think of me, Abbu, it's so important to me. I can't help it."

Sabi's father is quiet but says he disagrees with the imam, adding, "You don't need to understand someone before loving them." This, as the episode title aptly points out, is "Sort of I Love You." It's not closure or a solution to the family strife, but it is a gesture for the frustrated protagonist.

To Sabi's shock, however, Sabi's father dies in the next episode, and this gesture is their last moment of semi-closeness. "Sort of Janazah" (1.08) explores the funeral with the responsibility of the Janazah prayer—performed by the oldest son. Sabi studies, but their churning feelings are not up to the traditional assignment and community's judgment. Sabi freezes, and their mom comes and stands with them. Their sister joins them too, offering love and solidarity. After, Sabi is uncertain what to feel and how much they love their father. Losing him is not just heartbreaking but emphasizes his fragility—the tower of disapproval looming over them has vanished. Now Sabi will have to live without thinking in terms of their father's approval.

Managing to sympathize with the broken, once-powerful father and to integrate him into the self allows the hero to succeed him, claiming his intellect and his position. Thus, we know our inner strength. Vader, Aslan, Merlin all crumble before the protagonists, leaving them to step into power. With this comes understanding and adulthood. "We move from a place of total abandonment to a place where we can never be abandoned. In that moment of knowing, soul and Self are one" (Woodman, *Ravaged Bridegroom* 126).

The Orville has an arc featuring Topa, a girl child born to an all-male race. As the government orders surgery performed on the baby, an intersex allegory is clear. One father, Klyden, supports the surgery, while the other, Bortus, is more progressive after watching the video *Rudolph the Red-Nosed Reindeer* and considering the human celebration of diversity. When older, Topa feels dysphoria and despair. Bortus and the crew aid her in having the babyhood surgery reversed, but Klyden leaves them, despite his family's pleas. Heartbreakingly, he wishes Topa had never been born ("A Tale of Two Topas" 3.05). However, when Topa is kidnapped and tortured, Klyden returns in a panic. He tells her, sobbing, "You ... were almost lost, because of people who believed as I did. I ... I ... I thought I hated you. But even then, I never wished you harm. I simply ... did not know how to live with you. I allowed a lifetime of prejudice to cloud my judgment. That must change. I must change. I want you to know that I accept you, Topa, exactly as you are. And I am proud ... to call you my daughter" ("Midnight Blue" 3.08). This humbling as the father repents of exiling his child often appears at this step of the quest.

Lucy Holland's *Sistersong* retells the folktale of the wicked sister who killed the good one over a man and whose crime was revealed when her sister's bones were made into a harp. In this version, the siblings Riva, Keyne, and Sinne genuinely love one another, and the middle one longs to live as a boy. Keyne studies and trains as a warrior with the witch Mori, who sometimes appears as the wizard Myrdhin. Their father, King Cador, has turned to Christianity, so his ability to summon the land's magic has faded. (This, of course, symbolizes the father being led astray and all of society weakening as a result.) The family priest Gildas considers Myrdhin and Keyne pagans equivalent to the enemy. Still, Keyne feels he must speak up to save his father from throwing away their forces in battle. When Keyne's father lashes out physically, Keyne, now the stronger one, catches his arm. In battle, Keyne saves the day, but the king is struck, his jaw shattered. In such a classic moment, the all-powerful protector is vanquished or revealed as a lie. Now the young hero must take over. Kenye takes his place as king and stands up to the priest at last. In fact, his father appoints Keyne as his heir before all his lords, apologizes to him, and dies. After that, the crowd arrives. One lord defies Keyne and calls him a woman. Keyne claims his power and retorts, "You are wrong. My name is Constantine ap Cador of

Dumnonia. I am your lord by blood and by right—and you owe me allegiance" (364). Of course, this statement holds power and the assurance of self-naming. Moreover, naming himself the famous Constantine links the protagonist with this legend for readers.

Other stories find that speculative elements can offer tools for healing. In "The Shape of My Name" by Nino Cipri, the hero has time travelers in the family. The short story is in second person, written like a letter from child to mother. "How can I ever make you understand how much I disliked that name?" the child protests. "It felt like it belonged to a sister whom I was constantly being compared to, whose legacy I could never fulfill or surpass or even forget" (176). Instead, the child makes up a new name each day: "Doc, Buck, George, Charlie. Names that my heroes had, from television and comics and the matinees in town. They weren't my name, but they were better than the one I had" (177). The mother disapproves: "You just looked on, lips pursed in a frown, and told Dara you wished she'd quit indulging my silly little games" (177). The child gets to explore the future—surgery, more medical and social choices. At last, he returns to the past and tells his mother she has a son—already. "I left before I could introduce myself to you: my name is Heron, Mama. I haven't forgiven you yet, but maybe someday I will. And when I do, I will travel back one last time, to that night you left me and Dad for the future. I'll tell you that your apology has finally been accepted, and will give you my blessing to live in exile, marooned in a future beyond all reach" (188). Here, time travel offers a chance to reconcile with the mother of the past from the perspective of the child of the future, if that's what the child most desires.

Public Acknowledgment: Cemetery Boys *(Novel)*

In the celebrated teen novel *Cemetery Boys* by Aiden Thomas, Yadriel longs to be initiated as a brujo, a man of his community who can raise the dead, not as a woman healer. "When Yadriel had refused to be presented to Lady Death for his quinces as a bruja, they wouldn't let him go through it as a brujo. It was out of the question. It wouldn't work, they'd told him" (24). Considering the concept to be blasphemous and too new, the family won't even let him try.

When his father refuses, he performs the ritual himself with a secretly constructed portaje spirit blade constructed by his best friend Maritza. The ritual succeeds, and he is accepted by Lady Death. In her eyes, he is a brujo. Granted, trans stories where an all-powerful goddess or spirit discerns the hero's true identity are a staple, implying acceptance from nature, the divine, and the mentor hidden deep within, in contrast to the wider community. Indeed, Yadriel craves the external ceremony because it will mean public, official acceptance of his identity. Being called by the right name and pronouns, and more often, the wrong ones, in his daily life feels shallow to him when he knows his family and friends are humoring him. Their disbelief that he can fulfill the requirements of the men's rite of passage undermines his confidence daily.

Such heroes are close to their families and communities and don't wish to leave them but to make a place for themselves within the space. Their inner child seeks complete acceptance through performing the tribal rituals. In this tradition, ritual, like legal documents, feels incontrovertible—a larger affirmation of the self from outside. This, of course, bolsters the vulnerable feelings within.

Such a public forum offers more affirmation than casual daily encounters. It also marks a rite of passage, allowing the young character to transition to this new state of being. Alex Gino's beloved children's book *George* features a child who longs to reveal she's really a girl. Further, she adores the heroine of *Charlotte's Web* and fantasizes about showing her mother how wonderful she is as her in the school play. As the story goes on, her teacher won't let her be Charlotte, dismissing her with, "I have too many girls who want the part. Besides, imagine how confused people would be" (70). As George struggles, her best friend Kelly, cast as Charlotte, lets George take her place at that evening's performance. This reveals her to the community, giving her a moment of pure public acceptance. "George reveled in every moment, sharing her voice with the audience and watching them watch her as they waited for her next words" (156). After, the compliments flow, and the principal, in contrast to her teacher, remarks, "You can't control who your children are, but you can certainly support them, am I right?" and tells George her door is always open (160). Her mom unbends a little and starts to explore how to move forward with her daughter. While Kelly takes George on a wonderful girls' day out, George's real story arc is not this gift but the role she worked for and earned herself. With it, she proved herself to her family and community and received some acceptance.

Aida Salazar's luminous children's book, *The Moon Within*, offers a ceremony: the mother burns sage and announces:

Our child has arrived at a new truth.
   A real self. an authentic self, the reality always meant to be
      Marco is his true name. Magda is part of his historia, the earlier chapters of girlhood [126].

She and Marco's father explore how, in pre–Colombian culture, such a child would have been honored as *xochihuah*, the one who bears flowers. With this, they stretch back to these roots and celebrate them.

7. Return and Acceptance

Yadriel worries over his family, but Julian, his ghostly love interest, points out that Lady Death has accepted him, and he is a practicing brujo, whether others admit it. Next, Julian pushes Yads to explain why this acceptance isn't enough, asking why Yadriel still insists on seeking their official confirmation. Julian describes a trans classmate and adds that what she does "doesn't mean other people get to decide who she is. And the same goes for you" (Thomas, *Cemetery* 185). Still, Yadriel hesitates. "It wasn't enough to have summoned Julian, to have been bound to his portaje or for Lady Death's blessing to flow through him with its golden light. He needed to do *everything* the men could do before asking the brujx to accept him into the community. He couldn't leave any gaps for them to question" (185). Without official, irrefutable confirmation, his society will keep questioning him, and because they reflect his internal turmoil, he will keep questioning himself.

At last, confronted with his son's abilities at the climax, his father instantly accepts what Yadriel's become. In a "small and defeated" voice, he apologizes for doubting and assures his son he'll be initiated formally with the others (239). Yadriel saves the day and finds love, sacrificing himself in a show of power unseen for generations. He is not just a brujo, but the ultimate brujo. The treacherous villain is his own uncle, who, like Yads, has been seething with rejection.

"Initiation ceremonies are a powerful force throughout the world, guiding newcomers through the entire monomyth cycle from leaving home through death and apotheosis.... Central to this is the ordeal—the battle with the Self in the dark nadir of the cosmos" (Frankel, *From Girl to Goddess* 163). Yads has already done this, battling his uncle's dark plans and then sacrificing himself and using untold magic to save his uncle's victims. These victims are young men like himself—saving them symbolizes gathering together the scattered and wounded masculine aspects of the self, restoring them to the community in a triumphant return to life. Yads rises from death filled with new understanding. Thus, he proves to everyone that he transcends their abilities and commitment.

His final great achievement is to be welcomed by his community as a practicing brujo. The ceremony goes off properly as Yadriel's loved ones watch him in awe. As his father adds, "Our traditions should grow and change with every generation. Just because we follow the ancient ways doesn't mean we can't also grow.... Growth isn't a deviation from what we've done before but a natural progression to honor all those who make this community strong" (Thomas, *Cemetery* 339). Thus, his ceremony not only confirms who he is but fixes the mistakes that made his uncle so resentful and opens the door for the next generation to find acceptance. By fighting for his own rights, Yads has repaired his larger world, representing his entire self.

"Potion and Practices" by gwynception constructs an alternate reality where being trans is normalized and magic smooths transition. Violet Rage, an "Outlier," finds a matriarch and bargains for a transforming potion. There are tests, like awareness of all three worlds. The matriarch takes her to a realm with "unconditional warmth and care and hope," unlike the world of her birth (53). All is beautiful and nurturing, with a supportive shadow that provides companionship.

> She spent months that grew into years of waiting and learning and waiting and studying and practising under the Lady.... Violet learned of her own nature as an outlier, apparently all this information necessary for the job. She learned of her nonexistent existence. How her being wasn't really being.... The matriarch said at times the outliers were born out of negation or as a reaction. They would simply cease to exist outside of the context that gave them their apparent existence. Though thought to be rare for an outlier to escape their original context, their original home world or realm, there had been an infinite number, continuously and exponentially growing, of outliers who had escaped their original context [57].

An initiation ceremony follows as she descends into an inner chamber and meets an outlier like herself. A fern creature permeates her mind. "You know the feeling in the air?" Violet asks. "Somewhere where there's a vortex of magic—places of gathering?" When the fern observes that she's run from these places, she adds, "I have to hide though—I don't even exist in some people's eyes."

The fern tells her, "And yet you do. Your experience is unique unto yourself, but you are not alone. You have an infinite fractaling of selves and others out there. You are spirit, you are strength, you are resilience, you are resistance" (62). This acceptance gives Violet the affirmation she needs to finish transforming.

Oliver Jones's "Becoming Prom King" likewise describes the joy of such acknowledgment: As he explains, his teachers and friends had nominated and voted for him out of respect: "They planned to make it happen because they knew how much it would mean to me—not the concept of being the most popular (I certainly wasn't), but the concept of earning that title" (14). While this moment doesn't make up for snide comments and mockery, they chose Oliver to receive this special accolade. "I was so surprised, but so proud. I don't think I've ever experienced a more gender euphoric moment: undeniably, indisputably, I was male" (15). This was the purest form of gender validation he had ever received and a joyous moment of celebration.

Master of the Two Worlds: Good Omens *(Television)*

Mastery of two worlds is a journey step that trans heroes enjoy in different ways. Some protagonists become captains of both worlds in that

7. Return and Acceptance

they embrace their gender alongside treasured traits that others frame as "wrong." For example, Callie of *Sir Callie and the Champions of Helston* can do magic, which is culturally linked with womanhood in Helston. Callie is neither a woman nor a man and wishes to be a knight. With time, Callie meets more gender-nonconforming peers and fights transphobia and misogyny more directly. As they come into themselves, they also become more comfortable using their magic. As such, they are choosing to master both worlds—the sword fighting they find affirming and the link with their real family—alongside the magic. Callie and their friends show off this balance in a utopian moment as they play on the beach: "All the little things that don't or shouldn't matter drop away from us, like rain sliding off oil skin. Magic or no magic, boy or girl, neither or both. What difference does any of it make in the end?" (Symes-Smith 324). Their different magics rise: one green, one pink, one blue. "Our magic tumbles and dances like young creatures, careless and ignorant of the dangers of the real world because none of it matters right here and now. *That's how we should be* is my first thought" (326). After fighting for their friends' freedom, Callie wins a boon, which they use to make this youthful microcosm into a utopian reality. They insist, "Make it fair. Totally fair. Girls can fight and boys can be magical; Anyone can do both. Pretending that everyone split down the middle in two groups is ridiculous.... You'll just make people more miserable and turn them into enemies" (372). This decree creates a better world in which the children can celebrate all their abilities.

The Story of Silence by Alex Myers shows the medieval girl raised as a boy wanting to acknowledge both sides of the self. As a mentor, Merlin tells Silence, "You stand at the proper juncture for magic. You fit the spaces between, the nowheres, the anywheres, wherein lies possibility" (440). Silence uses this lesson to understand that choosing nature or nurture "would be wrong, limiting. Would make them always half, never both" because both are a part of Silence (440). At the story's conclusion, Silence gives the moral of the story: "Most of us insist on being one thing and denying all else ... we are not one thing. We are multitudes. And it isn't simply about what we do, but who we are, and how we understand ourselves. I'm beginning to work this out, what I am becoming, how I will keep on becoming" (445).

Likewise, the heroines of the film *Tangerine* brag about their duality and use it as a tool—for sex work but also beyond that. Alexandra faces down a belligerent client, emphasizing, "You forget I got a dick too." She takes pride in her unconventionality and lack of assimilation. Further, all the iPhone shots used to film the piece allow a closer focus on faces, challenging films that reduce trans characters to their body parts. This symbolism supports the characters' vivaciously living as all they are.

A more literal balance appears in the BBC's beloved miniseries adaptation of Terry Pratchett and Neil Gaiman's novel *Good Omens*.

One might rightfully raise the question of the genders and transness of the *Good Omens* characters because the topic has not been directly discussed in the text as of the end of season one. In the show, the protagonists, Crowley the demon (David Tennant) and Aziraphale the angel (Michael Sheen), are presented as eternal companions without deep romantic or platonic connections to humans. Further, they present at different times in different genders. In fact, Crowley takes on the form of Nanny Ashtoreth, complete with lipstick and curls, while Aziraphale comes down to earth in the body of a middle-aged, highly maternal sex worker, Madam Tracy. Both women are heavily made-up and campy in their appearance, bolstering a queer reading. Screenwriter and book author Neil Gaiman tweeted: "I wouldn't exclude the ideas that they are ace, or aromantic, or trans. They are an angel and a demon, not as male humans, per the book. Occult/Ethereal beings don't have sexes, something we tried to reflect in the casting. Whatever Crowley and Aziraphale are, it's a love story." Tweets such as this indeed leave somewhat open the question whether the two use this or that label, but make it clear that the two are queer, to use a human term.

After a frantic quest to prevent the apocalypse that their respective sides demand, the pair triumph. However, at the end of the first season, Crowley and Aziraphale are in serious trouble with hell and heaven. The demon community plans to kill Crowley after a "fair trial," using a bath of holy water. The angels plan a similar fate for Az, this time using demon fire. But as Crowley soaks in the bath, nothing happens. When Aziraphale steps into the whirling demon fire, Aziraphale is perfectly unscathed. Their peers look on with awe and terror, believing that their deities must have intervened to grant Crowley and Aziraphale extra powers and protection. Aziraphale breathes fire at them, while Crowley campily complains about the lack of a rubber duck. "It may be worse than we thought," Gabriel says, as Beelzebub concludes below, "He's not one of us anymore" (1.06). Apparently, the angel and demon have become so close that each has absorbed the other's immunities.

The two are set free and surmise that, at least for some time, they will be left alone. It is then revealed that the two did not have these powers. In fact, the pair have received a prophecy: "When alle is fayed and all is done, ye must choofe your faces wisely, for soon enouff, ye will be playing with fyre" (1.06). They have put this wisdom to use and switched places, each playing the other well enough to fool the two armies. This symbolizes their closeness, trust, and mutual understanding. Crowley was the one the angels had taken, and of course—as a demon—demon fire was not dangerous for him. Aziraphale was the one who, looking like Crowley, was dipped in the holy water bath and requested a duck. This achievement emphasizes their well-rounded growth. As Campbell explains, "Freedom to pass back and forth across the world division, from the perspective of the apparitions of time to that of the casual deep and back—not contaminating the principles of the one with those of the other, yet permitting the mind to know the one by virtue of the other—is the talent of the master" (*Hero* 196). The Cosmic Dancer flits about, wielding a deep understanding of different realms. Through friendship, the *Good Omens* heroes have transcended their upbringings to do the same.

Having outwitted their societies, the two go off to celebrate their survival with lunch at the Ritz, as they often do. Aziraphale tells him, "I like to think none of this would have worked out if you weren't, at heart, just a little bit a good person." His friend replies, "And if you weren't, deep down, just enough of a bastard to be worth knowing" (1.06). Here, Crowley and Aziraphale have managed to win back the human world, which they love. They gained mastery of it in the sense that they found a place in it for themselves, each on their own, and even a place for their loving relationship to blossom happily. Mastery of two worlds emphasizes wielding the skills one has rejected in the self—in this case, demon or angel—in others, the dark side, a society, or behaviors of a specific gender.

Beyond this, they have gained mastery of not one but two extra worlds. Crowley, through Aziraphale's help, has gained the awe of the demon world and breathed fire at some very impressed angels. Aziraphale, with Crowley's help, has gained the reverence of angels who previously scorned him and taken a bath in the demon's world. The two assert that this brave scheme and their relationship have bought them freedom from prosecution or pursuit for a while and, of course, the chance to enjoy the world they helped to save and its tea crumpets. This embracing of supposedly mutually exclusive sides in the world and in the self is a step toward happiness and wholeness. This is true of the tension between one's unique gifts and conforming to join society in stories such as *Frozen*. It can also be about the false binary of gender. As Pearson and Pope explore the female hero's quest, they explain how she incorporates both sides of the gender divide, as many enlightened heroes do:

> Having affirmed a commitment to the discovery of the true self in exiting from the garden, and having discovered that she has within her both male and female attributes, the female hero discovers and affirms the full humanity obscured by traditional sex roles. She learns to be autonomous and to achieve without exploiting or dominating others; and she learns nurturance that is not accompanied by a denial of the self. With the achievement of this unified vision, the hero is prepared to return to the kingdom and to enjoy a new relationship with the world [219].

For trans heroes, this wholeness is often already known, leaving the end of the story less about dichotomy and its resolution, as it is more often for cis heroes. The trans hero may know that male and female, man and woman, are not binary differences but are a few of many categories and practices.

Freedom to Live? Fierce Femmes and Notorious Liars (Novel)

At this point in the story, many cisgender characters receive their real treasure: the freedom to live happily and, as often goes without saying, to live as themselves: safely, celebrated, and surrounded by loved ones. This is rarely the case for trans characters, which often mirrors the impossibility of safety for trans people living in unsafe, hateful environments. Some stories envision a safer, happier, and better world. For example, *Pet* paints a beautiful and painful picture of a loving community. This community, horrified to find out it had not been as safe as it had believed, begins rebuilding to change and to learn how to promote this safety. Becky Chambers and R. B. Lemberg have created imagined worlds with safety for the entire gender spectrum, and other stories suggest a balance is possible.

Yoon Ha Lee's *Tiger Honor* centers on Sebin, a young, genderfluid tiger spirit from the Juhwang Clan. Loyalty to their family is one of their top priorities. They dream of joining the Thousand World Space Forces and someday getting to command a spaceship. They very much look up to their Uncle Hwan, who does just that. Sabin idolizes their uncle and wishes to be more like him: "It was because of Uncle Hwan that I longed to be accepted by the space forces—to someday become a battle cruiser Captain just like him" (6). They are accepted in their own right but learn that the Thousand World Space Forces planned to use them to monitor and perhaps bait their uncle, declared a traitor, to make a move. An official apologizes for this and welcomes Sebin as a cadet after all. This is more than a career move for Sebin. It means being admitted into an organization they have been idolizing since they were very young. Moreover, it stands for being recognized for who they are, not only in relation to their family but simply as themselves.

As discussed in previous chapters, becoming disillusioned with family is not only a common step in the hero's journey but particularly common and prominent for trans people. So many trans and otherwise non-binary people are disowned and abused by family; it is virtually a cliché. Sebin's story reflects this trope and the commonly accompanying trope of found family. Sebin's wish to join the Thousand World Space Forces morphs from a desire to prove their family is honorable and worthy to a desire to prove themselves and their abilities—a desire to stand on their own, and perhaps more importantly, a desire to find a different system to belong to that will accept and appreciate them. With time, the Thousand World Space Forces may become a home to Sebin, even if not a perfect one.

A different option, based more on realism, is offered in Kai Cheng Thom's *Fierce Femmes and Notorious Liars*. This book tells the story of an unnamed protagonist who grows up in a dangerous, unsupportive town. She runs away, calling herself an escape artist. When she first comes to the City of Smoke and Lights, she's delighted to find herself in a haven for the first time: "So the stories are true: the City of Smoke and Lights is full of fierce, fabulous femmes. Dangerous trans women, hot as blue stars. You can find them anywhere if you know how to look, and believe me I am looking. Can't take my eyes off them: these visions of what I could be. What I am becoming" (37). The heroine moves into a tiny apartment here and considers it a sanctuary. She describes loving it "with fierce, starving joy" from the first moment (43).

At last, the protagonist ends up with a cute, well-to-do trans guy who loves and uplifts her. She finds herself looking at his apartment—now her apartment as well. It is everything convenient and upper-middle class. She breaks his TV when a rich, right-wing trans woman appears on it—and expects him to be angry, but he is not. He is understanding and kind about it. And so she leaves. It is not her story, she feels. It is not the freedom she wanted to have. She explains:

> Oh please. Don't look so surprised now, you knew this was coming. I told you from the very beginning ... that this was the story of how I became the greatest escape artist in the whole goddamn world. It is not the story of how I ran away from home like a little trans baby princess Cinderella, got rescued by a handsome transgender prince, and vanished happily into the vast palace of the middle class. ... Really. You still don't know why I'm leaving. Honey. It's because I ran away to find myself, and so that I am never, ever, stuck in a story that someone else wrote for me. Because I said goodbye to my body full of bees and heart full of ghosts, and now it is time to fill my body and my heart with something new. I'm putting on my short skirt and my candy red heels and I'm flying away to see if I know who I am, what I might still become, so I can find out how far I can get, and if I could find my way back drawing a map of myself in the stars [185–186].

While the story intentionally leaves the ending as a shock, the protagonist claims to have foreshadowed it. The protagonist has never felt as if she has found herself in the middle class, academia, or with the fierce femmes she loves. For her, freedom to live does not mean safety—it means movement, exploration. She wants "freedom from," rather than "freedom to." Another text by the same author provides a clearer explanation:

> Safety is, I believe, an inherently classed, raced, and gendered experience that frequently runs the risk of being used for regressive ends—ironically, for restricting the freedoms of the vulnerable, those who are never really safe. Often, we see the call for safety actually reinforce the power of oppressive institutions, like the police and the prison system, in our lives. When we choose safety over liberation, our movements fail [Thom, *I Hope* n.p.].

The protagonist feels that not only might safety be fake but also might turn into the oppression of others. As the greatest escape artist, she is not willing to throw other vulnerable people under the bus for safety. She prefers to escape and find out who she may still discover she is. In our world, when some transgender protagonists find a happy ending, safety is dissonant with the knowledge of other trans people being in danger. Even when people choose to enjoy or reject their happy ending, to try to use privilege to uplift others—if there is privilege to be had—in worlds like ours, all our trans people don't share our fortune.

It should be noted that not all characters can bear to leave the fantasy world. "Nothing is Pixels Here" by K. M. Szpara has a young person dwelling in safety in an online gaming space only to be horrified at being downloaded into the wrong body. Ash's avatar was generated in his self-image, letting him live online as himself from age five on. Now, the jarring shock of return is a horror. "I'd never heard the word 'transgender' before. I didn't know there was a condition that could trap you in someone else's body," he thinks (95). He finally retreats to the online world, unwilling to leave it for a long process of medical procedures to regain what he already has here. The author explains, "For Ash, existing in his physical body is too hard—which is not weak to admit. He knows who he is, and that person exists in the SimGrid" (Szpara, "Author Spotlight" 284). The magic world online is where Ash felt safe as a rejected child "for whom reality is too much to handle" (284).

Other stories have happier endings with community support, emphasizing different paths for the hero. In Capetta's *The Brilliant Death*, Teodora, who goes by Teo, finds an opportunity when her father is poisoned and a family representative must go to the capital. "There was nothing false about stage magic. If I became a boy, it would be real. Another version of me, as true as this one" (52). Cielo, a strega (witch), is Teo's mentor and switches gender and appearance constantly. Cielo asks, "Is it strange to be stuck as one thing? ... To look at yourself and see the same face over and over, when you're constantly changing?" (105). Teo stares into a mirror and orders the magic to change her. Moments later, nobles attack. "I had to be careful, since I was so exposed, and yet I wouldn't have traded this feeling. As a girl, I had been given rules and restrictions and responsibilities. I drank my new freedom recklessly, like tipping an entire bottle of liquid

7. Return and Acceptance 177

genziana down my throat" (113). After, Teo is struck by how city dwellers clear the streets and defer. Cielo and Teo also discuss the persecution of the strega, with Cielo noting, "We're *not* like them. Or rather, we are and we aren't. People hold a deep fear of complication" (125). When Teo returns home, he makes demands like a boy, and his father is surprised but acquiesces. His father offers to make him his heir but cannot elevate a woman or a known strega. Teo is disappointed. "I had found truth in knowing I was not one fixed thing, and now I couldn't imagine living *only* in a boy's form because it was easier to wield power as a man. Besides, if I had learned one thing from trying to keep my magic in the shadows for so long, it was that I couldn't spend a lifetime hiding part of myself. *Any* part" (323). Theo goes off with Cielo instead, and they find freedom outside the family hierarchy.

In the sequel, *The Storm of Life*, Cielo and Teo continue their romance, often switching forms during lovemaking. "I like it when you are Teo, whatever that means," Cielo says sweetly (353). After their shape-changing lovemaking, Teo dons a mix of clothes, and they hold hands in public, unafraid of scandal. They secretly marry, then finally tell Teo's delighted family. Cielo is offered the throne but asks the families to accept Teo instead. He tells them how Teo has already proven themselves in battle as a leader. Cielo adds that Teo shouldn't have to rule as a man: "While Teo does have a delightfully boyish side, I will not stand for anyone making demands on how we must appear" (353). Instead, Cielo insists that the nobles accept the truth about them both. The loving couple adopts Teo's nephew and returns much of their magic to the land to heal it. They will keep some though—Cielo insists, "You and I could never be plain Vinalians" (361). With family, kingdom, magic, and honesty all aligned, they usher in a wonderful future together. This is a more complete ending, celebrating how they have found true acceptance integrated into their society and ruling it together.

Other heroes find success in the magic world and never return. Found abandoned as a baby and wearing a lizard t-shirt, Kivali dreams of the lizard aliens ushering her to a place where she feels fully at home in *Lizard Radio* by Pat Schmatz. One vital day when kids are bullying and beating her for wearing boys' boots and going back and forth on her clothes, she starts dreaming of a better world. "That was the day when I truly believed the saurian stories. I was lizard-dropped and only the lizards could save me. One day they'd come and help me do whatever good deed I'm supposed to do here on Earth, and then they'd take me away to the land of Lizard Radio where everyone is like me" (183). Indeed, in this futuristic world where transitioning is common, one character explains, "My little cousin was born a he and now she's a beautiful she. They tested her up before Grade One and she scored in the midthirties. Girl for sure. Transition complete by Grade Three, and she passed through PDGT in about six weeks. Easy for her" (26). However, Kivali still feels trapped between genders. Her score was indeterminate, and she was told to choose by her tenth birthday. She called herself female but still isn't comfortable with the choice. She describes herself as "still not getting 'girl' right—and not wanting to" and having to wear hair ribbons to signal to passersby that she's female instead of wearing a more ambiguous hairstyle (85). As she concludes, "Every choice sets off a world of possibilities. Every choice cuts off a world of possibilities" (86). In safety, at least she has the space to explore who she is.

Since our world has so many flaws, some heroes find themselves cast as world creators. L. A. Knight's "To Rest and to Create" takes place in a reality where many young people travel through magic portals to save worlds and become heroes. Rich kids get extra access, as do those who can manage to apply for scholarships, but, as the narrator explains, "I missed the window, so instead of popping off through a portal to go save the magical world of my heart, I flinch from the shriek of car horns slamming down the street, the cacophony of water crashing on fiberglass rooftops" (126). The narrator is disabled and autistic and thus has trouble finding a job in an ableist environment. As they huddle up outside, in fact, they tumble into a secondary world. There, a mysterious non-binary mentor reveals this is a House of Choosing, which leads young people to the right magical worlds. Xe adds that they're specifically seeking a world maker. "We need someone who can make the Doors. Who can find the seeds of different worlds and bring them blooming to life, then carve the Door that leads there. You can do it. You felt a world just now" (131). In this new job, the narrator will create whatever doors they wish and live in the perfect world for them, or they will continue traveling. The narrator is relieved, concluding, "I am so tired all the time, and so sick of having to worry. I want to escape, to sink into a place of safety and beauty and rest. I want to give that to other people and help them escape too" (138). At last, they have this chance.

Becoming a Community Elder: Pose *(Television)*

Trans journeys sometimes feature older heroes, not just adolescents (even though there is not enough such representation). As they continue the mythic life cycle, these questors become mentors, finding fulfillment through guiding the next generation. Author Kylie Ariel Bemis's "Dreamborn" has the narrator, Ume, become a mentor in their indigenous fantasy

7. Return and Acceptance

community. The narrator guides a child, Kiwu, through her own process and thus feels satisfaction, pride, and love:

> "You can be a girl," I said to her.
> "Really?" Her eyes lit up. Her dream-marks shimmered.
> "You are lameshi, like me," I said.
> "Like you?"
> "Yes. There are only a few of us for every thousand births. But that's why we're sacred" [117].

The child asks, "How do I become a girl?" and is told she already is. Ume will also supply her with hormonal teas, helping her body as well as her self-affirmation. These fill the role of the magic sword, doll, or talisman generally given from mentor to hero-child, though in this case, the gift is more immediately practical. Meanwhile, this relationship helps Ume as well. Ume relates her joy at becoming a mother and protector to this child. Thus, the relationship nurtures and urges development and connection for them both. She tells her student the myths of their people and makes the girl feel loved as she is.

Some mentors are called upon while they're still barely out of childhood. In Meredith Russo's *If I Was Your Girl*, Amanda relies on Virginia, a college-age trans friend from a past support group. Virginia educates and encourages Amanda and supports Amanda's cisgender mother, despite experiencing more marginalization than Amanda—being Black and not passing. In fact, when she visits Amanda, Amanda hides her from her new, cis friends. An age gap isn't sufficient to account for requiring this of Virginia, let alone an age gap so small.

Once, many world cultures offered godparents and mentors to teach children life skills. "Nowadays, our culture offers fewer mentors as teachers are overburdened with pupils and personal contact fades into emails and statistics. The mentor offers different wisdom than the parents, but wisdom that is no less valuable" (Frankel, *From Girl to Goddess* 37). The oldest myths emphasize all the skills such outside perspectives can offer, and modern fantasy, especially that with found families, helps model such mentorship.

The FX series *Pose* (2018–2021) explores the found families of New York's Black and Latino '80s–'90s ball culture and the elders who run the competing houses. It centers the largest number of transgender characters and writers/directors on television to date. After an HIV diagnosis in episode one, Blanca (MJ Rodriguez) realizes she needs to live her life. She leaves the House of Abundance with its tyrannical mother, Elektra (Dominique Jackson), who she feels is constraining her, and creates a new one, which she names House Evangelista. She recruits Damon (Ryan Jamaal Swain), a homeless teenage dancer, and Angel (Indya Moore), a sex worker, and challenges her former house mother to a competition at the ball. She loses, with nines to her former mother's tens. However, afterward, the master of ceremonies and host, Pray Tell (Billy Porter), tells her that she has great potential. Ricky (Dyllón Burnside), another young homeless dancer, joins her house, and Blanca realizes she has a purpose greater than winning competitions: to take in the people with nowhere to go.

Historically, when houses took over ball culture in the '80s, house mothers really did work as surrogate parents. Many LGBTQ+ youths had been kicked out or run away and received little love and support from their biological families. Still, such mentoring and advocacy could be exhausting. As one example reveals, Rupert Raj became a trans elder the year he began to transition, at age nineteen. He provided information, referrals, counseling, and peer support while also doing training workshops for psychiatrists, social workers, doctors, researchers, and policymakers (Malatino, *Trans Care* 19). He finally had to take an indefinite medical leave due to, as he put it, "work-related stress, an unhealthy workplace culture, chronic burnout, vicarious traumatization, clinical depression and generalized anxiety requiring psychotropic medication and ongoing psychotherapy" (Malatino, *Trans Care* 20). He had been aware of this toll for some time; for a 1987 issue of the trans men's magazine *Metamorphosis*, he penned a feature editorial entitled "Burn-Out: Unsung Heroes and Heroines in the Transgender World," with a list of fourteen trans mentors who had had to stop after many years of unpaid advocacy. As he ended the article, "I have been serving the transgender community in a variety of capacities (administrator, educator, researcher, counselor, peer supporter, local convener, public relations/liaison officer, networker, editor, writer, chairman of the Board—you name it, I've been it) for the past 15 1/2 years *without any form of monetary remuneration whatsoever*" (qtd. in Malatino, *Trans Care* 21). It's a massive burden, which many young, untrained people must manage, since no one else is taking it.

What is described here is more than a support system of disinterested friends; it is those who take an adoptive parenting role, actively watching over others. It's a great responsibility. Thom observes:

> In her poetry, Leah Lakshmi Piepzna-Samarasinha asks the question "What kind of elder do you want to be?" It's a question that haunts me. I know what I wanted from an elder. Guidance. Connection. Teaching. I wonder if I know how to give these things to another person. I look at the young people in my life and see how intense their longing is. It is a longing that mirrors my own. How do you become an elder when you barely had any yourself? In community, we romanticize our elders, but we have little idea of what generational responsibility actually entails, or how to form intergenerational relationships grounded in both intention and integrity [*I Hope* n.p.].

7. Return and Acceptance

Throwing herself into the role of mother, Blanca marches into the School of Dance and argues for Damon to audition, even after the deadline. In episode two, she explains gay sex and gives Damon brochures on safe practices. This contrasts with his birth father's talk, which he describes as awful and pointless. Through the first season, she gathers them all for home-cooked weekly dinners. She makes them all a special Christmas with their dream gifts and cares for Damon when he's sick. After all her hard work, she ends the season appointed Mother of the Year. Season two starts with her signing Damon up to teach a Vogue class at the YMCA and getting Angel into a modeling contest, which begins a successful career. A photographer takes dirty pictures of Angel, and Blanca is the one to storm in and retrieve them. "This is not happening on my watch," she declares. "Do you hear me? With what I got planned? With what you deserve in this world? Hell no. Hell no. We getting what's yours" ("Acting Up" 2.01). When they visit the beach, Angel is only willing to go into the water if Blanca holds her hand and promises not to let go.

Blanca also expands from her family to the larger world. After her HIV progresses to AIDS, she orders her family to join ACT UP's die-in protest. When she's kicked out of a gay bar, she stubbornly keeps returning. Blanca insists she'll "do something about it … so my children's world is fairer than the one I grew up in" (2.01). Of course, she's met with setbacks as the AIDS death count increases and her protests are ignored. After she embraces activism in "Acting Up" (2.01), she tells Angel, "Maybe I'm going a little crazy. Quitting a good job and thinking I could create some kind of immortality to … see through my house and my … my children. Maybe it's better to dream small or not dream at all. At least then you can die with some dignity still intact." Still, for them, she keeps trying. These moments of discouragement, along with grief at her mortality and occasional illnesses, emphasize her growth arc. She is not a perfect leader but struggles as she grows into the role. She also continues to squabble and compete with Elektra, once her own mentor-mother and now her rival.

Blanca's protectiveness outside her tiny family is emphasized when she brings in more strays, including Elektra herself, when she becomes homeless. Blanca lets her move in and finds her a good job as a restaurant hostess, returning the woman's dignity. This reversal of roles emphasizes Blanca's strength, eclipsing her former mother. When Elektra's daughter Candy (Angelica Ross) is killed and her co-house mother Lulu (Hailie Sahar) can't handle it, Blanca goes with her to the hotel to search for her and then claims the body and prepares it for the funeral. She also greets her birth parents kindly and commiserates with them.

The elders make an effort to teach their history too. In season two, voguing goes mainstream thanks to Madonna's song. Pray Tell launches the ball of the season premiere by telling his young people (and the television audience) the history of voguing and how it came from their community. *Pose* co-creator and showrunner Steven Canals observes how many people aren't taught LGBTQ+ history and how the show endeavored to change that: "Specifically in the case of the HIV/AIDS epidemic, and the crack epidemic of the '80s, and '90s—which is the environment I grew up in, in housing projects in the Bronx—we were there on the front line. We were on the ground dealing with the ramifications of all of this and we had no support from anyone" (qtd. in Goldberg n.p.).

In "Blow" (2.07), Lulu is stripping and taking drugs while devastated by Candy's death. Damon and Ricky are out of work and just watch television all day. As Blanca worries, Pray Tell surprises her with his observation.

> **Pray Tell:** I remember when I first found my way to New York City. Things were really bad, but we survived.
> **Blanca:** How?
> **Pray Tell:** The elders. When the going gets tough, it's up to the elders to light the way.
> **Blanca:** And where are these elders at now?
> **Pray Tell:** You looking at 'em right here.
> **Blanca:** Oh, excuse me? Oh, no, sir. I refuse that title.
> **Pray Tell:** Mm-hmm. Being a survivor is a blessing and a curse. And we're surviving, and we have to help those kids.

At this point, she's about thirty and he's forty-five, but they and the mothers and MC Council are the only community leaders shown. Queer elders are often too young for the responsibility, but no one else is there to intervene. "It's funny; when I was your age, we had lots of older, wiser men to look up to, aspire to. Now we're just an endangered species," Pray Tell observes (2.07). The AIDS crisis has wiped out a generation. Accordingly, Pray and Blanca assign the three lost young people a project: to wrap Blanca's cruel landlord's mansion in a giant condom to spread awareness of AIDS protection. In the process, Elektra gets Lulu a job to help pay for the custom balloon. Pray Tell and Ricky connect, as Pray insists that Ricky get tested and go with him. As they labor, the three are filled with pride and excitement at how well the project works. The young people end the episode by making a family dinner and showing off their new responsibility. However, the same episode sees Pray struggle with a romance with Ricky, something the mothers tell him has an unfair power differential. As he tries to give Ricky everything—nondemanding love, support for having HIV when he has little help himself—he's seen questioning the best way forward. Historically, this was a common struggle. AIDS served as a great impetus to expand found families as sources of support. "Sometimes

7. Return and Acceptance

a family of friends was transformed into a group of caregivers with ties to one another as well as the person with AIDS" (Weston 183).

Pray's grief at watching so many young people die chips away at him, as does his own health. As Pray loses hope in a series of endless funerals, he tells his partners he's done with the ball scene: "Y'all know the balls ain't what they used to be. We've lost too many icons, and ... and all these young kids ain't got no home training. And these cash prizes and these ... tacky lip syncs. I just can't...."

His fellow MC retorts, "The children ... they depend on us, Pray."

But Pray, who's been drinking and falling into despair, tells them, "I know. I know. I'm sorry. I love y'all. I really do. But I don't have anything left to give" ("On the Run" 3.01). Canals explains that they were "hyper-aware" of the greater story around HIV and the sacrifices the community had to make. "We made the decision that Pray Tell would be the character for us to tell that story through. Telling a story of the fullness of what it means to be diagnosed with AIDS to know that you have a finite amount of time left, and then what are the choices that you're going to make moving forward in life" (qtd. in Goldberg n.p.). This is the "queer temporality" discussed by Fisher and colleagues, and many others living at a faster pace with less time than many.

Blanca, meanwhile, gets her calling. Nurse Judy encourages her to enter nursing school because the patients respond so well to her empathy and experience with AIDS. Blanca is surprised: "You know how many times I've sat in these halls over the years? Waiting in fear for a diagnosis? It never crossed my mind that a woman like me could have the answers" ("On the Run" 3.01). At ACT UP, Blanca's fellow members plan to scatter the ashes of their fallen loved ones on the mayor's lawn to protest the government and medical corporations' mistreatment. (This references a real protest in which the ashes were spread on the White House lawn.) As the activist there insists, "Who here thinks that their loved ones would want their ashes to be a part of this history? Guys, we have lost thousands and thousands of people, and they are just sitting ... in urns, inactive. Well, if you ask me, they were revolutionaries who died for a cause. They are calling out, beyond the grave, to be in service. And they want to be active in our final fight" (3.08). Even after they've been lost, the elders defend the dying youth. Other *Pose* moments, like the Gay Men's Chorus wearing black for its overwhelming losses, underscore how the community of elders has been lost.

The series jumps ahead to 1998, carrying everyone through the darkness to an uplifting ending. Blanca has become a nurse and has found a happy relationship. Elektra is a rich philanthropist, Lulu is a tax accountant, and Angel is a stay-at-home mother with modeling gigs. Damon mentors young people by running a dance studio and has been inducting European teens into House Evangelista. Ricky has inherited Pray's legacy as a mentor as the Father of the House of Evangelista, with Blanca as grandmother—truly a grand elder at last. Canals explains that Blanca was always intended as the audience's guide and thus would survive the show. Still, "Blanca was going to have to deal with some form of a loss before being able to get to the other side of everything that we've seen her deal with—poverty, violence, etc." (Goldberg n.p.). Her lessons from all the losses have made her the true elder and guide for the next generation.

As a nurse, she's shown telling a young woman, Safaree, that she's HIV positive, much more gently than some nurses were shown doing on the show. As Blanca adds, bringing in her experience, "When I found out that I was HIV positive, there weren't any drugs that were available. AIDS was a death sentence. But now people are living long and healthy lives, as long as we keep taking our meds and listening to what the doctors say.... I'm proof you are gonna be okay if you follow the protocols" ("Series Finale Part 2" 3.08). She signs the younger woman up for the AIDS Drug Assistance Program, then invites her to a ball where her family dresses her up and inducts her into Evangelista. There, Elektra gives Blanca a special award and salutes her as legendary, explaining, "To be a legend isn't simply about competing and collecting trophies. It's about how you represent this community. And I have seen this woman work tirelessly, not only for family but for all of us." Blanca ends the series by repeating Pray Tell's words to the next mother, who is raising the next group. Pray Tell chimes in beside her, emphasizing the power of legacy:

> BLANCA: You want a reason to continue? It's standing right there in front of you.
> PRAY TELL: There it is, right there.
> BLANCA: Houses are homes to all the little boys and girls who never had one. And they gonna keep coming here to New York City. Sure as the sun rises. So, what you got to do is.... Work harder. Reach higher. And dream big until you...
> PRAY TELL: Triumph. Until you triumph.
> BLANCA: It won't happen today, but one day. And when you do, I'm-a be right in there ... cheering you on ["Series Finale Part 2" 3.08].

The Golden Globe– and Peabody-winning show broke other barriers. Rodriguez made history by becoming the first trans woman to win Best Actress in Television at the 2019 Imagen Awards. The greatest moment of mentorship is what the show provides for the audience, encouraging them to step up and protect those being left behind. In the second season, as the show embraces activism, each episode ends with a quote from a queer elder of color whose legacy paved the way for existing communities.

Repeating their words keeps them alive. Pray Tell's actor Billy Porter concludes that the show truly empowered everyone that participated in it and showed them how to seize the day even when there are no opportunities: "These characters had nothing and they chose life anyway. That is the power of the theme of it that surpasses anything. I have never in my life felt more empowered than I do in this very present moment. My fear of failure is gone; it already happened. I chose myself inside of it and transcended it" (Goldberg n.p.).

The crone, as well as often being a symbolically post-gender figure, often bridges the boundary between life and death, helping people to cross over, sometimes in both directions. This sacred magic appears in stories across cultures but has especial meaning in the context of genocide. Such terrible injustices, usually never made right and sometimes hidden from acknowledgment, finally find voice when they're given a pathway to power. Moray adds: "Be open to their wisdom as it comes through in dreams, in symbols, or in unexpected synchronicities. You will know them by their continued dedication to the work they began while living. As you fine-tune your awareness and attention to the surprising magick of the Mighty Trans Dead, the relationships will deepen" (30). While the ancestors might be lost, one can still feel their supportive presence.

Teaching the Next Generation: The Adventures of Priscilla, Queen of the Desert *(Film)*

The hegemonic hero may rise to become a respected, well-compensated mentor or teacher for a new hero's future adventure. Such positions often come with making a good and stable living and finding respect in the community. For example, in the later seasons of *My Little Pony: Friendship is Magic*, Twilight Sparkle mentors her protégé, Starlight Glimmer, and opens a school. It seems she never had, and still does not have, money or class issues; however, by this point, she is not only a respected educator but has become literal royalty.

For trans characters, this is more complicated. Quite a few take on the role of mentor, even reluctantly, because the notion that with age comes privilege is very much erroneous. For example, Steven of *Steven Universe Future* initially treats patients and mentors Gems new to the planet. After Steven's adventures and trauma, perhaps Steven would have preferred to take the time to be himself to find out what brings him joy and who he is on his own. Indeed, Steven finally decides to step away from activism and explore his own company. In this tradition, Jebi, of Yoon Ha Lee's *Phoenix Extravagant*, helps the people fighting against colonization. However, when the battle is over, Jebi opts out of remaining there as a mentor or fighter. They and their found family leave the planet to live alone on the moon, away from it all. They do continue to help in their way, storing historical artifacts for their people, but they remove themselves from the everyday tasks.

Danielle ends her journey in *Sovereign* deciding to use the money the supervillain gathered to help young people who are like she used to be: "I was thinking we'd put up a free clinic that provides the full range of transition services to anyone who asks. Or a halfway house for queer runaways who need to start a new life away from their family" (Daniels 308). She also wants one of the young superheroes to stay and provide more personal support for them all. Likewise, as London watches children play in *Love and Other Disasters*, London decides that they want to make the world better:

> A summer camp for LGBTQ+ kids. A cooking camp, to be specific. London would find a place in the woods and teach queer and trans and gender nonconforming kids of all ages how to cook.
> Telling marginalized kids that they were loved, that it would get better, was all well and good, but it didn't necessarily change their realities. Giving people a skill, on the other hand, making them feel like they were good at something, was useful and empowering.
> That was what their nonprofit would be [Kelly 292].

Often, even well-intentioned cis people are not equipped to be mentors. Other times, mentorship is put in the hands of kind-hearted trans people who may not be quite resourced and prepared to handle it. This reflects a problematic, if often desperate, notion in the trans community that anyone at all older is responsible for taking on mentor or parental roles. This is perhaps based on notions such as that of the privileged "it gets better" campaign of the 2010s. These promote the fanciful hope that one becomes upwardly mobile simply because of older age. However, as repeatedly demonstrated by research (Harless n.p.), this does not reflect the reality of trans people, particularly not women, genderqueer, and those marginalized beyond being trans. Indeed, one might suggest that young and more privileged people should give support to those who suffered longer and, at times, more severe oppression fighting for rights. Despite hopeful or irresponsible notions, such experiences often result in neurodivergence (Towns 16). Being marginalized further for this often means even less privilege, fewer resources, and less energy to provide any care.

There are fewer potential mentors because some trans people who would have been older don't make it to that age. Another representation nearly absent from literature and awareness are late-blooming transgender people and people outside of the binary. They, as well as other trans people, are only now finding out who they are and are not in a position to be required to mentor others.

One aspect of this is that care work falls to those most marginalized, and they are less likely to receive appreciation for it. An example appears in *The Adventures of Priscilla, Queen of the Desert*. Bernadette is one of three performers taking a road trip through Australia to a series of shows. She is the only trans woman in the group, along with Adam and Mitzi (Tick), who are gender-nonconforming queer men. Her queerness and femininity, honed for longer than those of her companions, set her up as a role model and mentor. "Perhaps it is because Bernadette has had to fight so hard and for so long to secure her female gender identity, both physiologically and in the eyes of society, that she appears the height of composed femininity" (Challinor 24). Without question, this struggle has toughened her into a protective warrior.

Bernadette is the oldest of the three, hardened yet kinder, from a life of dealing with transphobia. As the mentor, she teaches the others how to avoid paying for alcohol, but this playful moment is far from all she teaches them. The three stand out for their outsider status in most scenes. As such, they need one another for protection and care, especially in the wilderness: "Visually and spatially they are confined to interiors: clubs, dressing rooms, a telephone box, and domestic spaces in inner city Sydney. ... Similarly, the transgendered figure also hovers at the threshold between a series of opposites, blurring borders and destabilizing the boundaries between self and other" (K. Brooks 86).

When Bernadette, Adam, and Mitzi team up, the story emphasizes their partnership as a source of support as well as the interior and exterior journeys each of them embarks on. All have struggled to gain acceptance from peers, family, and society, as numerous flashbacks reveal. All offer reassurance here as well as camaraderie. "Tick turns to Bernadette as a mentor-figure as he struggles with his uncertainty over taking on the role of a husband once more" (Challinor 23–24). She tells Tick, "You're the world's best husband and given the chance you'd probably be a perfectly good father too." This is his arc, heading toward taking on that role. Thus, his journey into the wilderness suggests a fleeing of responsibility, until Bernadette can help reassure him and strengthen his resolve. This also connects with her own lost chances, letting her live through Tick with sympathy and humor, if not through her own experiences:

> TICK: Ever wanted kids?
> BERNADETTE: Sure, but I've learned not to think about it.
> TICK: Do you think an old queen's capable of raising a child?
> BERNADETTE: Well, Elizabeth did a pretty good job. Prince Charles is a wonderful boy.

The bus they are driving breaks down, emphasizing how much they are all symbolically lost in the wilderness, now made literal as well. Three separate camera shots emphasize the overpowering size of the Australian outback, which threatens to devour them all. They curse loudly as they discover the homophobic slur "AIDS fuckers go home" marking their vehicle.

> As socially abject subjects Tick, Adam, and Bernadette refuse the forces, metonymically represented by the landscape, which seek to contain them within a binary frame. Instead of remaining static and having their identities defined or elided or misled by the hostile landscape, they embrace dynamism and movement and thus earn, however briefly, legitimacy [K. Brooks 86].

Celebrating their nonconformity, Adam paints the bus lavender, while Tick dresses in a lurid outfit of scaly green and dances, standing out against the dull landscape as glowing and bright. As they travel through the landscape, "their constant movement opens up a space where nature/culture, man/woman, male/female, animal/human are blurred" (K. Brooks 86). Bernadette, who has fought society the longest and made the most profound change, stands out as a guide here in her bright white gown, as well as a beacon of hope, comfort, and civilization against the encroaching hostile wilderness.

Next, the three end up in a small town. Bernadette and Mitzi have a quiet dinner, while Adam defiantly goes to the video rental store. A man hits on him there, and he agrees to let him show him around town. However, when he and his friends realize he is queer, the fun evening turns into physical assault and attempted group rape.

While Bob, the local straight man, tries ineffectually to rescue Adam from the mob, Bernadette unleashes her rage and her self-assured power: She tells the biggest aggressor, "Oh stop flexing your muscles you big fucking pile of budgie turd! I'm sure your mates would be much more impressed if you just went back to the pub and fucked a couple of pigs on the bar." She knees him in the groin, and he collapses. She has taken back all the power with a "There, now you're fucked," which ironically fulfills and exceeds his brutish demand for sex by besting him physically.

After Bernadette has rescued him, Adam views her with more respect, moving beyond his juvenile antagonism to acknowledge the wisdom and strength she offers. She then comforts a sobbing Adam in their motel room, softly musing,

> It's funny. We all sit around mindlessly slagging off that vile stinkhole of a city. But in its own strange way, it takes care of us. I don't know if that ugly wall of suburbia's been put there to stop them getting in or us getting out. Come on. Don't let it drag you down. Let it toughen you up. I can only fight because I've learnt to. Being a man one day and a woman the next isn't an easy thing to do.

Bernadette is there for Adam because someone has to be. She knows what it's like to experience such things alone. Their relationship is complex and jagged; earlier in the film, he antagonizes and deadnames her, picking on her as the most feminine of their group. "Adam's irrepressible love of the dramatic, his juvenile attitude, and his obnoxious behavior regularly push the limits of Bernadette's patience" (Challinor 24). Moreover, he's using social power to harm those more marginalized. Still, Bernadette helps him without enjoying the status that comes with mentoring, for characters who already have more privilege.

As Leetal discusses in zir work on trans care (under review), trans characters are repeatedly put in the role of caretaker. When trans characters are cared for, the responsibility often falls onto more marginalized trans characters. As Malatino discusses in *Trans Care*, "Transing care also means grappling with the fact that the forms of family and kinship that are invoked in much of the feminist literature on care labor and care ethics are steeped in forms of domesticity and intimacy that are both White and Eurocentered, grounded in the colonial/modern gender system" (7). As Eden Kinkade adds in a review of Malatino's work,

> A concept of trans care, then, would need to extend beyond and unsettle a feminist care ethic, while remaining attentive to how gendered, racialized, and classed structures and norms configure care differently for a diversity of trans subjects. Reworking this concept of care might then be a step toward both recognizing and naming the failures of care that result in transphobic discrimination and violence while also fostering the kinds of relations that enable the survival and flourishing of trans [407].

Defending and comforting Adam with trash talk, with physical violence, with protection and commiseration stretches across these roles while acknowledging their position in a hostile system.

For Tick, the story has a happy ending: throughout their journey, Tick worries that his wife and son will reject him for being a drag queen. However, he is delightfully surprised when his son Benji is fully supportive. "The compassion and uncompromising acceptance from his son reassures Tick that he can be a father, without having to give up his lifestyle or hide who he is" (Challinor 25). In a similar happy ending, Bernadette remains in Alice Springs with her new man, Bob, while the others return to Sydney. After their wild adventure, Bernadette and Tick have each found domesticity in civilization, while Adam has healed his willful anger. Bernadette's mentoring of the next generation has helped all three find peace.

The adult questor's desperation to protect the younger ally is psychologically meaningful because this figure represents the inner child—the youthful part of the self sacrificed by society. This figure is often seen as one of the inner voices of an older questor, especially one who has reached the age of elder. In *Seven Suspects*, Bobbi thinks of teen Roberta while looking around her lovely bedroom: "I try not to push my issues on her, but truthfully, I experience these things with her as if I'm finally living the childhood I never had, the one where I was a girl with long hair and pretty dresses and slept in a cozy cotton nighty and was doted on by parents who loved me and thought I was cute" (16). Their special thing is Bobbi doing her hair and makeup. As Bobbi investigates a stalker, she spends extra effort keeping Roberta safe, not only from the criminal but even from the details. Roberta's innocence is precious to her too, and she's desperate to keep her safe. When her friend starts saying nasty things about her trans aunt, Bobbi is crushed once more. "My heart is in my throat. I don't want her to see me as a blight on her life. This was supposed to happen in junior high, with the advent of puberty and social errors. I've been through the ridicule and stigmatizing a million times, so I shouldn't feel so crushed but I love this little girl more than life itself" (26). She represents Bobbi's vulnerable, sweet side, desperate for protection.

In episode one of *Hit & Miss*, after finding she's been left in custody of her lover's four children, assassin Mia hesitates to kill. "Has he got any kids?" she asks of her next job. Her boss observes that parenthood changes people. When she hears there's no money to pay the bills, however, she does the job. Ryan, her own son, is named for her deadname. "Mum named me after you?" "Maybe. I hope so" (1.01). When she sees him, she channels her own childhood vulnerability and wants to adopt them all. She teaches him to defeat the local bully, and they end the episode tangling with him and his mean-spirited dad. When she's at her lowest point after her childhood tormentor has found her, Ryan beats in her door to bring Mia her boyfriend and to remind her of family responsibilities. Ryan also calls Mia "Dad" for the first time (1.06). She smiles and hugs him. At the end of the series, he also saves her, like a guardian spirit. Parenting, in all sorts of combinations and relationships, provides two-way comfort and fulfillment in the emerging family.

Final Thoughts

The past handful of years have seen a dangerous amount of backlash and hate aimed at transgender people. From hundreds of bills aimed at basically every aspect of the existence of trans and otherwise non-binary people to anti-trans activists like J.K. Rowling working to exclude transgender assault survivors from care or ban ordinary people from bathrooms, conditions have been increasingly grim.

> The transgender revolution still has a long way to go. Trans people are significantly more likely to be impoverished, unemployed and suicidal than other Americans. They represent a sliver of the population—an estimated 0.5%—which can make it harder for them to gain acceptance. In a recent survey conducted by the Public Religion Research Institute, 65% of Americans said they have a close friend or family member who is homosexual, while 9% said they have one who is transgender. And as the trans movement has gained momentum, opponents have been drawn in to fight, many of them social conservatives who cut their teeth and fattened their mailing lists opposing same-sex marriage. But perhaps the biggest obstacle is that trans people live in a world largely built on a fixed and binary definition of gender. In many places, they are unwelcome in the men's bathroom and the women's. The effect is a constant reminder that they don't belong [Steinmetz n.p.].

According to the 2011 National Transgender Discrimination Survey, nearly 80 percent of young trans people have experienced harassment at school, 90 percent of employees have faced it at work. Nearly 20 percent said they had been denied a place to live, and almost 50 percent said they had been fired, not hired, or denied a promotion because of their gender status. A chilling 41 percent have attempted suicide, compared with 1.6 percent of the general population (Steinmetz n.p.). Clearly, the battle for equality and respect has much further to go.

At times such as these, many trans and otherwise non-binary people have been forced to take up the mantle of being heroes. One hopes there will soon no longer be a need for such champions who suffer to protect themselves and their society. We hope for a world where trans and otherwise non-binary heroes can live plots about baking, not fighting for survival. Since that is not the world we live in, we hope trans and otherwise non-binary people find interest and validation in this book. Surviving as a non-binary or otherwise trans person is revolutionary, particularly for multiply marginalized people, such as BIPOC, disabled, overweight, old, or very young people. Your joy is subversive. Your being here makes the whole world better. We thank you for it.

Currently, the rise in stories with trans characters is creating many new texts to analyze alongside the older classics. "We are in a place now," Laverne Cox observes, "where more and more trans people want to come forward and say, 'This is who I am.' And more trans people are willing to tell their stories. More of us are living visibly and pursuing our dreams visibly, so people can say, 'Oh yeah, I know someone who is trans.' When people have points of reference that are humanizing, that demystifies difference" (qtd. in Steinmetz n.p.). Already, fiction is offering a dazzling spectrum of representation and bringing forward inspiring heroes of all types. Many readers, especially kids and teens, are finding representation. Further, as Cox adds, "seeing trans people loved, uplifted, and well regarded in film and television can endear you to step in when you see a trans person being harassed on the street, and to make sure the trans people in your life are supported in ways that affirm their humanity" (*Disclosure*). As to how such fiction should progress, J. Skyler responds:

> Having cisgender creative teams actually do their research prior to publishing a story is essential and having publishers hire trans people to create and develop trans characters is paramount. It is so much more logical to entrust these stories to writers and artists who have the lived experience—who can craft realistic portrayals of transgender individuals inspired by their own personal journeys—rather than wholly depending on cisgender men and women to hopefully get it right, only to lament when they don't. I must also reiterate, placing all of your eggs in one basket with a single trans character is futile. There should be multiple transgender characters with differing points of view (race, class, disability, religion, orientation) at the forefront of multiple books. Otherwise, discussions like this will simply be recycled as time goes on ["Trans Representations"].

Glossary

affect: the sense of impulse that is intuitive, often physical, before it is put into words as an emotion. See the work of Joshua Javier Guzmán.

AIDS/HIV: a disease that literally decimated the American gay and trans community (and elsewhere) between 1987 and 1998, while the government did strikingly little to intervene. There are better treatments now, but no cure.

ally: a person who supports a marginalized group, educates oneself about how to do it respectfully, and does so on the group's terms.

aromantic, aro: a person who identifies as having little or no romantic feeling.

asexual, ace: a person who identifies as not feeling sexual attraction.

assigned at birth: when most people are born, they are assigned a gender on their birth certificate, socially, and so on. This assignment is generally a hit-or-miss practice, which may be incorrect and harmful. Some people may refer to the gender they were arbitrarily assigned at birth versus their real gender.

BDSM: a term used to describe aspects of sex or other consensual exchanges that involve dominance, submission, and control. The acronym stands for bondage and discipline, domination and submission, sadism and masochism.

binarism: hate or harm against those outside of the gender binary.

binder: a clothing item worn to make one's chest flatter.

BIPOC: Black, Indigenous, and People of Color (used to refer to members of non-white communities).

bisexual, pansexual, polysexual, pan, or poly: attracted to multiple genders.

butch: a queer person who presents masculine and identifies as butch.

cis, cisgender: a person who is comfortable with the gender they were assigned at birth.

closeted, in the closet: a term used to refer to people who have not revealed their sexual or gender identity/identities either to themselves or others.

cross-dressing/drag: when people try on gender expressions (ways of dressing, hairstyling, etc.) often different from the one they live in—as art, for fun, to make a point about gender, etc.

deadname: (noun) a name someone used in the past that is misaligned with one's gender in the present. (verb) to use that name, usually causing harm.

demigirl, demi: demigirl means being somewhat girl (or woman), but not entirely or exactly. Demiboy and demi are used similarly.

dysphoria: a sense of discomfort or suffering that may come from incongruity or invalidation of one's gender.

egg: a trans person who does not know they are trans yet. (cracking one's egg: bringing on one's realization that they're trans.)

elder: a person, in this context queer or trans, who is more experienced and is able to guide people new to the trans/queer experience.

euphoria, gender euphoria: a sense of peace or delight that may come from validation of one's gender.

femme: a queer person who presents feminine and identifies as femme.

fluid, genderfluid: moving between genders. a type of gender(s) outside the binary.

found family: a family one chooses, and develops relationships with, rather than a family one is born into.

heteronormative, cisheteronormative: supporting or being an uncritical part of the system that privileges straight and cisgender people.

Indigiqueer, Two-Spirit: LGBTQ+ Indigenous people might identify as either or both, emphasizing that their cultural history differs from the Western model.

intersex: a general term used for a variety of conditions in which a person is born with a reproductive or sexual anatomy that appears outside the typical definitions of female or male.

LGBTQ+: lesbian, gay, bi, trans, queer, genderqueer, pan, poly, asexual, ace, aromantic, aro, and other queer identities. Some intersex, Indigiqueer, and others may choose to identify using this, and it is theirs to use but not mandatory to them.

misgendering: treating one as a gender they are not, often through the use of pronouns.

non-binary, genderqueer: a person who isn't 100 percent and consistently a man or a woman. For example, a person who has more than one gender, no gender, a gender different from male or female, etc. It should be noted that some people who fit this definition do not identify using these words and therefore are not genderqueer or non-binary.

non-binary trans: a term sometimes used to clarify that a person or character is both trans and non-binary. While non-binary people belong under the trans umbrella (unless they wish to identify otherwise), there is still sometimes bigotry against this inclusion. This term is sometimes used as shorthand to sidestep any questions.

privilege: an immunity or right granted to particular groups. The attributes of the privileged group are treated as societal norms—others are judged against their standards.

pronouns, neopronouns: a linguistic form referring to someone or something, such as *I, you,* and *it.* Some transgender people use less-common pronouns such as singular *they* or newer (neo) pronouns such as *zir*, because pronouns are often gendered (*she, he*), and most people prefer to be addressed in ways that respect their genders. Some people use gender-neutral pronouns, such as *ze/hir/hirs, zie/zir/zirs, ey/em/eirs, per/per/pers, hu/hum/hus,* or *they/them/theirs*. Some people use no pronouns at all and may only use their first name or the first letter of their first name. Introducing oneself with pronouns emphasizes a desire to not assume the gender of another person but to let them introduce themselves as using she, he, they, etc.

queer: lesbian, gay, bi, trans, queer, genderqueer, pan, poly, asexual, ace, aromantic, aro, and other LGBT+ identities. Some intersex, Indigiqueer, and others may choose to identify using this, and it is theirs to use but not mandatory to them. Unlike *LGBT+, queer* implies breaking society's heterosexual norms and resisting assimilation. For more in-depth discussion, see Heather K. Love's work on the topic.

questioning: in the process of understanding and exploring what their sexual orientation and/or gender identity and gender expression might be.

sexual orientation: describes who one is attracted to; different from gender identity; who one is.

stealth: living without sharing that one is trans.

TERF: an acronym for transgender-excluding radical feminism. A name taken by a type of second wave (so named) feminist who opposes transgender people. A common form of transphobia.

trans, transgender: a person who was assigned a wrong or inaccurate gender at birth.

transition: choosing to declare oneself and live as a particular gender or as genderfluid. This does not necessarily involve medical intervention.

transphobia, transmisia: hatred of trans people, practices, communities, rights.

Resources

Texts for Beginners

Brill, Stephanie, and Rachel Pepper. *The Transgender Child: A Handbook for Families and Professionals.* Cleis Press, 2008.
Ehrensaft, Diane, PhD. *Gender Born, Gender Made: Raising Healthy Gender-Nonconforming Children.* The Experiment, 2011.
———. *The Gender Creative Child: Pathways for Nurturing and Supporting Children Who Live Outside Gender Boxes.* The Experiment, 2016.
Erickson-Schroth, Laura. *"You're in the Wrong Bathroom!" and 20 Other Myths and Misconceptions About Transgender and Gender-Nonconforming People.* Beacon Press, 2017.
Gender Spectrum. genderspectrum.org.
Getty, Stuart. *How to They/Them: A Visual Guide to Nonbinary Pronouns and the World of Gender Fluidity.* Sasquatch Books, 2020.
GLSEN. https://www.glsen.org/activity/glsen-safe-space-kit-solidarity-lgbtq-youth.
Haefele-Thomas, Ardel. *Introduction to Transgender Studies.* Harrington Park Press, 2019.
Malatino, Hil. *Queer Embodiment: Monstrosity, Medical Violence, and Intersex Experience.* University of Nebraska Press, 2019.
———. *Trans Care.* University of Minnesota Press, 2020.
Naidoo, Jamie Campbell. *Rainbow Family Collections: Selecting and Using Children's Books with Lesbian, Gay, Bisexual, Transgender, and Queer Content.* Libraries Unlimited, 2012.
Nanda, Serena. *Gender Diversity: Crosscultural Variations.* Waveland Press, 2014.
National Center for Transgender Equality. transequality.org/issues/families.
Santos, Rita. *Beyond Gender Binaries: The History of Trans, Intersex, and Third-Gender Individuals.* Rosen Publishing, 2019.
Stryker, Susan. *Transgender History.* Seal Press, 2017.
Travers, Ann. *The Trans Generation: How Trans Kids (and Their Parents) Are Creating a Gender Revolution.* New York University Press, 2018.

Anthologies and Collections

Anders, Charlie Jane. *Even Greater Mistakes.* Tor, 2021.
———. *Six Months, Three Days, Five Others.* Tor, 2017.
Barzak, Christopher, and Liz Gorinsky, editors. *Queers Destroy Fantasy! Special Issue. Fantasy Magazine*, no. 59, Dec. 2015.
Benaway, Gwen, editor. *Maiden, Mother, Crone: Fantastical Trans Femmes.* Bedside, 2019.
Buchanan, Andi C., and Lauren E. Mitchell, editors. *Capricious, Issue 9: Gender Diverse Pronouns.* Createspace, 2018.
Clark, C.L., and Neon Hemlock, editors. *We're Here: The Best Queer Speculative Fiction 2021.* Hemlock Press, 2022.
Driskill, Qwo-Li, editor. *Sovereign Erotics: A Collection of Two-Spirit Literature.* University of Arizona Press, 2011.

197

Fitzpatrick, Cat, and Casey Plett, editors. *Meanwhile, Elsewhere: Science Fiction and Fantasy from Transgender Writers*. Topside Press, 2017.

Gil, Joamette, editor. *Heartwood: Nonbinary Tales of Sylvan Fantasy*. P&M Press, 2019.

Griffith, Nicola, and Stephen Pagel, editors. *Bending the Landscape: Science Fiction*. Overlook Press, 1998.

Guran, Paula, editor. *Far Out: Recent Queer Science Fiction and Fantasy*. Nightshade, 2021.

Jones, Michael M., editor. *Scheherazade's Facade: Fantastical Tales of Gender Bending, Cross-Dressing, and Transformation*. Circlet Press, 2012.

Kehrli, Keffy R.M., editor. *GlitterShip* Year 1 and Year 2. GlitterShip, 2017–2018.

LaValle, Victor, and John Joseph Adams, editors. *A People's Future of the United States*. Random House, 2019.

Lemberg, R.B. *Geometries of Belonging*. Fairwood Press, 2022.

Mandelo, Brit. *Beyond Binary: Genderqueer and Sexually Fluid Speculative Fiction*. Lethe Press, 2012.

McGuire, Seanan, editor. *Queers Destroy Science Fiction! Special Issue. Lightspeed*, no. 61, June 2015.

Monster, Sfé R., editor. *Beyond: The Queer Sci-Fi & Fantasy Comic Anthology*. Beyond Press, 2015.

Nicholson, Hope, editor. *Love Beyond Body, Space, and Time: An Indigenous LGBT Sci-Fi Anthology*. Bedside Press, 2016.

Oliveira, Isabela, and Jed Sabin, editors. *It Gets Even Better: Stories of Queer Possibility*. Speculatively Queer, 2021.

Plett, Casey. *A Dream of a Woman*. Arsenal Pulp Press, 2021.

———. *A Safe Girl to Love*. Topside Press, 2014.

Rogue, Lydia, editor. *Trans-Galactic Bike Ride: Feminist Bicycle Science Fiction Stories of Transgender and Nonbinary Adventurers*. Elly Blue Publishing, 2020.

Szpara, K.M., editor. *Transcendent*. Lethe Press, 2016.

Takács, Bogi. *The Trans Space Octopus Congregation*. Lethe Press, 2019.

Takács, Bogi, editor. *Transcendent 2*. Lethe Press, 2017.

———. *Transcendent 3*. Lethe Press, 2018.

———. *Transcendent 4*. Lethe Press, 2019.

Wagner, Wendy N., editor. *Queers Destroy Horror! Special Issue. Nightmare Magazine*, no. 37, October 2015.

Whitehead, Joshua, editor. *Love after the End: An Anthology of Two-Spirit & Indigiqueer Speculative Fiction*. Arsenal Pulp Press, 2020.

Children's Picture Books

Baldacchino, Christine, and Isabelle Malenfant. *Morris Micklewhite and the Tangerine Dress*. Groundwood Books, 2014.

Cart, Jennifer, and Ben Rumback. *Be Who You Are!* AuthorHouse, 2010.

Ewert, Marcus, and Rex Ray. *10,000 Dresses*. Triangle Square, 2008.

Fierstein, Harvey, and Henry Cole. *The Sissy Duckling*. Simon & Schuster, 2005.

Ford, JR, and Vanessa Ford. *Calvin*. Illustrated by Kayla Harren. G.P. Putnam, 2021.

Gonzalez, Maya Christina, and Matthew SG. *They, She, He: Easy as ABC*. Reflection Press, 2019.

Hall, Michael. *Red: A Crayon's Story*. Greenwillow Books, 2015.

Herthel, Jessica, and Jazz Jennings. *I Am Jazz*. Dial Books, 2014.

Hoffman, Sarah, and Ian Hoffman. *Jacob's New Dress*. Illustrated by Chris Case. Albert Whitman & Co. 2014.

Kilodavis, Cheryl, and Suzanne DeSimone. *My Princess Boy*. Aladdin, 2010.

Love, Jessica. *Julián Is a Mermaid*. Candlewick, 2018.

Lukoff, Kyle, and Kaylani Juanita. *When Aidan Became a Brother*. Lee & Low Books, 2019.

Lukoff, Kyle, and Luciano Lozano. *Max and the Talent Show*. Reycraft Books, 2019.

Lyons, Maddox, and Jessica Verdi. *I'm Not a Girl*. Illustrated by Dana Simpson. Roaring Brook Press, 2020.

Neal, Trinity, and Art Twink. *My Rainbow*. Kokila, 2020.

Newman, Lesléa, and Maria Mola. *Sparkle Boy*. Lee & Low Books, 2017.

Patterson, Jodie, and Charnelle Pinkney Barlow. *Born Ready: The True Story of a Boy Named Penelope*. Crown Books, 2021.

Pessin-Whedbee, Brook, and Naomi Bardoff. *Who Are You? The Kid's Guide to Gender Identity*. Jessica Kingsley Publishers, 2016.

Pitman, Gayle E., and Violet Tobacco. *My Maddy*. Magination Press, 2020.

Rhodes-Courter, Ashley, and MacKenzie Haley. *Sam Is My Sister*. Albert Whitman & Co., 2021.

Savage, Sarah, and Joules Garcia. *She's My Dad! A Story for Children Who Have a Transgender Parent or Relative*. Jessica Kingsley, 2020.

Silverman, Erica, and Holly Hatam. *Jack (Not Jackie)*. Little Bee, 2018.

Thom, Kai Cheng, and Kai Yun Ching. *From the Stars in the Sky to the Fish in the Sea*. Illustrated by Wai-Yant Li. Arsenal Pulp Press, 2017.

Thorn, Theresa, and Noah Grigni. *It Feels Good to Be Yourself: A Book about Gender Identity*. Henry Holt, 2019.

Children's Middle Grade Fiction

Beam, Chris. *I Am J*. Little, Brown, 2011.

Bunker, Lisa. *Zenobia July*. Viking, 2019.

Clarke, Cat. *The Pants Project*. Sourcebooks, 2017.

Darling, Abbey, and Amy Eleanor Heart, editors. *99% Chance of Magic: Stories of Strength and Hope for Transgender Kids and Other Humans*. Heartspark Press, 2020.

Gephart, Donna. *Lily and Dunkin*. Penguin, 2016.

Gino, Alex. *George*. Scholastic, 2015.

Hennessey, M.G. *The Other Boy*. Harper, 2016.

Leali, Michael. *The Civil War of Amos Abernathy*. Harper, 2022.

Lee, Yoon Ha. *Tiger Honor*. Disney Hyperion, 2022.

Locke, Katherine, and Nicole Melleby. *This Is Our Rainbow: 16 Stories of Her, Him, Them, and Us*. Knopf, 2021.

Lukoff, Kyle. *Different Kinds of Fruit*. Dial, 2022.

———. *Too Bright to See*. Dial, 2021.

Moser, Rabbi Leiah. *Magical Princess Harriet: Chessed: World of Compassion*. Dag Gadol, 2018.

O'Neill, Kay. *The Tea Dragon Festival*. Oni Press, 2019. (Graphic Novel Series)

Polonsky, Ami. *Gracefully Grayson*. Hyperion, 2014.

Riley, Ronnie. *Jude Saves the World*. Scholastic, 2023.

Riordan, Rick. *The Hammer of Thor*. Hyperion, 2016.

Salazar, Aida. *The Moon Within*. Arthur A. Levine, 2019.

Shappley, Kai, and Lisa Bunker. *Joy to the World*. Clarion Books, 2023.

Symes-Smith, Esme. *Sir Callie and the Champions of Helston*. Labyrinth Road, 2022.

Wang, Jen. *The Prince and the Dressmaker*. First Second, 2018. (Graphic Novel)

Wittlinger, Ellen. *Parrotfish*. Simon & Schuster, 2007.

Young Adult/Teen Novels

Anders, Charlie Jane. *Dreams Bigger Than Heartbreak*. Tor Teen, 2022.

———. *Promises Stronger Than Darkness*. Tor Teen, 2023.

———. *Victories Greater Than Death*. Tor Teen, 2021.

Axelrod, Jadzia. *Galaxy: The Prettiest Star*. DC Comics, 2022. (Graphic Novel)

Brewer, Z. *Into the Real*. Quilltree, 2020.

Callender, Kacen. *Felix Ever After*. HarperCollins, 2020.

———. *Lark & Kasim Start a Revolution*. Amulet Books, 2022.
Capetta, Amy Rose. *The Brilliant Death*. Viking, 2018.
———. *The Storm of Life*. Viking, 2020.
Capetta, A.R. *The Heartbreak Bakery*. Candlewick Press, 2021.
Constantine, Alysia, editor. *Short Stuff: A Young Adult LGBTQ+ Anthology*. Interlude, 2020.
Daniels, April. *Dreadnought*. Diversion Publishing, 2017.
———. *Sovereign*. Diversion Publishing, 2017.
Davis, G. Haron. *Transmogrify! 14 Fantastical Tales of Trans Magic*. HarperTeen, 2023.
Devine, Eric. *Look Past*. RP Teens, 2016.
Edgmon, H.E. *The Fae Keeper*. Inkyard Press, 2022.
———. *The Witch King*. Inkyard Press, 2021.
Ellor, ZR. *May the Best Man Win*. Roaring Brook, 2021.
Emezi, Akwaeke. *Pet*. Make Me a World, 2019.
Fitzsimmons, Isaac. *The Passing Playbook*. Dial Books, 2021.
Gillman, Melanie. *Stage Dreams*. Lerner, 2019. (Graphic Novel)
Glass, Joe. *The Pride Omnibus*. Dark Horse Books, 2021. (Graphic Novel)
Gow, Robin. *A Million Quiet Revolutions*. Farrar, Straus and Giroux, 2022.
Hartman, Rachel. *In the Serpent's Wake*. Random House, 2022.
———. *Tess of the Road*. Random House, 2018.
The Kao. *Magical Boy Vol. 1*. Graphix, 2021. (Graphic Novel)
———. *Magical Boy Vol. 2*. Graphix, 2022. (Graphic Novel)
Katcher, Brian. *Almost Perfect*. Delacorte, 2009.
Lam, Laura. *Pantomime*. Pan Books, 2016.
Lee, C.B. *Not Your Villain*. Duet Books, 2017.
Lee, Emery. *Meet Cute Diary*. HarperCollins, 2021.
MacGregor, Maya. *The Many Half-Lived Lives of Sam Sylvester*. Astra, 2022.
McLemore, Anna-Marie. *Blanca & Roja*. Feiwel and Friends, 2018.
———. *Lakelore*. Feiwel and Friends, 2022.
———. *Self-Made Boys: A Great Gatsby Remix*. Feiwel and Friends, 2022.
———. *Venom & Vow*. Feiwel and Friends, 2023.
McSmith, Tobly. *Act Cool*. Quill Tree Books, 2021.
———. *Stay Gold*. HarperTeen, 2020.
Mitchell, Saundra, editor. *All Out: The No-Longer-Secret Stories of Queer Teens Throughout the Ages*. Inkyard, 2020.
———. *Out Now: Queer We Go Again!* Inkyard, 2020.
———. *Out There: Into the Queer New Yonder*. Inkyard, 2022.
Novoa, Gabe Cole. *The Wicked Bargain*. Random House, 2023.
Russo, Meredith. *If I Was Your Girl*. Flatiron Books, 2016.
Salvatore, Steven. *And They Lived*. Bloomsbury, 2022.
Schmatz, Pat. *Lizard Radio*. Candlewick Press, 2015.
Steele, Hamish. *DeadEndia: The Watcher's Test*. Nobrow, 2018. (Graphic Novel)
Stevenson, Noelle. *Nimona*. HarperTeen, 2015. (Graphic Novel)
Stoeve, Ray. *Between Perfect and Real*. Amulet Books, 2021.
Thomas, Aiden. *Cemetery Boys*. Swoon Reads, 2020.
———. *The Sunbearer Trials*. Feiwel & Friends, 2022.
Thomas, Leah. *Violet Ghosts*. Bloomsbury, 2021.
Van Otterloo, Ash. *The Beautiful Something Else*. Scholastic, 2023.
Vaughan, Brian K., et al. *Runaways: Escape to New York*. 2006. Marvel, 2017. (Graphic Novel)
Walker, Suzanne, and Wendy Xu. *Mooncakes*. Oni Press, 2019. (Graphic Novel)
Whitby, S.J. *Cute Mutants Vol 1: Mutant Pride*. 2020. (Graphic Novel)
White, Andrew Joseph. *Hell Followed with Us*. Peachtree Teen, 2022.
Williams, Stephanie, et al. *Nubia & the Amazons*. DC Comics, 2022. (Graphic Novel)

Works Cited

Primary Sources

The Adventures of Priscilla, Queen of the Desert. Directed by Stephan Elliott, PolyGram Filmed Entertainment, 1994.
Anders, Charlie Jane. "Don't Press Charges and I Won't Sue." *Far Out: Recent Queer Science Fiction and Fantasy*, edited by Paula Guran, Nightshade, 2021, pp. 255–272.
———. "The Visitmothers." *Trans-Galactic Bike Ride: Feminist Bicycle Science Fiction Stories of Transgender and Nonbinary Adventurers*, edited Lydia Rogue, Elly Blue Publishing, 2020, pp. 89–94.
Anders, Charlie Jane, et al. "Permanent Sleepover." *Marvel Voices Pride #2*. Marvel, 2023.
Aoki, Ryka. *Light from Uncommon Stars*. Tor, 2021.
Baudreau, Jenn. *Return of the Dragon Guard*. Kindle Scribe, 2019.
Beam, Chris. *I Am J*. Little, Brown, 2011.
Bemis, Kylie Ariel. "Dreamborn." *Maiden, Mother, Crone: Fantastical Trans Femmes*, edited by Gwen Benaway, Bedside, 2019, pp. 108–126.
Binnie, Imogen. *Nevada*. Farrar, Straus and Giroux, 2022.
Boy Meets Girl. Directed by Eric Schaeffer. Wolfe, 2014.
Bunker, Lisa. *Zenobia July*. Viking, 2019.
Burt, Stephanie, and Rachel Gold. "Battlement of Straw," *Decoded Pride #1: Special EBook Edition*, edited by Sara Century and S.E. Fleenor, Decoded Pride, 2020.
Callender, Kacen. *Felix Ever After*. HarperCollins, 2020.
Capetta, Amy Rose. *The Brilliant Death*. Viking, 2018.
———. *The Storm of Life*. Viking, 2020.
Capetta, A.R. *The Heartbreak Bakery*. Candlewick Press, 2021.
Carriger, Gail. *Defy or Defend*. Gail Carriger LLC, 2020.
Chambers, Becky. *A Psalm for the Wild-Built*. Tor, 2021.
Chant, Austin. *Peter Darling*. Less Than Three Press, 2017.
Charmed. Created by Jennie Snyder Urman et al., Poppy Productions, 2018–2022.
Cipri, Nino. "The Shape of My Name." *Far Out: Recent Queer Science Fiction and Fantasy*, edited by Paula Guran, Nightshade, 2021, pp. 173–188.
Clare, Cassandra. *Lord of Shadows*. McElderry Books, 2017.
———. *Queen of Air and Darkness*. McElderry Books, 2018.
Cowboys. Directed by Anna Kerrigan, Limelight, 2021.
Daniels, April. *Dreadnought*. Diversion Publishing, 2017.
———. *Sovereign*. Diversion Publishing, 2017.
"The Dark in The Dark." *The Watch*, written by Simon Allen & Amrou Al-Kadhi, directed by Emma Sullivan, season 1, episode 6, BBC, 2021.
Dead End: Paranormal Park. Created by Hamish Steele, Netflix, 2022.
Deaver, Mason. "Genderella." *Transmogrify! 14 Fantastical Tales of Trans Magic*, edited by G. Haron Davis, HarperTeen, 2023, pp. 239–270.

dePackh, Selene. "In Her Mind's Eye." *Recognize Fascism: A Science Fiction and Fantasy Anthology*, edited by Crystal M. Huff, World Weaver Press, 2020, pp. 160–174.
Devine, Eric. *Look Past*. RP Teens, 2016.
"The Doctor Falls," *Doctor Who*, directed by Rachel Talalay, written by Steven Moffat, season 10, episode 12, BBC One, July 1, 2017.
Doom Patrol. Created by Jeremy Carver, Berlanti Productions, 2019–.
Edgmon, H.E. *The Fae Keeper*. Inkyard Press, 2022.
———. *The Witch King*. Inkyard Press, 2021.
"Elliot." *Two Sentence Horror Stories*, written by Stephanie Adams-Santos, directed by Chase Joynt, season 3, episode 2, The CW, 2021.
Emezi, Akwaeke. *Freshwater*. Grove Press, 2018.
———. *Pet*. Make Me a World, 2019.
A Fantastic Woman. Directed by Sebastián Lelio. Sony, 2017.
Fitzsimmons, Isaac. *The Passing Playbook*. Dial Books, 2021.
4400. Developed by Ariana Jackson, The CW, 2021–2022.
Gino, Alex. *George*. Scholastic, 2015.
Glass, Joe. *The Pride Omnibus*. Dark Horse Books, 2021.
Gold, Rachel. *Just Girls*. Bella Books, 2014.
Good Omens. Created by Neal Gaiman, Amazon Studios, BBC Studios, 2019.
Gow, Robin. *A Million Quiet Revolutions*. Farrar, Straus and Giroux, 2022.
Gun Hill Road. Directed by Rashaad Ernesto Green, Motion Film Group, 2011.
gwynception. "Potion and Practices." *Maiden, Mother, Crone: Fantastical Trans Femmes*, edited by Gwen Benaway. Bedside Press, 2019, pp. 50–64.
Hall, Alexis. *The Affair of the Mysterious Letter*. Ace, 2019.
———. *A Lady for a Duke*. Forever, 2022.
Hancox, Lewis. *Welcome to St. Hell*. Scholastic, 2022.
Harris, Joanne. *The Testament of Loki*. Saga Press, 2018.
Hartman, Rachel. *In the Serpent's Wake*. Random House, 2022.
———. *Tess of the Road*. Random House, 2018.
Heartstopper. Created by Alice Oseman, Netflix, 2022.
Hedwig and the Angry Inch. Directed by John Cameron Mitchell, New Line Cinema, 2001.
Hess, Al. *World Running Down*. Angry Robot, 2023.
Hit & Miss. Created by Paul Abbot, Sky Atlantic, 2012.
James, Renee. *A Kind of Justice*. Oceanview Publishing, 2016.
———. *Seven Suspects*. Oceanview Publishing, 2017.
Jones, Oliver. "Becoming Prom King: How My Classmates Showed Their Support for My Transition Gender." *Gender Euphoria: Stories of Joy from Trans, Non-Binary and Intersex Writers*, edited by Laura Kate Dale, Unbound, 2021, pp. 7–17.
The Kao. *Magical Boy Vol. 1*. Graphix, 2021.
———. *Magical Boy Vol. 2*. Graphix, 2022.
Kelly, Anita. *Love & Other Disasters*. Forever, 2022.
Kelly, Ava. "A Sudden Displacement of Matter." *Trans-Galactic Bike Ride: Feminist Bicycle Science Fiction Stories of Transgender and Nonbinary Adventurers*, edited Lydia Rogue, Elly Blue Publishing, 2020, pp. 95–114.
Kemp, Juliet. "Riding for Luck." *Trans-Galactic Bike Ride: Feminist Bicycle Science Fiction Stories of Transgender and Nonbinary Adventurers*, edited by Lydia Rogue, Elly Blue Publishing, 2020, pp. 19–34.
Kinkaid, Eden. "Toward a Trans Ethos of Care." *TSQ: Transgender Studies Quarterly*, vol. 8, no. 3, Aug. 2021, pp. 406–08. Silverchair, https://doi.org/10.1215/23289252-9009024.
Knight, L.A. "To Rest and to Create." *We're Here: The Best Queer Speculative Fiction 2021*, edited by C.L. Clark, Neon Hemlock Press, 2022, pp. 125–138.
Lai, Lee. "This Far." *Heartwood: Nonbinary Tales of Silvan Fantasy*, edited by Joamette Gil, P&M Press, 2019, pp. 171–182.
Lake, Joss. *Future Feeling*. Soft Skull, 2021.
Lanning, Courtney. *Funky Dan and the Pixie Dream Girl*. Riverdale Books, 2021.

Works Cited

Larson, Rich. *Annex*. Hachette, 2018.
Lee, C.B. *Not Your Villain*. Duet Books, 2017.
Lee, Emery. *Meet Cute Diary*. HarperCollins, 2021.
Lee, Yoon Ha. *Phoenix Extravagant*. Solaris, 2020.
―――. *Tiger Honor*. Disney Hyperion, 2022.
Lemberg, R.B. *The Four Profound Weaves*. Tachyon, 2020.
―――. "Grandmother Nai-Leylit's Cloth of Winds." *Geometries of Belonging*, Fairwood Press, 2022, pp. 15–67.
Loki. Created by Michael Waldron, Marvel Studios, 2021–.
Lynn, S.T. *Cinder Ella*. LoveLight Press, 2016.
Ma Vie en Rose. Directed by Alain Berliner. Sony, 1997.
Mardoll, Ana. "Daughter of Kings." *No Man of Woman Born*, Acacia Moon, 2018, pp. 74–103.
―――. "Tangled Nets." *No Man of Woman Born*, Acacia Moon, 2018, pp. 1–21.
Marvel's Runaways. Created by Josh Schwartz and Stephanie Savage, Hulu, 2017–2019.
The Matrix. Directed by Lana Wachowski and Lilly Wachowski. Warner Brothers, 1999.
McLemore, Anna-Marie. *Blanca & Roja*. Feiwel and Friends, 2018.
―――. *Self-Made Boys: A Great Gatsby Remix*. Feiwel and Friends, 2022.
McSmith, Tobly. *Act Cool*. Quill Tree Books, 2021.
Milks, Megan. *Margaret and the Mystery of the Missing Body*. Feminist Press, 2021.
Moraine, Sunny. "The Cloak of Isis." *Scheherazade's Facade: Fantastical Tales of Gender Bending, Cross-Dressing, and Transformation*, edited by Michael M. Jones, Circlet Press, 2012, pp. 133–158.
Morrison, Grant, writer, and Richard Case, artist. "Crawling from the Wreckage." *Doom Patrol* #19–20, 1987. DC Comics, 1992.
―――. *Doom Patrol Book 3* #51–63, 1992. DC Comics, 2017.
―――. "Down Paradise Way." *Doom Patrol* #35, 1990. DC Comics, 2005.
Mrs. Doubtfire. Directed by Chris Columbus, Twentieth Century Fox, 1994.
Myers, Alex. *Continental Divide*. University of New Orleans Press, 2019.
―――. *The Story of Silence*. Harper Voyager, 2021.
My Little Pony: Friendship Is Magic. Created by Lauren Faust, Hasbro Studios, 2010.
Neustifter, Blue. "Unknown Number." Azure, 2021.
Nimona. Directed by Nick Bruno and Troy Quane, Netflix, 2023.
O'Neill, Kay. *The Tea Dragon Festival*. Oni Press, 2019.
Orange Is the New Black. Created by Jenji Kohan, Lionsgate, 2013–2019.
The Orville. Created by Seth MacFarlane, Fuzzy Door Productions, 2017–.
Our Flag Means Death. Created by David Jenkins, HBO, 2022–.
Pollack, Rachel. *The Body of the Goddess: Sacred Wisdom in Myth, Landscape, and Culture*. Vega, 2003.
Pollack, Rachel, and Ted McKeever. "The Teiresias Wars." *Doom Patrol* #75–79, Vertigo, 1994.
Polonsky, Ami. *Gracefully Grayson*. Hyperion, 2014.
Pose. Created by Ryan Murphy et al., Color Force, 2018–2021.
Pratchett, Terry. *The Fifth Elephant*. 2000. HarperCollins, 2014.
Rent. Directed by Chris Columbus. Sony, 2005.
Riordan, Rick. *The Hammer of Thor*. Hyperion, 2016.
The Rocky Horror Picture Show. Directed by Jim Sharman, Twentieth Century Fox, 1975.
Russo, Meredith. *If I Was Your Girl*. Flatiron Books, 2016.
Rustad, A. Merc. "Our Aim Is Not to Die." *A People's Future of the United States*, edited by Victor LaValle and John Joseph Adams, One World, 2019, 27–48.
Salazar, Aida. *The Moon Within*. Arthur A. Levine, 2019.
Salvatore, Steven. *And They Lived*. Bloomsbury, 2022.
Schmatz, Pat. *Lizard Radio*. Candlewick Press, 2015.
Schrieve, Hal. *Out of Salem*. Triangle Square, 2019.
Sex Education. Created by Laurie Nunn, Netflix, 2019.
She-Ra and the Princesses of Power. Created by N.D. Stevenson, Dreamworks, 2018–2020.

Sklar, David. "Lady Marmalade's Special Place in Hell." *Scheherazade's Facade: Fantastical Tales of Gender Bending, Cross-Dressing, and Transformation*, edited by Michael M. Jones, Circlet Press, 2012, pp. 187–200.

Solomon, Rivers. *Sorrowland*. Farrar, Straus and Giroux, 2021.

Somebody, Somewhere. Created by Hannah Bos and Paul Thureen, HBO, 2022–.

Sort Of. Created by Bilal Baig and Fab Filippo, CBC, 2021–.

Spider-Man: Across the Spider-Verse. Directed by Joaquim Dos Santos et al., Sony Pictures, 2023.

Spitzer, Leora. "Sea Glass at Dawn." *It Gets Even Better: Stories of Queer Possibility*, edited by Isabela Oliveira and Jed Sabin, Speculatively Queer, 2021, pp. 66–78.

Steele, Hamish. *DeadEndia: The Watcher's Test*. Nobrow, 2018.

Stevenson, Noelle. *Nimona*. HarperTeen, 2015.

Steven Universe. Created by Rebecca Sugar, Cartoon Network, 2013–2019.

Steven Universe Future. Created by Rebecca Sugar, Cartoon Network Studios, 2019.

Stoeve, Ray. *Between Perfect and Real*. Amulet Books, 2021.

Supergirl. Created by Ali Adler et al., Berlanti Productions, 2015–2021.

Symes-Smith, Esme. *Sir Callie and the Champions of Helston*. Labyrinth Road, 2022.

Szpara, K.M. "Nothing Is Pixels Here." *Queers Destroy Science Fiction! Special Issue*, edited by Seanan McGuire, *Lightspeed*, no. 61, June 2015, pp. 86–96.

———. "You Can Make a Dinosaur, but You Can't Help Me." *Uncanny Magazine* 23, 2018. https://www.uncannymagazine.com/article/you-can-make-a-dinosaur-but-you-cant-help-me.

Tacchi, Francesca. "High Tide." *Transmogrify! 14 Fantastical Tales of Trans Magic*, edited by G. Haron Davis, HarperTeen, 2023, pp. 105–130.

Tangerine. Directed by Sean Baker, Duplass Brothers, 2015.

Tenser, Margarita. "Chosen." *Transcendent*, edited by K.M. Szpara, Lethe Press, 2016, pp. 119–122.

Thom, Kai Cheng. *Fierce Femmes and Notorious Liars: A Dangerous Trans Girl's Confabulous Memoir*. Metonymy Press, 2016.

———. "I Shall Remain." *Maiden, Mother, Crone: Fantastical Trans Femmes*, edited by Gwen Benaway, Bedside, 2019, pp. 97–107.

Thomas, Aiden. *Cemetery Boys*. Swoon Reads, 2020.

———. *The Sunbearer Trials*. Feiwel & Friends, 2022.

Tootsie. Directed by Sydney Pollack, Columbia Pictures, 1982.

Torch Song Trilogy. Directed by Paul Bogart, New Line Cinema, 1988.

Transamerica. Directed by Duncan Tucker, Belladonna Productions, 2006.

The Umbrella Academy. Created by Steve Blackman and Jeremy Slater, Borderline Entertainment and Irish Cowboy, 2019–.

Vaughan, Brian K., et al. *Runaways: Escape to New York*. 2006. Marvel, 2017.

Wachowski, Lana, Lilly Wachowski, and J. Michael Straczynski, creators. *Sense8*. Netflix, 2015–2018.

Walker, Suzanne, and Wendy Xu. *Mooncakes*. Oni Press, 2019.

Wang, Jen. *The Prince and the Dressmaker*. First Second, 2018.

Wasserstein, Izzy. "Ports of Perceptions." *Transcendent 4: The Year's Best Transgender Speculative Fiction*, edited by Bogi Takács, Lethe Press, 2019, pp. 73–74.

Whitby, S.J. *Cute Mutants Vol 1: Mutant Pride*. 2020.

Williams, Stephanie, et al. *Nubia & the Amazons*. DC Comics, 2022.

Wittlinger, Ellen. *Parrotfish*. Simon & Schuster, 2007.

Secondary Sources

Adair, Cassius. "Licensing Citizenship: Anti-Blackness, Identification Documents, and Transgender Studies." *American Quarterly*, vol. 71, no. 2, 2019, pp. 569–594. Project MUSE, https://doi.org/10.1353/aq.2019.0043.

Adams, James Eli. "Monstrosity." *Victorian Literature and Culture*, vol. 46, no. 3–4, Nov.

Works Cited

2018, pp. 776–79. Cambridge University Press, https://doi.org/10.1017/S1060150318000815.

Aguilar, Matthew. "DC's Stephanie Williams Talks Creating a New Origin for Nubia and Teases Role in *Trial of the Amazons*." *ComicBook.com*, 17 Feb. 2022. https://comicbook.com/dc/news/dc-stephanie-williams-talks-nubia-new-origin-role-trial-of-the-amazons-wonder-woman-diana-yara.

Ashley, Wendy. "The Angry Black Woman: The Impact of Pejorative Stereotypes on Psychotherapy with Black Women." *Social Work in Public Health*, vol. 29, no. 1, Jan. 2014, pp. 27–34. Taylor and Francis+NEJM, https://doi.org/10.1080/19371918.2011.619449.

B., Rob. "Interview with April Daniels." *SFF World*, 23 Jan. 2017. https://www.sffworld.com/2017/01/aprildaniels-interview.

Battis, Jes. "Trans Magic: The Radical Performance of the Young Wizard in YA Literature." *Over the Rainbow Queer Children's and Young Adult Literature*, edited by Michelle Ann Abate and Kenneth Kidd, University of Michigan Press, 2011, pp. 314–329.

Bell-Metreau, Rebecca. *Transgender Cinema*. Rutgers University Press, 2019.

Bergado, Gabe. "*Pet* Author Akwaeke Emezi on Making a Better World for Their Protagonist, a Black Trans Girl Named Jam." *Teen Vogue*, 13 Sept. 2019. https://www.teenvogue.com/story/akwaeke-emezi-pet.

Bettelheim, Bruno. *The Uses of Enchantment: The Meaning and Importance of Fairy Tales*. Vintage Books, 1989.

Bird, Jackson. "*Harry Potter* Helped Me Come Out as Trans, But J.K. Rowling Disappointed Me." *The New York Times*, 21 Dec. 2019. https://www.nytimes.com/2019/12/21/opinion/jk-rowling-twitter-trans.html.

Bronski, Michael, et al. "*You Can Tell Just By Looking*": And 20 Other Myths about LGBT Life and People, vol. 9, Beacon Press, 2013.

Brooks, Daphne A. *Liner Notes for the Revolution: The Intellectual Life of Black Feminist Sound*. Harvard University Press, 2021.

Brooks, Karen. "Homosexuality, Homosociality, and Gender Blending in Australian Film." *Antipodes*, vol. 13, no. 2, 1999, pp. 85–90. JSTOR, http://www.jstor.org/stable/41956954.

Brown, Adelia. "Hook, Ursula, and Elsa: Disney and Queer-Coding from the 1950s to the 2010s," *The Macksey Journal*, vol. 2, no. 43, 2021. https://mackseyjournal.scholasticahq.com/article/27887-hook-ursula-and-elsa-disney-and-queer-coding-from-the-1950s-to-the-2010s/attachment/74928.pdf.

Brown, Bill. *Other Things*. University of Chicago Press, 2020.

Busnardo, Rachel. "Steven Universe: A Gender Fusion Buffet on Cartoon Network." *The Thought Erotic*, 2 Mar. 2016. https://thethoughterotic.com/2016/03/02/steven-universe-agender-fusion-buffet-on-cartoon-network.

Campbell, Joseph. *The Hero with a Thousand Faces*. Princeton University Press, 1973.

Campbell, Joseph, with Bill Moyers. *The Power of Myth*, edited by Betty Sue Flowers, Doubleday, 1988.

Chace, Alexandra. "Necrotic Machines/Zombie Genders: Transfeminine Disruptions of Feminist Progress." Thesis, Georgia State University, 19. https://oa.mg/work/2946407729.

Challinor, Lauren. "An Examination of Gender Roles in *The Adventures of Priscilla, Queen of the Desert*." *ESSAI*, vol. 11, no. 13, 2013. http://dc.cod.edu/essai/vol11/iss1/13.

Cornum, Lou, and Maureen Moynagh. "Introduction: Decolonial (Re) Visions of Science Fiction, Fantasy, and Horror." *Canadian Literature*, vol. 240, 2020, pp. 8–19.

Damaske, Damion. "8 Ways *The Matrix* Is a Trans Allegory." *CBR*, 21 Jan. 2022. https://www.cbr.com/ways-matrix-trans-allegory.

Danter, Stefan. "Destructive Villain or Gigantic Hero? The Transformation of Godzilla in Contemporary Popular Culture." *The Supervillain Reader*, edited by Robert Moses Peaslee and Robert G. Weiner, University of Mississippi Press, 2020, pp. 190–202.

DiEdoardo, Christina A. "Nietzsche and a Trans Woman Walk into a Prison." *Orange Is the New Black and Philosophy*, edited by Richard Greene and Rachel Robison-Greene, Open Court, 2015, pp. 29–39.

Disclosure. Directed by Sam Feder, Netflix, 2020.

Dueben, Alex. "Smash Pages Q&A: Stephanie Burt and Rachel Gold." *Smashpages*, June 25, 2020. https://smashpages.net/2020/06/25/smash-pages-qa-stephanie-burt-and-rachel-gold.

Duggan, Lisa. "Making it Perfectly Queer." *Theorizing Feminism*, edited by Anne C. Herrmann and Abigail J. Stewart, Routledge, 2018, pp. 215–231.

Earle, Joshua. "Deadnames and Missing Chiralities: A Response to Steve Fuller's 'The Problem of Cishumanism.'" *Social Epistomology*, 21 Mar. 2022. https://social-epistemology.com/2022/03/21/deadnames-and-missing-chiralities-a-response-to-steve-fullers-the-problem-of-cishumanism-joshua-earle.

Ellis, Sigrid. "Science Fiction Has Always Been Queer." *Queers Destroy Science Fiction! Special Issue*, edited by Seanan McGuire, Lightspeed, no. 61, June 2015, pp. 360–361.

Estés, Clarissa Pinkola. *Women Who Run with the Wolves*. Ballantine Books, 1992.

Estrella, Ariel. "Tones of the Caparazón, or the Lizard Brain's Response to Misgendering by Folks Who Should Know Better." *Trans Love: An Anthology of Transgender and Nonbinary Voices*, edited by Freiya Benson, Jessica Kingsley Publishers, 2019, pp. 168–181.

Evans, Judith. *Feminist Theory Today: An Introduction to Second-Wave Feminism*. Sage, 1995.

Ferguson, Roderick A. *Aberrations in Black: Toward a Queer of Color Critique*. University of Minnesota Press, 2004.

Fisher, Simon Elin, et al. "Trans Temporalities." *Somatechnics Journal*, vol. 7, no. 1, 2017. https://ssrn.com/abstract=3065691.

Foxwood, Orion. "Queer-Fire Witchery: The Rainbow-Flame that Melts the Soul-Cage: The Emerging Fluidity of Consciousness." *Queer Magic: Power Beyond Boundaries*, edited by Lee Harrington and Tai Fenix Kulystin, Mystic Productions Press, 2018, 285–293.

Frankel, Valerie Estelle. *Chosen One*. Smashwords, 2016.

———. *From Girl to Goddess: The Heroine's Journey Through Myth and Legend*. McFarland, 2010.

———. *The Villain's Journey: Descent and Return in Science Fiction and Fantasy*. McFarland, 2022.

Galupo, M. Paz, et al. "Transgender Friendship Experiences: Benefits and Barriers of Friendships across Gender Identity and Sexual Orientation." *Feminism & Psychology*, vol. 24, no. 2, 2014, pp. 193–215. https://doi.org/10.1177/0959353514526218.

Gelderloos, Peter. *How Nonviolence Protects the State*. South End Press, 2007.

Goldberg, Lesley. "*Pose* Series Finale: Billy Porter and Steven Canals on the Show's Legacy and Tragic Yet Hopeful Conclusion." *Hollywood Reporter*, 6 June 2021. https://www.hollywoodreporter.com/tv/tv-features/pose-series-finale-billy-porter-steven-canals-explain-how-it-ended-1234963320.

Gould, Joan. *Spinning Straw into Gold*. Random House, 2006.

Gross, Aeyal. "Theories and Discourses of Rights and Democracy: A Comparative Inquiry." S.J.D. diss., Harvard Law School, 1996.

A Group Interview "Gay Soul Making: Coming Out Inside." *Gay Spirit: Myth and Meaning*, edited by Mark Thompson, St. Martin's Press, 1987, pp. 237–254.

Guzmán, Joshua Javier. "3. Affect." *Keywords for Gender and Sexuality Studies*, New York University Press, 2021, pp. 13–17.

Haefele-Thomas, Ardel. *Introduction to Transgender Studies*. Harrington Park Press, 2019.

Halberstam, Jack. *The Queer Art of Failure*. Duke University Press, 2020.

Hall, James A. *Jungian Dream Interpretation*. Inner City Books, 1983.

Harless, C. "The Report of the 2019 Southern LGBTQ Health Survey." *Campaign for Southern Equality*, 2019. https://southernequality.org/wp-content/uploads/2019/11/SouthernLGBTQHealthSurvey%E2%80%93FullReport.pdf.

Harrison, Jack, et al. "A Gender Not Listed Here: Genderqueers, Gender Rebels, and OtherWise in the National Transgender Discrimination Survey." *LGBTQ Public Policy Journal at the Harvard Kennedy School*, vol. 2, no. 1, Apr. 2012, p. 13.

Hernandez, C.M. "Forging an Iron Woman: On the Effects of Piracy on Gender in the 18th Century Caribbean." *Vanderbilt Undergraduate Research Journal*, 2009, 5. https://doi.org/10.15695/vurj.v5i0.2812.

Hillman, James. "Anima II." *Spring: An Annual of Archetypal. Psychology and Jungian Thought*, 1974, pp. 113–146.

Works Cited

Himes, Mavis. *The Power of Names*. Rowman & Littlefield, 2016.
Hopcke, Robert H. "Gay Relationship as a Vehicle for Individuation." *Mirrors of the Self: Archetypal Images that Shape your Life*, edited by Christine Downing, St. Martin's Press, 1991, pp. 137–143.
Huang, Stephanie. "Art Versus Artist: What's a Poor Reader to Do?" *Mercer Street*, 2022. https://wp.nyu.edu/mercerstreet/2021-2022/art-versus-artist-whats-a-poor-reader-to-do.
Johnston, Dais. "Is Loki Genderfluid? 'It's always been there,' Tom Hiddleston Tells *Inverse*." *Inverse*, 8 June 2021. https://www.inverse.com/entertainment/loki-gender-fluid-marvel-tom-hiddleston.
Jung, Carl. "Concerning Rebirth." *Collected Works*, translated by R.F.C. Hull, Princeton University Press, 1990, pp. 113–147.
———. "Conscience, Unconscious, and Individuation." *Collected Works*, translated by R.F.C. Hull, Princeton University Press, 1990, pp. 275–289.
Kaufman, Roger. "Terminators, Aliens, and Avatars: The Emergence of Archetypal Homosexual Themes in a Filmmaker's Imagination." *The Films of James Cameron: Critical Essays*, edited by Matthew Kapell and Stephen McVeigh, McFarland, 2011, pp. 167–185.
Keegan, Cáel M. "In Praise of the Bad Transgender Object: Rocky Horror." *Flow Journal*, 28 Nov. 2019. https://www.flowjournal.org/2019/11/in-praise-of-the-bad.
———. *Lana and Lilly Wachowski: Sensing Transgender*. University of Illinois Press, 2018.
Kenson, Steve. "The Queer Journey of the Wheel." *Queer Magic: Power Beyond Boundaries*, edited by Lee Harrington and Tai Fenix Kulystin, Mystic Productions Press, 2018, pp. 253–263.
Kichler, Rosalind. "'What Has Kept Me Alive': Transgender Communities and Support." *Journal of Homosexuality*, vol. 69, no. 14, Dec. 2022, pp. 2463–82. Taylor and Francis+NEJM, https://doi.org/10.1080/00918369.2021.1943277.
Koehler, Mimi. "Q&A: Esme Symes-Smith, Author of *Sir Callie and the Champions of Helston*." *The Nerd Daily*, 7 Nov. 2022. https://thenerddaily.com/esme-symes-smith-author-interview.
Kogod, Theo. "Who Is Wonder Woman's New Trans Amazon—and Why Is She So Important?" *CBR*, 28 Oct. 2021. https://www.cbr.com/wonder-woman-trans-amazon-bia-explained.
Lamm, Zachary. "The Queer Pedagogy of Dr. Frank-N-Furter." *Reading Rocky Horror: The Rocky Horror Picture Show and Popular Culture*, edited by Jeffrey Andrew Weinstock, Palgrave Macmillan, 2008, pp. 193–206.
Leetal, Dean. "Revisiting Gender Theory in Fan Fiction: Bringing Nonbinary Genders into the World." *Transformative Works and Cultures*, vol. 38, Sep. 2022. https://doi.org/10.3983/twc.2022.2081.
Love, K. Heather. "Queer." *Transgender Studies Quarterly*, vol. 1, no. 1–2, 2014, pp. 172–176.
Maier, Sophia V., et al. "Get the Frac In! Or, the Fractal Many-festo: A (Trans)(Crip)t." *Peitho*, vol. 22 no. 4, Summer 2020. https://cfshrc.org/article/get-the-frac-in-or-the-fractal-many-festo-a-transcript.
Malatino, Hil. *Queer Embodiment: Monstrosity, Medical Violence, and Intersex Experience*. University of Nebraska Press, 2019.
———. *Trans Care*. University of Minnesota Press, 2020.
———. "The Transgender Tipping Point: The Social Death of Sophia Burset." *Feminist Perspectives on Orange Is the New Black*, edited by April Kalogeropoulos Householder and Adrienne Trier-Bieniek, McFarland, 2016, pp. 95–110.
McCormack, O. "Perspective 'The Matrix' Has Always Been a Trans Story, and Now Audiences Can't Ignore It." *Washington Post*, 23 Dec. 2021. https://www.washingtonpost.com/gender-identity/the-matrix-has-always-been-a-trans-story-and-now-audiences-cant-ignore-it/.
Miller, Kiri. "Gaming the System: Gender Performance in Dance Central." *New Media & Society*, vol. 17, no. 6, 2015, pp. 939–957.
Moray, Pavini. "The Glitterheart Path of Connecting with Transcestors." *Queer Magic: Power Beyond Boundaries*, edited by Lee Harrington and Tai Fenix Kulystin, Mystic Productions Press, 2018, pp. 28–33.

Morrell, Jessica. *Bullies, Bastards and Bitches: How to Write the Bad Guys of Fiction*. Writer's Digest, 2008.

Nanda, Serena. *Gender Diversity: Crosscultural Variations*. Waveland Press, 2014.

@neilhimself. "@HeleneFosse I wouldn't exclude the ideas that they are ace, or aromantic, or trans. They are an angel and a demon, not as make humans, per the book. Occult/Ethereal beings don't have sexes, something we tried to reflect in the casting. Whatever Crowley and Aziraphale are, it's a love story." *Twitter*, 8 Jun. 2019, 10:46 a.m., twitter.com/neilhimself/status/1137370226931228672.

Packer, Sharon. *Superheroes and Superegos: Analyzing the Minds behind the Masks*. ABC-CLIO, 2010.

Pearson, Carol. *Awakening the Heroes Within*. HarperOne, 1991.

Pearson, Carol, and Katherine Pope. *The Female Hero in American and British Literature*. R.R. Bowker, 1981.

Perera, Silvia Brinton. *Descent to the Goddess*. Inner City Books, 1981.

Pilford-Bagwell, Adam. "The Matrix as Transgender Metaphor." *Birth Movies Death*, 10 Apr. 2017. https://birthmoviesdeath.com/2017/04/10/the-matrix-and-dysphoria-blues.html.

Quatrini, Amerigo. "On J.K. Rowling's Discourse on Transsexual Issues, An Analysis of the Language Used on Rowling's Twitter and the Sociolinguistic Implication of Hate Speech." *International Journal of Languages, Literature and Linguistics*, vol. 8, no. 2, June 2022, pp. 89–99. DOI.org (Crossref), https://doi.org/10.18178/IJLLL.2022.8.2.328.

Ragussis, Michael. *Acts of Naming: The Family Plot in Fiction*. Oxford University Press, 1986.

Sanchez, Melissa E. "This Field That Is Not One." *Journal for Early Modern Cultural Studies*, vol. 16, no. 2, 2016, pp. 131–146.

Schmidt, Victoria Lynn. *45 Master Characters: Mythic Models for Creating Original Characters*. Writer's Digest, 2007.

Scott, Darieck. "I am Nubia: Superhero Comics and the Paradigm of the Fantasy Act." *Keeping it Unreal: Black Queer Fantasy and Superhero Comics*, New York University Press, 2022, pp. 47–88.

Scott, Suzanne, and Ellen Kirkpatrick. "Trans Representations and Superhero Comics: A Conversation with Mey Rude, J. Skyler, and Rachel Stevens." *Cinema Journal*, vol. 55 no. 1, 2015, p. 160–168. Project MUSE, https://doi.org/10.1353/cj.2015.0060.

Serano, Julia. *Whipping Girl: A Transsexual Woman on Sexism and the Scapegoating of Femininity*. Hachette UK, 2016.

Shibusawa, Naoko. "Where is the Reciprocity? Notes on Solidarity from the Field." *Journal of Asian American Studies*, vol. 25, no. 2, 2022, pp. 261–282.

Singer, Marc. *Grant Morrison: Combining the Worlds of Contemporary Comics*. University Press of Mississippi, 2012.

Spade, Dean, et al. "Building an Abolitionist Trans and Queer Movement with Everything We've Got." *Captive Genders: Trans Embodiment and the Prison Industrial Complex*, edited by Eric Stanley and Nat Smith, AK Press, 2011, pp. 15–40.

Steinmetz, Katy. "The Transgender Tipping Point." *Time*, 29 May 2014. https://time.com/135480/transgender-tipping-point.

Stryker, Susan. "My Words to Victor Frankenstein above the Village of Chamounix: Performing Transgender Rage." *The Transgender Studies Reader Remix*. Routledge, 2022, pp. 67–79.

———. *Transgender History*. Seal Press, 2017.

Symonds, Dominic. "Drag, Rock, Authenticity and In-Betweenness: Hedwig and the Angry Inch." *Twenty-First Century Musicals: From Stage to Screen*, edited by George Rodosthenous, Routledge, 2018, pp. 18–33.

Szpara, K.M. "Author Spotlight." *Queers Destroy Science Fiction! Special Issue*, edited by Seanan McGuire, *Lightspeed*, no. 61, June 2015, pp. 283–285.

Thom, Kai Cheng. *I Hope We Choose Love*. Arsenal Pulp Press, 2019.

Towns, Jennifer. "Insidious Trauma, Heteronormative Steeping, and Help-seeking: Exploring the Rural Non-Heterosexual Experience." *Journal of Social, Behavioral, and Health Sciences*, vol. 14, no. 1, 2020.

Tudor, Alyosxa. "Terfism Is White Distraction: On BLM, Decolonising the Curriculum, Anti-Gender Attacks and Feminist Transphobia." *Engenderings*, 22 June 2020. SOAS, https://eprints.soas.ac.uk/id/eprint/33114.

Urban, Bek, et al. "Social and Contextual Influences on Eating Pathology in Transgender and Nonbinary Adults." *Eating Disorders* 31.4 (2023): 301–319.

Uspenskiy, Andrey. "'Wumben, Wimpund, Woomud': An Exploration of Social Censure in the Internet Age." *The Morningside Review*, vol. 18, Sept. 2022. https://journals.library.columbia.edu/index.php/TMR/article/view/8292.

Vogler, Christopher. *The Writer's Journey*. Michael Wiese Productions, 1998.

von Franz, Marie Louise. "The Process of Individuation." *Man and His Symbols*, edited by Carl Jung. Doubleday, 1964, pp. 157–254.

Walker, Mitch. "The Double." *Mirrors of the Self: Archetypal Images that Shape your Life*, edited by Christine Downing, St. Martin's Press, 1991, pp. 48–52.

———. "Visionary Love: The Magickal Gay Spirit Power." *Gay Spirit: Myth and Meaning*, edited by Mark Thompson, St. Martin's Press, 1987, pp. 210–236.

Wallace, Michelle. *Black Macho and the Myth of the Superwoman*. Verso, 1999.

Weldon, Glen et al. "*Sort Of* Is Back and Still Great." *NPR*, Dec. 5, 2022. https://www.npr.org/transcripts/1140146457.

Weston, Kath. *Families We Choose*. Columbia University Press, 1991.

White, Abbey. "*Dead End: Paranormal Park* Creator Hamish Steele on Crafting the Animated YA LGBTQ-Inclusive Horror Series." *Hollywood Reporter*, 16 June 2022. https://www.hollywoodreporter.com/tv/tv-features/netflix-dead-end-paranormal-park-hamish-steele-interview-1235165517.

Whitmont, Edward C. "The Persona: The Mask We Wear for the Game of Living." *Mirrors of the Self: Archetypal Images that Shape your Life*, edited by Christine Downing, St. Martin's Press, 1991, pp. 14–18.

Wood, Frank, et al. "Visibly Unknown: Media Depiction of Murdered Transgender Women of Color." *Race and Justice*, vol. 12, no. 2, 2022, pp. 368–386. https://doi.org/10.1177/2153368719886343.

Woodman, Marion. *The Pregnant Virgin: A Process of Psychological Transformation*. Inner City Books, 1985.

———. *The Ravaged Bridegroom*. Inner City Books, 1990.

Index

ableism 18, 72, 78, 112–113
abuse 4, 15, 16, 49, 60, 72, 73, 77, 79, 82, 100, 102, 119–122, 158, 161
Act Cool 14, 57
activism 3, 43, 45, 58, 100, 106, 159, 180–183, 191
adolescence 19, 25, 131, 135
adoption 56, 71
The Adventures of Amina Al-Sirafi 47
The Affair of the Mysterious Letter 61–64
African 78
A.I. 42, 45, 93, 150
AIDS 181–184, 188
Akwaeke, Emezi 23, 77–80, 90
Alice in Wonderland 69, 135
alien 4, 30, 36, 37, 42, 49, 50, 66, 75, 106–108, 177
allies 3, 5, 14, 29, 59, 73, 74, 77, 78, 81, 82, 85, 109, 145, 160, 162
America 4, 58, 59, 77, 103, 108, 144, 164, 191
And They Lived 74, 90
Anders, Charlie Jane 50, 51, 127
angel 28, 38, 43, 68, 71, 77, 79, 80, 90, 126, 134, 172, 173
anim 88, 90, 93–94, 98
anima 82, 86–89, 96, 125
animus 82, 86–88, 96
Annex 139
anti-trans bills 59, 191
Arjuna 3
aromantic 172
art 21, 35, 36, 45, 46, 53, 90, 100, 139, 154, 175
Aruna Shende 51
asexual 172
ASL 78
assault 15, 18, 73, 100, 104, 106, 110–111, 116, 119, 188, 191
Australia 187–188
autism 45, 72, 178

Baig, Bilal 163
bathroom: attack 106, 116, 135; use 137, 191
Batman 53
"Battlement of Straw" 35, 38
BDSM 10
beauty salon 114, 118
Belgium 88
belly of the whale 121, 127–130, 138
Benjamin, Harry 17
Berlin 96
best friend 20, 25, 46, 77, 82, 85–89, 91, 112, 118, 167, 168; *see also* friendship
Between Perfect and Real 46
Bia of the Amazons 50, 53–55
Bible 3, 56, 80, 97, 128
bigotry 33, 73, 100, 110, 113
binary 1, 3, 4, 10, 11, 14, 17, 18, 25, 35–38, 41, 43, 50, 57, 66, 76, 87, 90, 100, 113, 144, 149, 173, 174, 186, 188, 191; *see also* heteronormativity
binder 19, 27, 90, 130
biological essentialism 144
Birdverse 46, 56, 147–150, 155
birth family 57, 70–72, 180–181; *see also* brother; child; father; mother; sister
Black experience 15, 40, 52–55, 61, 65, 100, 113, 118, 141, 159, 179; *see also* people of color
Black Lives Matter 100
Blanca & Roja 60
blog 34, 35, 69
body horror 127, 159; *see also* medical establishment
Boy Meets Girl 46, 85
Brazil 160
The Brilliant Death 176
brother 33, 34, 73, 74, 79, 85, 97, 140, 142, 148, 161
Buffy the Vampire Slayer 53, 143

Index

bullies 46, 47, 84, 99, 103, 112, 113, 135, 136, 177, 190
butch 23, 48

call to adventure 18, 23
camp 118, 126, 152, 172
Campbell, Joseph 1, 7, 17–19, 23, 57, 61, 62, 87, 121, 127, 129, 130, 143, 157, 161, 162, 173
Canals, Steven 182–184
Capetta, A.R. 23, 32, 176
capitalism 86, 115
care web 41
care work 72, 187
Cemetery Boys 45, 167–169
Chambers, Becky 24, 51, 174
Charmed 57–58
chat rooms 9
Chicago 159
child 4, 15, 19, 21, 25, 27, 29–31, 37, 43, 47, 48, 52, 54, 56, 63, 71–78, 81–84, 97, 102, 103, 111, 118, 123, 125, 131, 132, 137, 148–151, 164–168, 176, 179, 187; inner, 71–72, 133, 147, 150, 168, 189–190
Chile 59, 111
Chilling Adventures of Sabrina 99
chimera 36
"Chosen" 29
chosen one 10, 28, 30, 143
Christianity 106, 144, 166; *see also* fundamentalists
church 20, 48, 104, 128, 129
Cinder Ella 15, 95
Cinderella 18, 43, 46, 57, 78, 92, 175
Cipri, Nino 167
clinic 60, 127, 133, 186
"The Cloak of Isis" 44
clothes 10, 20, 21, 33, 46, 67, 83, 88–92, 99, 125–127, 130, 153, 164, 177, 188; *see also* costume; drag; dresses; hair; makeup; masks; sewing; suit; weaving; wig
Coagula 50, 154
college 15, 34, 58, 60, 62, 179
colonialism 3, 18, 119, 144, 185
comics 4, 29, 30, 53–55, 66, 68, 137, 143, 146, 167
coming out 16, 18, 19, 31, 39, 58, 59, 95, 99, 102, 105, 127
community of care 81
conformity 10, 11, 55, 101, 103, 124–126, 157
conservative 15, 34, 62, 89, 157, 159, 191
Continental Divide 130
conversion camp 14
conviction 116–117
cooking 24, 32, 35, 49, 186, 192
coping mechanisms 23

costume 21, 33, 89, 152
counterculture 42, 112, 159
Cowboys 74
Cox, Laverne 107, 117, 192
Coyote 3
crone 143, 145, 185
The Crying Game 103
Cute Mutants 14, 36, 76
cyborg 93

dance 13, 33, 68, 75, 76, 92, 126, 147, 161, 163, 179, 180, 184
DC Comics 50–53, 65, 154
Dead End Paranormal Park 60, 70–72
Deadendia 71
deadname 12, 19, 28, 56, 124, 133, 136, 138, 144, 145, 158, 189, 190
death 12, 29, 40, 44, 57, 59, 63, 79, 93, 111, 115–118, 126, 128–133, 135, 141–150, 155, 165, 166, 169, 181–185
Defy or Defend 33
demiboy 14
demon 71, 72, 172, 173
denial 15–19, 119, 155, 173
depression 91, 115, 121, 180
destiny 19, 29, 30, 37, 40, 54, 81, 83; *see also* chosen one
Different for Girls 103
dignity 159, 181
disability 18, 32, 109, 115, 119, 150, 178, 192; *see also* medical establishment; mental illness; neurodivergent
disclosure 104
discrimination 55, 59, 106, 107, 111, 112, 118–120, 191
Disney 18, 78, 152; *see also* fairytales
diversity 6, 47, 55, 68, 113, 144, 166, 189
divorce 54, 104, 114
doctors *see* medical establishment; surgery
Doctor Who 141
Doom Patrol 50, 65–69, 154–155
Double 7, 44, 51, 81–83, 93
drag 33, 51, 65–68, 89, 93, 127, 150, 161, 188, 189
dragon 5, 35–41, 49, 77, 90, 131–132
Dreadnought 14–17, 45, 60, 81, 146
"Dreamborn" 178
Dreamer 50, 106–110
dreams 13, 24, 45, 57, 58, 69, 87, 94, 97, 107, 115, 123, 133–135, 143–146, 152, 157, 174, 177, 179, 181, 184, 185, 192
dresses 24, 33, 43, 45, 50, 85, 88, 89, 94, 99, 123, 129, 130, 135, 144, 145, 152, 164, 184, 188, 190
drugs 50, 108, 115, 116, 122, 161, 182, 184

Index

Dungeons & Dragons 2
dysphoria 11, 27, 96, 127, 138, 166
dystopia 139; *see also* government; law

Eaton-Kent, Jo 123
ego 20, 87, 109, 162
elders 31, 32, 44, 49, 61, 147, 179–184, 190
empathy 72, 109, 114, 157, 161, 162, 183
England 152, 154
Estés, Clarissa Pinkola 20, 21, 144, 149, 150, 153
Estrella, Ariel 100
euphoria 27, 170

fairies 81, 84, 85
fairytales 29, 40, 43, 45, 46, 57, 63, 131, 134, 143, 144; *see also* Cinderella; dragon; goddess; king; knight; magic; prince; princess; Sleeping Beauty; Snow White
fandom 100
A Fantastic Woman 59, 111
fantasy 1–6, 18, 29, 37, 43, 54, 56, 59, 63, 66, 68, 87, 102, 123, 161, 176–179; *see also Alice in Wonderland*; fairytales; *Frozen*; *Game of Thrones*; *Lord of the Rings*; magic; magical world; *Narnia*; *Sir Callie*; *The Wizard of Oz*
father 3, 15–17, 21, 22, 24, 26, 30, 44–49, 59–63, 70, 72–75, 81, 84–88, 91–94, 100–106, 111, 125, 129, 133–137, 142, 148, 150, 151, 161, 164–169, 176, 177, 181, 187–190
fatphobia 18
fear of return 162
Felix Ever After 14, 96, 136
feminine 22, 66, 85, 87–90, 125, 152, 189
feminism 54, 55, 143
femme 32, 75, 100, 138, 141, 164
Fierce Femmes and Notorious Liars 18, 24, 56, 146, 174–176
fired 88, 191; *see also* unemployment
forest 5, 25, 60, 61, 79, 100, 101, 139
forgiveness 98, 106, 114, 119, 128, 151, 167
found family 5, 30, 31, 38, 41, 70–72, 94, 117, 152, 174, 186, 189
The 4400 61
Frankenstein 25, 38, 42, 113, 114, 117
freedom 5, 12, 21, 29, 47, 50, 55, 56, 60, 91, 137, 149, 156, 173–177
Freshwater 90
friendship 72, 78, 83–85, 88, 173; *see also* allies; anim; best friend; Double
Frozen 173
fundamentalists 14, 104, 126
Funky Dan and the Pixie Dream Girl 133–136
Future Feeling 86, 126

Gaiman, Neil 143, 144, 146, 172
Galaxy 50
Game of Thrones 56, 108
gaslighting 5, 55, 79, 101
gay *see* homosexuality
Gay Men's Chorus 183
gender expression 6, 22, 46, 49, 52, 54, 59, 70, 94, 111, 140; *see also* costume; drag; dresses; hair; makeup; masks; persona; suit; wig
gender roles 3, 5, 43, 44, 58, 81, 91–93, 101, 161, 173; *see also* binary
"Genderella," 46
genderfluid 5, 6, 51, 63, 83, 137, 149, 174
gender-nonconforming 81, 171, 187
George 168
ghost 50, 141, 145, 149, 185
Girl 46
GLAAD 4
goddess 19–22, 28, 29, 44, 45, 89, 124, 131, 132, 134, 149, 150, 167
Good Omens 170–173
Gothic 158
government 23, 45, 67–69, 77, 106, 159, 162, 166, 183
Gracefully Grayson 22
graphic novel 19, 37, 88, 111, 143
Greek myth 3, 43, 82
Gun Hill Road 103, 137
gwynception 169

hair 19, 30, 46, 74, 75, 94, 125, 126, 130, 137, 144–146, 152, 153, 163, 178, 190; *see also* wig
hate crime 110; *see also* bullies; discrimination
haven 13, 14, 18, 32, 34, 42, 47, 48, 54, 56, 61, 64–79, 97, 101, 107–110, 161, 167, 174–178
healing 21, 22, 33, 81, 83, 85, 122, 133, 137, 151
healthcare 118–119
Heartbreak Bakery 23, 32, 152
Heartstopper 46, 61
Hedwig and the Angry Inch 95–98
heteronormativity 43, 69, 70, 72, 162
Hiddleston, Tom 137
"High Tide" 44
Hijra 3
Hit & Miss 190
HIV 179–184
Hollyoaks 103
home 14, 16, 17, 20, 23, 25–28, 37, 47, 49, 61, 67, 70, 71, 73, 77, 84, 94, 99, 102, 105, 108, 118, 124, 139, 142–144, 158, 161, 163, 164, 169, 170, 175, 177, 181, 183, 188; *see also* ordinary world

Index

homecoming queen 105; *see also* prom; school
homelessness 116, 118, 150, 179–181
homosexuality 66, 82, 152, 191
hormones 11, 12, 17, 61, 119, 133, 179; *see also* medical establishment; testosterone
horror, medical 17; *see also* body horror
house mother 13, 49, 94, 180, 181
The Hunger Games 26
hybrid 36, 38, 56, 66, 79, 126

I Am J 59, 60
Ianthe 44–45
identity 3–5, 9–12, 15, 17, 19, 21, 22, 31, 39, 40, 43, 50, 53, 55, 70, 72, 82, 87, 91, 93, 95, 97, 101, 108, 109, 130, 131, 137, 150, 152, 157, 158, 167, 168, 187
If I Was Your Girl 15, 18, 60, 74, 103, 104, 179
"In Her Mind's Eye" 150
In the Serpent's Wake 18
India 131
indigenous 3, 178
innermost cave 5
internet 9, 10, 45, 69, 108, 129, 150, 176; *see also* blog; chat rooms; social media; YouTube
intersex 65, 137
intuition 24, 64, 77, 82
it gets better campaign 186

Jessie Drake 50
Jung, Carl 82, 87, 88, 139, 145
Just Girls 15

karma 64
kicked out 59, 60, 73, 86, 111, 180, 181
kidnapped 18, 121, 166
A Kind of Justice 116
king 3, 21, 30, 37, 71, 83, 84, 89, 123, 124, 141, 151, 153, 155, 156, 166
knife 47, 48, 130–132
knight 5, 90, 101, 155, 171

A Lady for a Duke 46, 61, 91, 92
"Lady Marmalade's Special Place in Hell" 150
Latino 179
law 16, 29, 57, 59, 104, 112, 119, 120, 168; *see also* government
Lee, Yoon Ha 18, 36, 174, 185
legacy 19, 49, 53, 167, 184
Lemberg, R.B. 147, 174
Light from Uncommon Stars 48
Lizard Radio 177
Loki 52, 90, 137–143
Look Past 126, 128, 129, 130
The Lord of the Rings 82, 88, 131
Los Angeles 28
Love and Other Disasters 24, 74, 186

Ma Vie en Rose 24, 59, 111
Macbeth 131
Madonna 181
magic 1, 3, 14, 24, 25, 29, 37, 51, 52, 58, 64, 71, 72, 79, 82, 83, 89, 90, 93, 101, 102, 112, 113, 125, 126, 134, 136, 140, 143, 147–153, 158–161, 166, 169–171, 176–179, 185
Magical Boy 19, 21
magical world 5, 24, 25, 47, 62–64, 144, 145, 161; *see also* fantasy; multiverse; underworld
makeup 13, 15, 19, 33, 42, 43, 95, 97, 125, 138, 163, 172, 190
Malatino, Hil 18, 36, 38, 40, 41, 81, 119–121, 180, 189
Margaret and the Mystery of the Missing Body 18, 32
marginalization 13, 31, 34, 100, 107, 108, 110–115, 119, 186, 187, 189, 192
marriage 3, 30, 43, 44, 46, 50, 65, 81, 89, 92, 94, 149, 155, 162, 163; laws 191; sacred 163
Marvel 30, 50, 51, 53, 137
Marvel Voices Pride 51
masculine 16, 21, 22, 66, 84, 87–90, 94, 124, 152, 161, 169; traits 84; *see also* butch
masks 36, 69, 98
The Matrix 9–12, 45
McLemore, Anna-Marie 61, 93
medical establishment 17, 32, 42, 60, 118, 119, 155, 158, 159, 183; *see also* body horror; clinic; disability; healthcare; hormones; mental illness; neurodivergent; surgery
Meet Cute Diary 31, 34
memoir 4, 139
mental illness 32, 42, 91, 112, 158, 159; *see also* disability; multiple personalities; trauma
mentor 5, 27, 29–35, 37, 40–44, 49, 55, 67, 72, 77, 78, 87, 114, 132, 141, 144, 167, 171, 176, 178–181, 184–187; *see also* dragon; goddess; monsters; shaman; wisewoman; witch
Merlin 31, 166, 171
Mexico 160
A Million Quiet Revolutions 15
mirror 66–68, 88, 94–98, 138, 139, 149, 160, 176

misgendering 5, 14, 61, 73, 94, 100–102, 129, 145, 149, 155
monsters 5, 19–21, 35, 36, 38, 40, 42, 53, 73, 77, 79, 80, 82, 83, 109, 111–117, 133, 135, 139; *see also* chimera; cyborg; dragon; Frankenstein; *Nimona*; *Pet*; sphinx; vampire; witch; zombie
The Moon Within 168
Mooncakes 151
The Mortal Instruments 28–29
mother 15, 16, 19–22, 25, 27, 38, 49, 58, 60, 70, 72–77, 87, 88, 90, 95, 100, 104, 105, 107, 108, 119, 123–125, 131, 134, 139, 143, 150, 163, 164, 167, 168, 179–184; *see also* goddess; house mother; stepmother
Mrs. Doubtfire 95
multiple personalities 90
multiverse 125
murder 48, 62, 103, 104, 109, 128–130, 147, 181
music 40, 49, 69, 92, 97, 112, 126
musicals *see Hedwig and the Angry Inch*; *Rent*
My Little Pony 185
Myers, Alex 130, 155, 171
mystery 5, 18, 62, 63, 128
Mystique 51, 53

naming 22, 52–56, 69, 89, 147, 167, 189
Narnia 130, 166
neurodivergent 112, 186
Nevada 23, 69
New York 13, 14, 57, 61, 69, 107, 146, 179, 182, 184
Nigeria 77
Nimona 51, 53, 111
No Man of Woman Born 131
non-binary 1–6, 24, 31, 33, 37, 38, 42, 45, 51, 66, 69, 75–77, 79, 93, 96, 111, 113, 123, 132, 147, 163, 165, 174, 178, 191, 192
nonconformity 43
nonviolence 36, 110
Normal 103
Not Your Villain 81
Nubia 52–55
oppression 14, 18, 55, 58, 81, 110, 112, 176, 186

Orange Is the New Black 117–122
ordinary world 4, 12, 14, 15, 18, 22, 64, 66, 129, 162; *see also* home
orphan archetype 15, 134, 164
The Orville 166
Othering 109, 113
Our Flag Means Death 45, 46
Out of Salem 111

Pakistani 163, 164
Paris 162
Parrotfish 12, 99
The Passing Playbook 46, 57
patriarchal 31, 137, 160; *see also* father; government
people of color 13, 15, 32, 119, 120, 147, 159, 192
persona 5, 9, 10, 13, 46, 53, 87, 89, 153
Pet 23, 76–80, 151, 174
Peter Darling 47, 151–154
Peter Pan 69, 152
Phoenix Extravagant 18, 23, 36, 55, 77, 151, 185
pirate 46–48, 63, 152–153
Plato 84, 96
Pollack, Rachel 43, 154
Porcelain 51
Porter, Billy 185
Pose 6, 13, 46, 49, 70, 94, 141, 178–184
"Potion and Practices" 169
poverty 13, 18, 86, 118, 184, 191
Pratchett, Terry 123, 172
prejudice 5, 14, 20, 24, 52, 55, 58, 77, 81, 98, 99, 111–113, 119, 159, 166; *see also* marginalization; transphobia
Pride parade 61, 158, 160, 161
prince 3, 4, 81, 82, 85, 89–94, 101–103, 139, 175
The Prince and the Dressmaker 87–88
princess 24, 33, 50, 88, 90, 143, 145, 175
Priscilla, Queen of the Desert 95, 185–187
prison 11, 109, 118–122, 127, 137, 149, 150, 176
privilege 18, 25, 30, 31, 41, 69, 70, 109, 110, 114, 119, 145, 150, 161, 176, 185, 186, 189
prize 151, 154
projection 82, 86, 87, 93, 96
prom 46, 125, 170
pronouns 6, 33, 35–38, 66, 75, 83, 93, 123, 124, 131, 164, 168; *see also* misgendering
A Psalm for the Wild-Built 24, 45, 76
Psycho 109
publicity 116, 121
Puerto Rican 150

queer communities 31, 32, 36, 47, 62, 72, 114, 158, 161; *see also* found family; safe spaces
queer reading 113, 152, 172

racism 18, 108, 113, 119
rage 86, 108, 113–117, 120, 132, 151, 188
rape 18, 24, 105, 115–117
rebellion 18, 56, 101; *see also* revolution
reincarnation 53, 54, 69, 143, 147, 150
Rent 145–146

Index

representation 4, 6, 9, 19, 36, 42, 119, 145, 178, 186, 192; *see also* tokenism
resurrection 125, 144
Return of the Dragon Guard 37, 77
revenge 48, 102, 105, 109, 113, 115–117, 120, 150
revolution 36, 37, 45, 126, 191
reward 4, 111, 153–156
Riordan, Rick 51
rite of passage 17, 26, 59, 125, 131, 132, 168–170
robot 46, 60, 76, 81, 154
The Rocky Horror Picture Show 42–44, 126
"Roja" 93
romance 6, 29, 33, 34, 42, 56, 72–74, 82–85, 87, 91–98, 103, 139, 145, 154, 162, 169, 172, 177, 182
Romeos 69, 103
Rowling, J.K. 100, 191
Rudolph the Red-Nosed Reindeer 166
ruler 124, 148, 177
Runaways 30, 51

safe spaces 46–47
San Francisco 158
Sandman 56, 143–146
school 14–17, 20, 25, 27, 32, 34, 35, 46, 47, 57, 59–61, 71, 99, 101, 104, 111, 112, 129, 144, 168, 183, 185, 191; *see also* bully; college
science fiction 1, 4, 5, 13; *see also Doctor Who*; *Light from Uncommon Stars*; *Lizard Radio*; *Loki*; *The Matrix*; *The Orville*; *Sense8*; *Sorrowland*; *Star Wars*; superheroes
"Sea Glass at Dawn" 38
Seattle 114
secret identity 20, 59–60
segregation 120, 121, 148
self-actualization 5, 6, 12, 23, 59, 82, 96, 111, 125, 143, 145, 150, 151, 162, 169, 173
self-doubt 143, 159
Self-Made Boys 61
self-portraits 90, 96
selkie 112
Sense8 56, 69, 157–158, 161–163
Sera 51
Seven Suspects 46, 99, 112–116, 190
sewing 46, 47, 78, 85, 88, 92, 123
Sex Education 74
sex worker 115, 118, 137, 171, 172, 180
sexism 24, 119, 171
sexual liberation 42, 43, 62
shadow 1, 5, 9, 13, 20, 44, 72, 86, 87, 96, 121, 124–128, 132, 138–143, 170, 173; definition 140

shaman 52
shape-shifting 5, 51, 53, 154
She-Ra 51
short story 38, 50, 131, 138, 147, 167
The Silence of the Lambs 109
Sir Callie and the Champions of Helston 24, 61, 74, 81, 99, 100, 171
sister 21, 28, 30, 50, 53, 54, 59, 82, 85, 87, 91, 107, 108, 118, 132, 163–167
Sistersong 166
slavery 18, 155
Sleeping Beauty 131
small town 104, 107, 128, 188
Snow White 95, 131
So Long Suburbia 46
social death 119, 121
social media 86, 110
society 5, 9–12, 18, 23, 27–29, 36, 38, 40, 43, 53, 56, 59, 61, 66, 72, 77, 80, 81, 85, 91, 95, 97, 102, 103, 108–111, 114, 115, 117, 120, 124–127, 130, 132, 135, 136, 144, 145, 148, 158, 162, 164, 166, 169, 173, 177, 187–189, 191
soldier 33, 91–93, 132
Solomon, Rivers 56
Somebody, Somewhere 46
Sorrowland 56
Sort Of 46, 69, 103, 163–166
Sovereign 127, 186
speech 19, 50, 76, 107, 108, 119, 133, 161
sphinx 37, 79
Spider-Man: Across the Spider-Verse 59
Star Wars 123, 127, 134–135, 166
stepmother 3, 15, 46, 95
stereotype 6, 12, 42, 51, 100, 113, 116
Steven Universe 6, 56, 73–76
Steven Universe Future 185
The Storm of Life 177
The Story of Silence 155, 171
Stryker, Susan 25, 37, 40, 113–117, 119, 158–159
suicide 14, 16, 18, 34, 73, 104, 114, 122, 150, 191
suit 10, 11, 22, 39, 45, 46, 68, 70, 83, 94, 125, 145
The Sunbearer Trials 23, 25
Supergirl 106–110
superhero 9, 11, 12, 16, 21, 26, 51–54, 59, 60, 68, 81, 108, 111, 146, 186; *see also* Aruna Shende; Bia of the Amazons; Batman; Coagula; DC Comics; *Doom Patrol*; *Dreadnought*; Dreamer; *Galaxy*; Jessie Drake; Loki; *Magical Boy*; Marvel; Mystique; *Not Your Villain*, Nubia; Porcelain; *Runaways*; Sandman; secret identity; Sera; She-Ra; *Steven Universe*;

Sovereign; *Spider-Man*; *Supergirl*; *Superman*; *Teen Titans Academy*; X-Men
Superman 9, 34
surgery 11, 12, 17, 27, 43, 90, 117, 133, 134, 145, 158, 166, 167
surveys 191
sword 30, 45, 83, 92, 103, 144, 167
Szpara, K.M. 136, 176

talisman 5, 45, 46, 47, 49, 50, 103, 151, 179; *see also* knife; mirror; sword
Tangerine 46, 171
The Tea Dragon Society 37, 151
Teen Titans Academy 51
telepathy 157
TERF 143, 145
Tess of the Road 18, 24, 76
The Testament of Loki 90
testosterone 12, 17, 27, 60, 94; *see also* hormones
theater 14, 22, 46, 62, 145, 168
therapist 2, 17, 85, 138, 151, 155, 180
They/Them 99
"This Far" 163
Thom, Kai Cheng 1–2, 18, 137, 175
threshold guardians 57, 59
Tiger Honor 174
time travel 61, 167
Tiresias 3
"To Rest and to Create" 178
Toilet Training 59, 111
tokenism 46, 51, 55, 79
Tootsie 95
Torch Song Trilogy 95
torture 66, 162, 166
trans panic 103, 115
Transamerica 155
Trans-Galactic Bike Ride 50
transition 11, 12, 15, 17, 29, 46, 58, 60, 85, 107, 127, 139, 147, 155, 164, 170, 177, 180
transphobia 4, 6, 14–18, 24, 25, 32, 42, 52, 60, 70, 73, 95, 98–100, 105, 107, 110, 113, 115–122, 126, 143, 145, 158, 187, 189; *see also* marginalization; prejudice
trauma 16, 18, 28, 35, 62, 90–92, 112, 117, 121, 128, 185

tricksters 3, 139
Trump, Donald 106
Two Sentence Horror Stories 112

unconscious 14, 20, 21, 62, 64, 79, 86, 88, 96, 121–124, 126, 131, 134, 138, 139, 150, 152, 157, 158
underworld 12, 25, 68, 105, 121–126, 131, 132, 146, 150, 151, 158, 172
unemployment 118, 191; *see also* fired
"Unknown Number" 46, 138

vampire 33, 63
victim-blaming 5, 111
violin 49
Vogler, Christopher 57, 58, 74, 133, 135, 139, 142
von Franz, Marie Louise 23, 62, 84, 85, 88, 123, 140, 151

Wachowski, Lana and Lilly 9–12, 157–158
Walker, Mitch 82, 83, 88, 93
The Watch 46, 123–126
weaving 147–149
Welcome to St. Hell 139
West Indian 78
White House 183
The Wicked Bargain 47
wig 46, 67, 98, 122
wilderness 5, 44, 141, 187, 188
wisewoman 148, 150
witch 58, 64, 81, 90, 101, 132, 166, 176
The Witch King 81–84
The Wizard of Oz 18, 69, 83, 123, 135, 136, 146
Wizards 113
Woodman, Marion 131, 134, 166
World Running Down 93

X-Men 51
xochihuah 168

YouTube 99, 129

Zenobia July 33
zombie 111, 112, 114

www.ingramcontent.com/pod-product-compliance
Lightning Source LLC
Chambersburg PA
CBHW052059300426
44117CB00013B/2206